The Collapse of British Rule in Burma

The Collapse of British Rule in Burma

The Civilian Evacuation and Independence

Michael D. Leigh

BLOOMSBURY ACADEMIC
LONDON • NEW YORK • OXFORD • NEW DELHI • SYDNEY

BLOOMSBURY ACADEMIC
Bloomsbury Publishing Plc
50 Bedford Square, London, WC1B 3DP, UK

BLOOMSBURY, BLOOMSBURY ACADEMIC and the Diana logo are trademarks of Bloomsbury Publishing Plc

First published in Great Britain 2018
Paperback edition published 2020

A catalogue record for this book is available from the British Library.

A catalog record for this book is available from the Library of Congress.

ISBN: HB: 978-1-4725-8973-6
PB: 978-1-3501-4757-7
ePDF: 978-1-4725-8974-3
eBook: 978-1-4725-8975-0

Typeset by Newgen KnowledgeWorks Pvt. Ltd., Chennai, India

Julie, the love of my life, to whom I owe everything

Contents

Illustrations

Maps

Tables

Acknowledgements

I am deeply grateful to all the following: U Set Paing Htet for his unfailingly stimulating and knowledgeable guidance; Diana Catto, Alastair Brown, Michael Brown and John Salkeld who allowed me to celebrate with them the lives of David Smith and P. G. G. Salkeld; also, Chris and Martine Smith for their kindness. I appreciated the generosity of Robin and Lois Knight, who introduced me to Kachin hospitality and who gave me so much information about the Darlington family. U Myint Thein Tun, Nan Shue La and U Khin Aung Nyunt were absolutely brilliant in guiding me through the backstreets of Myitkyina and for digging out many long-forgotten gems of its World War II history. It was a huge privilege to join in a joyous celebration of the life and work of the great Dr Cornelius North. His descendants, Hilary Mitchell, Robert, Essie, William and Cornelius North are fitting successors. My friend Dr Archie McAdam, has ensured that the outstanding work of his father, Major William McAdam in the Chindwin Valley will never be forgotten; Caroline Robinson and her colleagues at the Clear Mapping Co. produced excellent maps and Harriet Montgomery's chirpy technical guidance has been greatly appreciated. I owe a great deal to the insights of Dr Kevin Greenbank at the Cambridge Centre for South Asian Studies. Professor Richard Reid and his colleagues at the School for African and Asian Studies (SOAS) have been constant sources of inspiration, and I am eternally grateful to Professor Ian Brown, who launched me on this labour of love. I am also grateful to Diana Kennedy for the affectionate and lively descriptions of her father, Reginald Clarke, and to Ken Vorley whose father, J. S. Vorley OBE, was profoundly important in the story of the evacuation. Finally, thanks go to Murad Hemmadi, David Butler MBE, Dorothy Willies, Jean Ellis and so many others for their helpful, stimulating and challenging comments.

Abbreviations

ABDACOM	American-British-Dutch-Australian Command
AFO	Anti-Fascist Organisation
AFPFL	Anti-Fascist People's Freedom League
BBRC	Burma Banks Reconstruction Committee
BBTC	Bombay Burmah Trading Corporation Ltd.
BCCC	Burma-China Construction Company
BCMS	Bible Churchmen's Missionary Society
BDA	Burma Defence Army
BIA	Burma Independence Army
BOC	Burmah Oil Corporation
BISNCo Ltd	British India Steam Navigation Co Ltd
BFF	Burma Frontier Force
CIC	Commander in Chief
CNAC	China National Aviation Corporation
CO	Commanding Officer
GOC	General Officer Commanding
HSBC	Hongkong and Shanghai Banking Corporation
ICS	Indian Civil Service
IFC	Irrawaddy Flotilla Company
IMS	Indian Medical Service
ITA	Indian Tea Association
KOYLI	King's Own Yorkshire Light Infantry
PPC	Political Porter Corps
PVO	People's Volunteer Organization
PWD	Public Works Department
RAOC	Royal Army Ordnance Company
RETSCo	Rangoon Electric Tramway and Supply Company
SEAC	South East Asia Command
Steels	Steel Brothers & Co Ltd
YMBA	Young Men's Buddhist Association

Honours

KG	(Knight of the Garter)
PC	(Privy Counsellor)
GCB	(Knight Grand Cross of the Order of the Bath)
GCVO	(Knight Grand Cross of the Royal Victorian Order)
KCVO	(Knight Commander of the Royal Victorian Order)
OM	(Order of Merit)
CIE	(Commander of the Indian Empire); KCIE (Knight Commander of the Indian Empire); GCIE (Knight Grand Commander of the Indian Empire).[1]
CSI	(Companion of the Order of the Star of India); KCSI (Knight Commander of the Star of India); GCSI (Knight Grand Commander of the Star of India).[2]
KCMG	(Knight Commander of the Order of St Michael and St George)
KStJ	(Knight of the Order of St John),
OBE	(Order of the British Empire); MBE (Member of the British Empire)
VC	(Victoria Cross); MC (Military Cross); DSO (Distinguished Service Order)
	Note: No appointments have been made to the Order of the Indian Empire since 1947, and, no appointments have been made to the Star of India since 1948.

Foreword

Let us talk of graves, of worms, and epitaphs … and tell sad stories of the death of kings: How some have been deposed, some slain in war; some haunted by the ghosts they have deposed.

Shakespeare: *Richard II*, Act 3. Scene 2

Myitkyina is a town full of ghosts. This most northerly town in Burma sprawls in the broad curves of the Upper Irrawaddy. It is on the edge of civilization. Beyond it rise like walls the jungle-clad mountains that separate Burma from Assam and China. In Myitkyina one expects to bump into spectres of the past – exotic warriors, war lords, fierce resistance fighters and courageous heroes. Over many years, and in many conflicts, battalions of Kachin, Chinese, Burmese, British and Japanese troops have fought, advanced and retreated across the vast marchlands that surround Myitkyina. At the same time, the town has offered a last refuge for waves of civilians who have fled from dangers in Lower Burma.

In 1962, when General Ne Win brought a bamboo curtain down on Burma, a new sense of mystery shrouded Myitkyina. After that it was often a 'forbidden city', closed to visitors, dangerous, and beset by civil war. Glasnost descended on Burma after the momentous elections held on 8 November 2015. The mists rolled away from Myitkyina – and there it was, bathed in bright sunlight, full of life, vibrant, colourful, bristling with understated courage, unapologetic and unsentimental.

In January 2017, I flew into Myitkyina. I had never visited the town before and expected so much of it. I had dreamed of the moment, but there were no monuments to past tragedies and no plaques commemorated fallen heroes. Traders sold their wares in the bazaars, teashops prospered and young people went about their daily lives. They laughed, ate delicacies in Kachin restaurants, planned the future and wrote assignments for tutorials. It was as if nothing of particular importance had happened in this northern town of theirs.

However, the perception obscured one simple fact. Throughout its history, Myitkyina has witnessed many tumultuous events. One of the most electrifying sequence of calamities took place in a few short weeks in May 1942. A series of events played out at the airport, in the railway station, along the roads to the north out of town, in the panelled rooms of long-forgotten colonial-era buildings and in dingy gated alleyways, where British troops had once polished their boots.

In 2017 a few elderly survivors could still recall the traumas of those far-off colonial times. Their vivid recollections are like gold dust. These old men were without apparent rancour or self-pity. Soon they will have passed away, and with them will go their precious memories.

U Khin Aung Nyunt walked up to the tea stall on Myitkyina Railway Station at 10.00 am on 24 January 2017. He was on time – not a minute early and not a minute late. He had offered to take me on a journey back in time – and here he was in person – neat, calm, jovial, trim and bright as a button. He was 87 years of age, but his sprightly appearance belied his advanced years.[1]

I looked forward to hear about U Khin Aung Nyunt's life in Myitkyina 75 years ago. He did not disappoint. In 1942, Ko Khin Aung Nyunt (as he was then) was an eleven-year-old schoolboy. He lived through the tumultuous events of a remarkable year. His memories were vivid. It was appropriate that our journey began on Myitkyina Railway Station. It was here that Ko Khin Aung Nyunt had spent much of his time in 1942. His school had been closed from the beginning of April because of the war. His father was a Burma Railways worker on the station staff at Myitkyina. To keep his young son out of mischief the railwayman brought Khin Aung Nyunt to the station with him most days. The young boy ran errands, swept the platform, sold newspapers and opened doors for passengers. He observed what was happening on the station platforms at close quarters.

In May 1942, Myitkyina Railway Station was a lifeline for thousands of people. Trains were still running – but only just. Engines pulled behind them scores of carriages. The up-trains arrived from the south every day. They came from Rangoon Maymyo, Mandalay, Bhamo and Shwebo, The down-trains left for Mogaung. They were full of evacuees who were about to start walking to Assam through the Hukawng Valley. The up-trains were packed with evacuees and wounded troops who intended to fly to Assam from the Myitkyina airstrip. The new arrivals occupied every inch of space and clung to the carriage roofs and running boards. As the engines edged into the station, the carriage doors burst open to disgorge onto the platform hundreds of men, women and children. Most of them were Anglo-Burmese. U Khin Aung Nyunt recalled that they were neatly dressed in clean *longyis*, white shirts, blouses, colourful skirts and clean shoes. Once on the platforms, they stretched, dusted themselves down and gathered their bags. Then they walked towards the airstrip just a few miles away. This ritual was repeated several times a day, and it went on day after day. We talked about the people, what they were carrying, and how many of them were very quiet, not knowing what to expect.

Next U Khin Aung Nyunt took me on a tour of the town. We did not follow the tourist trail of markets, pagodas and new public buildings but instead, we peered into obscure places that had been significant in 1942 but which had been long since forgotten. Two friends of U Khin Aung Nyunt – very knowledgeable Kachin men – drove us down bumpy side roads, stopping here and there to paint elegant word pictures of the sepia scene in 1942.

Our first port of call was Myitkyina's small, bright and breezy modern airport. I learned that the runway is exactly where it was at the height of the civilian evacuation in 1942. Then it had been formed of baked earth that became a quagmire when the monsoon season began. The jungle presses up against the perimeter fence today, as it did in 1942, and distant mountains rise beyond the trees. I tried to imagine the terrifying roar of Japanese planes as they appeared over the trees on 6 May 1942 and the explosions as bombs thudded onto the airstrip and killed many evacuees.

We drove from the airport along a broad, straight concrete highway. It passed in front of the modern Myitkyina University building and seemed to lead nowhere. The road was several hundred yards long, it was empty apart from an occasional *tuk-tuk* and it suddenly came to an end. This was the highway that the Americans had built in 1945, not as a road but as the new runway onto which their heavy transport planes landed and from which they took off as they prepared for the reconquest of Burma.

We drove back into a pretty and leafy part of the town. This was the old colonial quarter – nothing remains now to suggest that this was once the case. We stopped at a large gate through which could be glimpsed some single-storeyed, nondescript government office buildings. This was where Government House had once stood. There was nothing left of it now, but it was just possible to imagine the scene on 6 May 1942 as R. S. Wilkie and his colleagues held their last, late night meeting before finally abandoning Myitkyina to Japanese units.

We turned down a rutted side street and were decanted into a very grubby Ministry of Works vehicle yard. Bits of old engines and rusting chassis parts were scattered around. The outline of faded military insignia on a crumbling brick wall gave it away. This unprepossessing edifice had once been the British garrison's barracks in 1942, and it was from here that Brigadier Upton and his tiny force of British troops had marched out of the town on the morning of 7 May 1942.

From there we drove out of the northeast quarter of the town for a short distance along the road towards Sumprabum and Putao (Fort Hertz). Spectacular jungle-clad mountains towered above us in the distance. Scratched and scuffed Chinese trucks with enormous tyres and shovels strapped to their sides lumbered past us en route to Kunming. The road to Putao was obviously still very rough. And then we turned back to Myitkyina. We drove for a short distance along the road that left the town to the northwest towards Maingkwan and Shingbwiyang. Army roadblocks prevented us from travelling beyond the municipal boundary. Military manoeuvres were taking place in Kachin State at the time. As we stood for a while, I gazed into the distance and imagined the scene 75 years ago, when hundreds of exhausted and frightened civilian evacuees shuffled along the road in 1942 on their way to Shingbwiyang and beyond. Abandoned cars and discarded personal belongings – boxes, bags, ornaments, sewing machines and furniture – had once been left by the side of the track by evacuees too weak to carry them further.

The Nahlon Bridge was our next port of call. It was on the outskirts of Myitkyina and, in 1942, it had been a notorious bottleneck on the road from Bhamo. Scores of trucks and cars had to be abandoned at the bridge by fleeing refugees. Many of the vehicles were pushed over the bridge into the dried-up bed of the Nahlon stream and set on fire. The continuous conflagration sent up clouds of suffocating, acrid black smoke. Alister Rose had arrived at the bridge in his Hillman Imp on 5 May 1942. He found a scene of utter chaos, but he managed to turn around and find an alternative route into Myitkyina. Today, the site of the bridge is tucked away down a deserted narrow road. The Nahlon Bridge itself has completely disappeared. Indeed, a house has been built over the stream where the bridge once stood. The bed of the stream was still clearly visible, but it was full of stinking rubbish. We stood and gazed down at the dry valley. A very old man emerged from a nearby house. Like U Khin Aung Nyunt he had been a small boy in 1942. He remembered the horrific scenes at the bridge in those far-off days, and he stretched out his arms (as if in benediction) to indicate how wide – or rather how narrow – the bridge had been in those days.

***

My visit to Myitkyina is seared upon my memory. My earlier book, *The Evacuation of Civilians from Burma: Analysing the 1942 Colonial Disaster* (2014) ends with the story of these events in Myitkyina in May 1942. This book picks up the story just where it left off and continues from May 1942 to January 1948.[2] Two questions come to mind. First, why was Myitkyina (of all the towns in Burma) so important, and second, what was so special about May of all months in1942?

The reasons for Mytkyina's significance are as follows: after the capitulation of Rangoon, Mandalay and Maymyo in 1942, the Kachin town of Myitkyina was Britain's last, fragile hold on civilian rule in Burma. Japanese forces had occupied the whole area south of the town and the civilian evacuation from Burma was now confined to the northern part of Burma *beyond* Myitkyina. By the end of April 1942, the airstrip in Myitkyina was the only operational runway in the whole of Burma. Myitkyina was now the only place from where civilian evacuees could fly to India or, more precisely, to Dibrugarh in Assam. It was a short flight of less than sixty minutes. The trek to Assam on foot could take as many days. By the end of April, each and every refugee trapped in Burma was desperate to reach Myitkyina.

This simple truth explains why the tragedy that occurred at the airstrip on 6 May 1942 was so devastating in the grand scheme of things.[3] Myitkyina was the fulcrum upon which rested Britain's future role in Burma. The fall of Myitkyina spelled the absolute and final end to the colonial project. Japanese troops marched into the town on 8 May 1942.

Myitkyina had always been a frontier town, a place where different races and ethnic groups mixed, traded and squabbled – Kachins, Shans Burmans, Nepalis, Chinese, Hmongs and Nagas. Between 1942 and 1948 the armies of Britain, Japan, China and the United States tramped in and out of Myitkyina.

The town was captured, recaptured, bombed and re-bombed several times over. It was not surprising that its reputation for being a wild and, lawless place has continued unabated.

Hugh Tinker includes a revealing document in his monumental work on the constitutional relationships in Burma between 1944 and 1948. The minutes of a Burma Executive Council meeting held in Government House, Rangoon, on 4 November 1946 reports the lengthy discussion on Myitkyina. The Director of Frontier Areas Administration reported that recently there had been a build-up of Chinese troops along the border of southwest Yunnan. It looked very likely that they were about to attack Myitkyina. Their pretext was to protect Chinese nationals who were resident in the town.[4] Danger, conflict and turbulence were then, as now, the trademarks of this remarkable town.

The second question was what was so special about May 1942? At first sight, the choice of May appears to be arbitrary. It was like any other month in this most turbulent of years. Nevertheless, it was the real turning point in the civilian evacuation. Up until April 1942, Europeans had been able to escape up-country in cars, lorries and trains. Now they had to walk great distances – just as the Indians had to walk. May marked the turning point. The dry season ended in May 1942 and the monsoon rains began. By May, the evacuation was confined to the northernmost part of Burma. By the end of April, British military forces in Burma were in full retreat. At the beginning of May, Sir Reginald Dorman-Smith escaped to India – so by May 1942 Burma was completely undefended and totally ungoverned.[5]

At a Cabinet meeting in Westminster, in May 1942, concerns were expressed about the handling of affairs in Burma. Churchill turned his fire on the hapless Governor and Sir Reginald Dorman-Smith's reputation began to suffer from this point on. Indeed, his reputation has never fully recovered since then.[6]

May 1942 was a turning point in one other way. Burmese nationalist fighters operated alongside the Japanese Army and in May 1942 they were able to boast that they had finally removed the colonial forces from Burma. During May 1942, General Aung San became a very well-known figure in Tokyo and in London.

At the Myitkyina Railway Station, in January 2017, U Khin Aung Nyunt took me on a journey through time and space. In this book, we will embark on a somewhat bigger journey through time and space. The journey will take us onwards from May 1942 and northwards from Myitkyina. The journey will end at the point when Burma achieved its independence on 4 January 1948.

Map 0.1 Outline map of Burma, circa 1942–1948

1

Introduction

Since pride must have a fall and break the neck of that proud man that did usurp his back?

Shakespeare, *Richard II* Act 5. Scene 5

Part One: Preamble to the Events that Occurred between 24 December 1941 and 6 May 1942

Fall followed pride with a vengeance in the dying days of British colonial rule in Burma. Burma is the unsung hero in this story – it is also the victim. The Burmese people suffered terribly in the war. It was a war in which they had no interest, one that was not of their making and one that destroyed their country. The land of Burma was the backdrop against which all the action took place. However, although Burma is the raison d'être for this book, it is *not* a history of Burma per se – nor is it a history of the Burmese people. Rather, it is a history of one corner of the British Empire and of the people who ruled and organized the colony. The colonial rulers also brought in other peoples from elsewhere in the Empire – mainly Indians and Eurasians. They settled in the land, performed menial tasks and oiled the wheels of commerce. They struggled out of Burma with their British 'sponsors' when Japanese forces invaded. What follows is an account of the fortunes of these colonial 'incomers' during the tumultuous years between May 1942 and January 1948.

The narrative in this book commences at the beginning of May 1942 and ends *precisely* at 4.00 am on 4 January 1948. It describes the second phase of the civilian evacuation, examines Anglo-Burmese negotiations, the financial implications of the war, and it ends as Burma became an independent nation. One event followed another with bewildering speed, and it is a sobering thought that Burma achieved full independence a mere six years after the last colonial evacuee had left the country.

Figure 1.1 Rangoon Docks in 1945. Credit: The British Library Board. Rangoon was devastated by successive bombardments. The docks were hit particularly hard. Japanese aircraft bombed the city from 23 December 1941 to February 1942. British forces demolished key installations on 7 March 1942. In April 1945, British forces returned. Lieutenant General Hyotaro Kimura evacuated the city on 23 April after which there was an orgy of looting and arson and much damage was done. Gurkha parachute troops and the 17th and 26th Indian Divisions recaptured the city on 6 May 1945.

Five factors underpinned this rush to the finishing line. First, Japanese forces traumatized the civilian population and routed the British Army. Second, Burmese nationalist leaders grew in confidence during and after the Japanese invasion. Third, the civilian evacuation was deeply disruptive and it undermined colonial morale. Fourth, Britain declined economically and diplomatically during the war, and fifth, Britain's post-war entanglements in Southeast Asia further sapped its strength.

This book has two main aims – to join the dots and to place the civilian evacuation in a wider context. Three of the factors just mentioned – namely, Britain's post-war weakness, the effect of its involvement in Southeast Asian post-war conflicts and the exploits of Burmese nationalist leaders – will be picked up in Chapters 8 and 10 respectively. The impact of the Japanese invasion will be discussed in this chapter, and questions relating to the evacuation will be examined in Chapters 2, 3, 4 and 5.

***

This book does not pretend to be a military history. Nevertheless the crushing victories and heavy defeats that followed one another in 1942 cannot be ignored. Indeed they exerted a powerful influence on everything that followed. Military defeats underpinned the decline of the British Empire and explained the breakneck speed with which colonial rule in Burma collapsed. Military issues will not be revisited later in the book, but their ongoing influence must not be underestimated.[1]

In fact the impending military debacle in Burma should have come as no surprise. Britain had been in grave danger from external aggression throughout 1940. Indeed senior British military commanders in Europe were reluctant to risk sending arms or men to Southeast Asia because they were urgently needed closer home. The United States was neutral; Belgium, Holland and France had collapsed and Britain stood alone. During May–June 1940 the British Expeditionary Force was trapped in Dunkirk and 350,000 troops came within a whisker of being lost. A few weeks later the Battle of Britain raged over southern England. It was another close-run thing. The Royal Air Force (RAF) could claim to have won the battle in the air by October 1940 but British cities would be continuously *blitzed* for months to come. Britain's coastal waters were unsafe because of German U-boat activity. By the beginning of 1943, a staggering 3,500 British and Allied merchant ships had been sunk and Britain had lost 1million tons of imports.[2]

However, the sense of impending doom that gripped Britain in 1940 was strangely absent in colonial Southeast Asia. Everyday life in Burma continued more or less normally until the beginning of December 1941, and until then Burmese towns were reported to be calmer than they had been for many a year. There were warning signs. Japanese officials directed a stream of hostile rhetoric against the colonial rulers in Burma. Their main bone of contention was the Burma Road. Japan demanded the closure of the road because it was being used to transport military supplies to Chiang Kai-shek's Chinese Nationalist forces in Kunming.

The fragile peace was shattered in December 1941. Three cataclysmic events occurred in quick succession. Each episode increased the likelihood of war in

Burma and in the region, generally. On 7 December 1941, Japanese aircraft attacked the US Pacific fleet in Pearl Harbor. Eighteen naval vessels (including nine front-line battleships) were sunk or damaged in the space of 90 minutes and 4,400 US citizens were killed or wounded. The incident caused a political tidal wave. America entered the war with a vengeance, and Japan unleashed a ferocious offensive across Southeast Asia. Malaya bore the brunt of the initial thrust as General Yamashita's 25th Army launched a brutal, unorthodox and fast-moving campaign.[3] By the end of January 1942, the number of allied soldiers who had been killed or imprisoned was put at 138,708, and Singapore fell on 15 February. It was a portent of things to come.

The second incident imperilled every European colony between the Dutch East Indies and India. At 12 noon on 10 December 1941, Japanese aircraft attacked the battleship HMS *Prince of Wales* and the cruiser HMS *Repulse* in open seas off the Malayan coast. Both vessels were sunk in a matter of minutes – *Repulse* at 12.33 pm and *Prince of Wales* at 1.18 pm. Admiral Tom Phillips and Captain John Leach, along with 840 officers and men, lost their lives in the action. It dealt the Royal Navy a terrible blow. It was no longer the supreme maritime force in the Indian Ocean. Singapore and Rangoon were exposed to attack from the sea and Churchill acknowledged that he had 'never received a more direct shock … Over all this vast expanse of waters', he later wrote, 'Japan was supreme, and we everywhere were weak and naked.'[4]

The third incident was specifically aimed at Burma. At 10 am on 23 December 1941, Japanese planes bombed central districts of Rangoon and the Mingaladon airfield to the north of the city. It was the first in a series of bombing raids that would continue for the next two months. The raids were as devastating as those carried out by the Luftwaffe on London, Coventry or Rotterdam. The Japanese planes returned to bomb Rangoon every day for the next two months. General Michio Sugawara masterminded the operation. He had at his disposal a fleet of Mitsubishi Ki-21 bombers (capable of flying at 300 mph), Mitsubishi Ki-30 light bombers and the superfast Nakajima Ki-27 fighter planes – 600 fighter aircraft in all.[5] Against them, the British could muster only 15 obsolete RAF Buffaloes and 12 American Volunteer Group (AVG) Tomahawks. The contest was hopelessly one-sided, although the handful of AVG and RAF pilots displayed conspicuous courage and punched above their weight. The first raids were launched from airfields in Thailand and

Indochina but, in due course, captured airfields in southeast Burma were used. The raids did what they were intended to do – they reduced the infrastructure around Rangoon to rubble and traumatized the civilian population – shock and awe: Sturm und Drang. The Japanese air raids on Rangoon brought the phony war to an abrupt end. It heralded a period of intense military activity. Japanese land forces invaded Burma at the beginning of January1942.

General McLeod and the British High Command in Burma had long insisted that there would be no Japanese invasion of Burma. They assumed that the Tenasserim frontier in southeast Burma was impenetrable and that it would not be possible to manoeuvre troops and heavy equipment across the trackless jungle-clad mountain ranges. They had to change their minds by the end of December, but even at that late stage General Shojiro Iida kept them guessing. A seaborne invasion seemed most likely, but failing that, an incursion from Thailand into the northern Shan States was a distinct possibility. Here there were roads of sorts – so in the end, McLeod decided to concentrate British forces in the Shan States. He retained only a small, token force in southeast Burma.[6]

General Iida called McLeod's bluff and took him by complete surprise. At 5.00 am on 20 January 1942 General Takeuchi and two regiments of the Japanese 55th Division entered Tenasserim in southeast Burma.[7] The Japanese troops were supported only by mules, oxen and elephants. They had moved quickly and silently across the Kra Peninsula, hacking through virgin jungle and constructing bridges across deep ravines. General Sakurai's 33rd Infantry Division followed close behind with artillery, engineers and two horse companies.[8] It was a brilliantly unorthodox operation. Afterwards it took Takeuchi's troops only eleven days to mop up the opposing forces in southeast Burma. Takeuchi seized Tavoy and its airfield before moving on to Moulmein, where his forces met remarkably little resistance.

An infamous episode took place on 23 February 1942. It altered the course of the war, and was not the proudest moment in British military history. Sittang Bridge was a strategic barrier. It was a barrier to the route to Rangoon and Lower Burma.[9] Major-General Smyth and the 17th Indian Division were deputed to defend the bridge. A series of poor decisions resulted in many of Smyth's troops being killed or taken prisoner. Valuable equipment was captured and the most important strategic position in Burma was lost. One of

Field Marshal Wavell's first acts, as he took charge of the forces in Burma, was to dismiss Smyth on the spot.[10]

Japanese forces were now able to advance across Burma at will. Rangoon fell on 7 March 1942 and with it went most of Lower Burma, including the Delta, Pegu, Toungoo, Bassein and southern Arakan. By 17 April, Japanese troops controlled the whole of central Burma from Akyab in the west to Taunggyi in the east. They were now also within easy striking distance of Lashio, Yenangyaung and Monywa. By 28 April, Mandalay, Maymyo and Bhamo had fallen, and by 8 May Monywa, Myitkyina, Kalewa and most of the northern frontier region were under Japanese control. Four months after Japanese forces had first entered Tenasserim the whole of Burma was at their mercy. Only the very far north of Burma lay beyond Japanese control. Already Japanese commanders felt strong enough to launch raids on northeast India.

Ordinary Burmans watched agog as columns of well-disciplined Japanese soldiers and bright-eyed young Burmese fighters marched side by side through their towns and villages and as British troops retreated in disarray. Japanese forces had achieved spectacularly, in the space of four months, what Burmese nationalists had only dreamt of doing for the past six decades. Between January and May 1942, the Japanese had put the British Army to flight and toppled the colonial government. By the end of December 1942, both the British Army and the colonial administration had been forced out of Burma. The genie was out of the bottle. Colonial rule had been exposed. It had been soundly beaten by an Asiatic power.

What had gone wrong from the British point of view? One thing was that British Army officers consistently underestimated the fighting qualities of Japanese combat troops. Wavell once described them as 'highly trained gangsters'.[11] A British field officer was reported to have told his men that Japanese soldiers were 'small, myopic [men] with a level of military achievement below that even of the Italians'. Such arrogance was dangerous. Japanese infantrymen were tough fighters. Many of them had been coal miners, farmers and factory workers in civilian life and now they often went into battle clad only in 'shorts, light shirts and plimsolls'.[12]

Senior British commanders had similarly underestimated their Japanese counterparts, with fatal consequences. Japanese commanders were often unorthodox, astute, intelligent tacticians, and they regularly outflanked their

British opponents. General Iida's brilliant invasion of Burma equalled the exploits of General Yamashita and his 25th Army's celebrated 'bicycle blitzkrieg'.[13]

For their part, British officers were often flat-footed and predictable. Moreover, the Army was riven by disunity – it lacked esprit de corps. This stifled originality and initiative. Disloyalty tended to come from the top. Churchill once famously described Wavell as 'a man competent to run a country golf club and little else'.[14] In turn Field Marshal Alan Brooke launched a blistering attack on Australian ministers because they (wisely – as it turned out) refused to send Australian reinforcements to Rangoon.[15]. Wavell became even more irascible after he broke two vertebrae on 10 February.[16] He flailed at anyone and everyone in his way, summarily sacking General McLeod and promoting General T. J. Hutton over him.[17] On 28 February 1942, he demoted Hutton, and appointed General Harold Alexander in his place. The very next day he dismissed Smyth.[18] It set McLeod and Hutton against one another.[19] Moreover, relations between the civilian and military authorities were equally bad. Lord Linlithgow (Viceroy of India) urged Wavell to dismiss General Hutton, and Wavell and Dorman-Smith endured a very prickly relationship.[20]

Japanese commanders were as surprised as anyone at the speed of their own successes. However, they were totally unprepared for a long-term occupation of Burma. They had to press Burmese nationalists into service to control the civilian population, and gratuitous cruelty soon became the order of the day. When the Japanese authorities granted limited independence to their Burmese subjects, they received few plaudits.[21]

It is difficult to decide whether the Japanese occupation was a triumph or a disaster. Joyce Lebra suggests that it stimulated 'endemic revolutionary forces [and] anti-colonial independence movements' in Southeast Asia.[22] Ienago Saburo argues that it 'weakened former rulers' but failed to liberate Asia.[23] In Burma, the Japanese invasion (if not the occupation) severely diminished Britain's credibility. Yet, the Japanese had no real strategy for the occupation of Burma – after all *liberating* indigenous populations had never been one of Japan's chief war aims. Although the Japanese granted limited independence to Burma in 1943, it was hedged around by so many pettifogging regulations that it gained little support from local people. Saburo suggests that Dr Ba Maw was being disingenuous when he claimed that the Japanese occupation 'marked the beginning of the end of all imperialism and colonialism'.

Notwithstanding the problematic nature of the Japanese *occupation* of Burma, the Japanese invasion of Burma in 1942 was a stunning success. It was the root cause of all that followed afterwards. As has already been said, it traumatized the civilian population, wrong-footed the colonial hierarchy and shattered forever the myth of British military infallibility. It was of little consequence that Japan was defeated in 1945. By then the damage had been done. The British Army, the British Governor, his officials and the entire colonial apparatus had been swept away by the end of 1942. What really mattered was that it had created a vacuum. Burmese nationalist leaders moved in to fill the gap. They regarded the defeat of Japan as a bonus but, having got rid of one empire in 1942, they had no wish to be stuck with another in 1945.

***

It is important here to discuss the nature of nationalism in Burma, and to trace its long and very painful journey up to the outbreak of World War II. The wartime and post-war exploits of the resurgent Burmese nationalist movement (the second of the five underlying factors cited earlier for the collapse of colonial Burma) will be discussed more fully in Chapters 8 and 10, but first some background information is necessary

In 1826, the British Army had grabbed its first big slice of Burmese territory and for the next 60 years imperial forces continued to chip away at the Konbaung dynasty's ancient heartlands. Burma was *formally* annexed as a British colony in 1885.[24] Burmans accepted British rule with sullen resignation and popular resentment seethed and simmered beneath the surface for more than 60 years. The pattern was that nationalist anger flared, died down, then flared again in a seemingly endless cycle. Sometimes nationalist sentiment manifested itself in open rebellion and sometimes in low-level resistance. Whatever form it took, dissent was never far away. However, it had been clear from the very beginning that British coercive forces were able to keep dissent firmly in check.

Between 1885 and 1937 Burmese nationalist leaders were in the shadow of their more illustrious Indian counterparts. Bal Gangadhar Tilak, Mohandas Gandhi, Jawaharlal Nehru and Subhas Chandra Bose were among those that made the running.[25] Gandhi in particular was a hero in Burma. His campaign of non-violent civil disobedience, the *Swaraj* Movement, and his anti-salt tax (*Satyagraha)* march in 1930 became models of subversion.[26] Gandhi's Young

India Movement and his transformation of the Congress from an elitist party to an organization of the people also attracted much interest in Burma.[27] It was at about this time also that the Indian National Congress began to demand independence with dominion status. Burmese and Indian nationalist movements began to dance to the same tune during the 1920s and 1930s. British police officers on both sides of the frontier collaborated in order to contain their activities.

Rural cultivators, students, Buddhist monks, students, factory workers, politicians and soldiers each took a turn in leading the Burmese nationalist movement. Armed uprisings, protests, political machinations, boycotts, strikes, demonstrations, dacoity and legal challenges were frequently deployed during the 1920s and 1930s. European residents were edgy because of the almost constant low-level disruption. They felt threatened even in the safety of their smart enclaves of Rangoon and in the protected civil lines of provincial towns.[28]

The nationalist movement in Burma, however, was *not* just a pale reflection of the Indian movement. It developed a distinctive style of its own, and it was led in turn by Buddhist activists, intellectuals, politicians, students, industrial workers and poor farmers. Its objectives were shaped by religious, political, economic and cultural ideals. A few nationalists demanded immediate independence, but all regarded the colonial government as the principal enemy.

Modern Burmese nationalism can be traced back to Young Men's Buddhist Association (YMBA), which was founded in 1906. It adopted some of Tilak's aggressive campaigning methods.[29] In 1920, the General Council of Burmese Associations provided a rudimentary local organization while the University Boycott (directed against the University Act) attracted idealistic, articulate university and secondary school students.[30] Confrontations between Burmese nationalists and the colonial authorities became continuous and ever more violent during the 1930s.[31] In the early 1930s, a millenarian mystic named Hsaya San led an economic rebellion of tenant cultivators. They had been the victims of foreclosure during the great Depression. Their rising was directed against colonial rule and it was often very violent. The Hsaya San Rebellion spread across large swathes of rural Burma, but the colonial police force was ready to meet violence with violence.

The *Dobama Asiayon* manifested nationalism in a very different way. It was instinctively secular and it swept the board in the 1930s. From its ranks rose a cadre of urbane, overtly political young intellectuals who called themselves *Thakins*.[32] Anti-colonial nationalist activity peaked during 1938 and 1939 when striking oil-workers in Chauk and Yenangyaung led a mass march to Rangoon. They gathered public support on the way. They encouraged Buddhist *pongyis*, workers, students and rural cultivators to join in a national strike.

Although the police service was stretched, government forces remained firmly in control and Indian Army regiments were drafted in to help. It exposed the truth that after decades of protest and growing popular support, the nationalist movement in Burma was no closer to gaining independence than it had been at the beginning.

Colonial coercion was simply too determined. Police and army units were too numerous, too generously resourced, too heavily armed and too well-served by paid informers to be seriously challenged. Subversion was routinely nipped in the bud and time and again Burmese nationalists had to resign themselves to many more years of colonial rule. It was generally assumed that the British grip on Burma was too strong to be broken.[33] In1940 the nationalist demonstrations – so noisy, persistent and strident during the1930s – suddenly subsided. The nationalist moment seemed to have gone. All became ominously quiet in Burma.

***

Part Two: Background to the Evacuation through Northern Burma after 6 May 1942

The civilian evacuation of 1942 was the third of five factors that ultimately led to the collapse of colonial rule in Burma. Of course it was the direct consequence of the Japanese invasion but more importantly it marked the de facto end of colonial rule in Burma.

Little more need be said for the moment about the events in Lower Burma between 23 December 1941 and 6 May 1942. They are described in detail in my book *The Evacuation of Civilians from Burma: Analysing the 1942 Colonial Disaster* (2014). Suffice it to say that European and Indian families had begun to trickle out of Burma before December 1941 and afterwards they continued to leave unobtrusively. They earned the opprobrium of those who stayed on until the bitter end and were sometimes labelled defeatists and cowards.

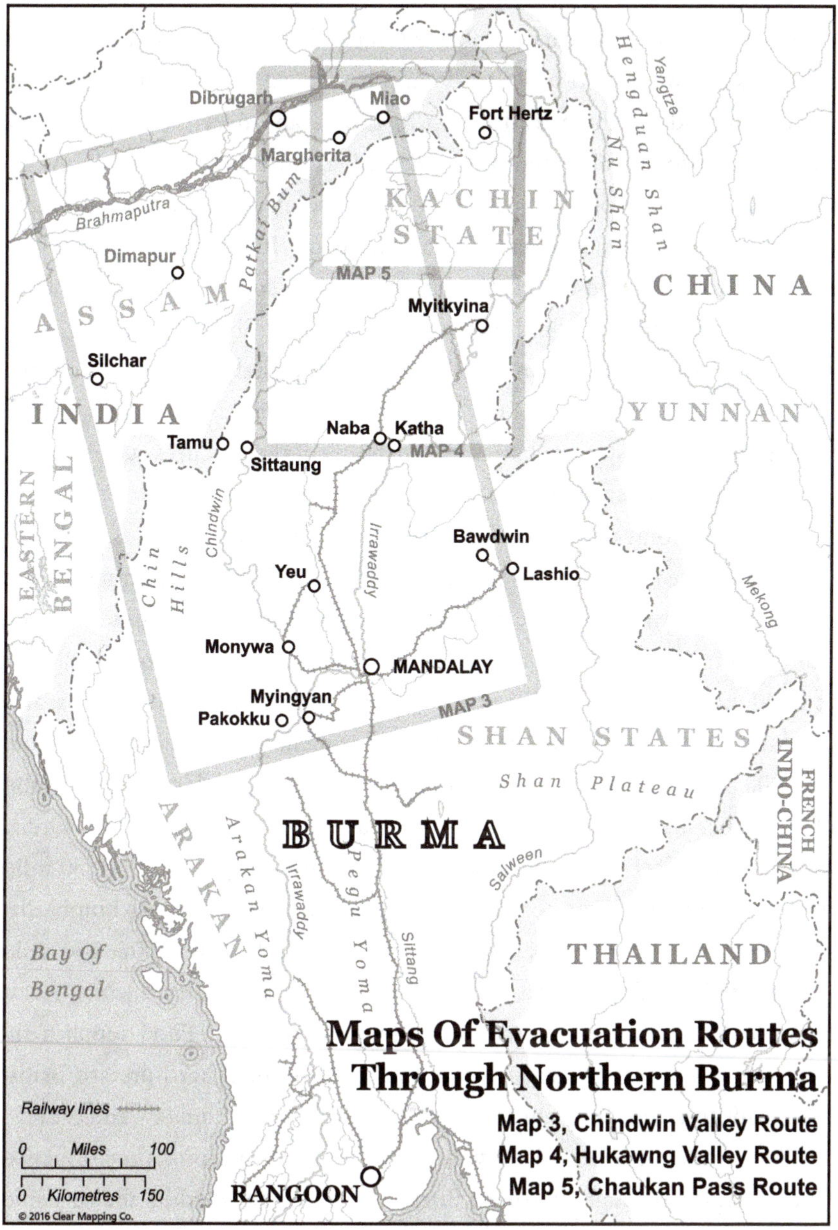

Map 1.1 Maps of evacuation routes through Northern Burma

The trickle of evacuees became a flood after the Japanese bombing raids on Rangoon started on 23 December 1941. Thousands of poor Indian workers were particularly vulnerable and they were among the first to flock out of the city. The exodus from Rangoon continued unabated for the next two months.

By the end of February, 70,000 evacuees had clambered onto ocean-going vessels in the Port of Rangoon and had sailed to ports in India. Many more thousands of them trudged up to Prome and over the Arakan Yoma via Taungup to Akyab where they escaped in unseaworthy vessels. At the same time, armadas of riverboats, trains, lorries, buses, cars and bullock carts transported refugees up to Mandalay and Maymyo. It was mistakenly believed that these towns would be safe havens. A relatively small number of (mainly) European women and children were flown from Shwebo to Chittagong. Meanwhile, extended Indian family groups straggled northwards for mile after mile. It was the height of the dry season so the roads were dusty and the springs, ponds and streams had dried up. Many of the evacuees succumbed to dehydration, heat exhaustion, malaria, cholera and smallpox.

The escape routes out of Lower Burma were closed one by one as Japanese troops advanced northwards at breakneck speed. By the beginning of May, nowhere in Burma was safe. Mandalay was bulging at the seams. Evacuees slumped on the streets, squatted in empty houses, slept in schools, collapsed in fetid hospitals and gathered in vast refugee camps. Food was scarce, drinking water ran low, sewers overflowed and cholera epidemics broke out. At 11.00 a.m. on 3 April, Japanese planes bombed Mandalay and set swathes of its timber buildings ablaze. Maymyo was bombed five days later, forcing the evacuees to set off northwards yet again. The airstrip at Shwebo (50 miles north of Mandalay) was bombed on 28 April and Monywa was bombarded on 30 April. Tens of thousands of evacuees made for Myitkyina 250 miles northeast of Mandalay. It was now the only place in Burma from which planes could fly to Assam. Conditions in Myitkyina were awful. Food supplies and clean water had run dangerously low and the handful of hard-pressed British administrators and troops in the town struggled to maintain law and order.

Chapters 2, 3, 4 and 5 will provide more specific detail about those evacuees who struggled through Northern Burma to Assam (or died by the roadside) after 6 May 1942. However, by way of preamble it is necessary to make several observations.

First, by May 1942 the task of reporting the civilian evacuation from Burma had become *especially* difficult. The desperate exodus through Northern Burma was beyond the reach of journalists, civil servants, cameras and broadcasters. Consequently, ramshackle narratives were constructed from unauthenticated

Table 1.1 Matrix of evacuation accounts, April–June 1942

Name	Group type	Route	From	To	Start	Finish	Days
Brown	Bulloch Bros	Chindwin	Sittang	Tamu	1 February 1942	12 May 1942	102
Wallace	Officials	Chindwin	Monywa	Dimapur	30 April 1942	14 May 1942	14
McAdam	Medical Officer	Chindwin	Monywa	Dimapur	14 March 1942	12 May 1942	29
Vorley	Officials etc	Chindwin	Naba	Dimapur	5 May 1942	23 May 1942	18
Beattie	Tea planter	Chindwin	Dimapur	Dimapur	7 February 1942	12 July 1942	155
Wilkie	Officials etc.	Hukawng	Myitkyina	Margherita	7 May 1942	09 June 1942	33
Rose	Businessmen	Hukawng	Myitkyina	Ledo	8 May 1942	16 June 1942	38
Russell	Missionaries	Hukawng	Sahmaw	Margherita	5 May 1942	02 June 1942	28
Brookes	Family group	Hukawng	Myitkyina	Margherita	08 April 1942	24 October 1942	200
North	BFF officer	Hukawng	Shingbwiyang	Margherita	Feb.42	Oct.42	250
Salkeld	Steel Brothers	Hukawng	Mandalay	Margherita	30 April 1942	09 June 1942	40
Rowland	Businessmen	Chaukan	Sumprabum	Margherita	05 May 1942	11 August 1942	98

fragments, frantic letters written under extreme duress, scribbled notes on rain-sodden paper, memos, citations, vague bits of data and very occasional snippets of film.

The late, great Peter Preston, editor of the *Guardian* newspaper, used to warn his journalists 'not to deliver tiny fragments of reportage [but] to add context to events [and] to show how one thing fits with another' (*The Observer*, 25 June 2017, p. 45). Historians should follow the same advice. However, it was easier said than done after 6 May in Northern Burma, at a time when the only available information was in such a fragmentary and disjointed form. I have been fortunate to be able to refer to a dozen or so excellent accounts of evacuees' experienced as they trekked through Northern Burma.

Most of the accounts are unpublished, a few of them were scribbled en route, and others were written up soon after the authors reached safety. Each of the accounts has an air of authenticity and authority, and together they provide a 365° view of the situation in Northern Burma. The authors were all evacuees, but most of them were also officials, surgeons and businessmen who helped hundreds of ordinary evacuees to escape. They all provide deep insights and broad visions, and offer compelling descriptions of life and conditions on the trek (Table 1.1).

Second, it had been the case from the beginning of the evacuation that the vast majority of the evacuees were Indians. Most of them were not great letter writers, keepers of diaries or scribblers in notebooks, whereas European and Eurasian evacuees were consummate correspondents. Because the majority of the evacuees were silent while a minority was heartily vocal, reportage of the evacuation tends to be lopsided and events are interpreted from a British perspective. That said, the documents give a sense of the fatigue, hunger, feelings of hopelessness, oozing mud, impenetrable jungles, mountain peaks, deep gorges, raging torrents, flimsy bridges, incessant rain, leeches, blood blisters and flies that afflicted *all* evacuees regardless of their ethnicity. From the European accounts three themes emerge. Most of them were dismayed that the British Army and British officials had left their posts prematurely. They were deeply grateful to the Indian Tea Association (ITA) for providing the support that the Government failed to provide, and they grudgingly admired the dogged resilience of many Indian evacuees.

Third, the accounts were chillingly synchronous, covering the period from February to August 1942 – the time when the Governor, Sir Reginald Dorman-Smith, was escaping from Burma. He was about to settle uneasily into the opulent splendour of the Viceroy's residence in Calcutta and then into the European summer retreat in Simla.

When Japanese planes bombed the Myitkyina airstrip on 6 May 1942, it brought all flights to Assam to an abrupt end. The last few British Government officials in Burma drove out of the town on 7 May, and when Japanese troops marched in on 8 May, it marked the end of British rule in Burma. Many evacuees were still trapped in northern Burma. They were desperate and afraid. There were several groups of British evacuees – dishevelled men who, until recently, had held senior posts in the upper echelons of colonial society. Among them were district commissioners, politicians, judges, police chiefs, prison governors, doctors, missionaries, headmasters, businessmen, lawyers, engineers, university professors and bankers. They had to trudge out of Burma alongside Indian manual workers and menials and Anglo-Burmese clerks. They rarely pulled together, for it was a case of every man for himself.

***

The frontier region between Burma and Assam was extremely forbidding. There were no motorable roads at any point along the frontier and most of the tracks were impassable during the monsoon season. Conditions deteriorated the further east one went towards Fort Hertz. The sheer remoteness and inaccessibility of the area meant that there was little likelihood that road improvements could be carried out to the track in time to assist the evacuation.

The frontier stretched for 300 miles from Imphal in the west to Fort Hertz in the east. Dense jungles, high mountains and turbulent rivers formed a natural barrier.[34] A vast wilderness of between 100 and 200 miles wide straddled the frontier. Within it there were no navigable rivers and no motorable roads. No vessels, lorries, cars, bullock carts, or even mule-transport could operate in this region, which for the most part lay beyond the reach of aircraft. It was completely unpopulated apart from a few isolated Kuki and Naga settlements. Persistent rumours about headhunters abounded, and malaria and other tropical diseases were rife. No crops grew in the frontier area and porters had to carry in every morsel of food consumed by the sudden influx of evacuees.

***

Three cross-frontier routes still remained open. The Chindwin Valley route was the most frequently used and by far the quickest route. Large numbers of civilian evacuees were already using the route and there were no immediate plans to upgrade the track. The situation changed in February 1942, when Japanese forces closed the Burma Road up the eastern flank of the country to Kunming. It focused the minds of military planners, who had to find a reliable escape route for British and Indian troops. They identified the Chindwin Valley route as the only viable alternative route out of Burma.

The rapid Japanese advance during February 1942 forced British and Indian troops to retreat along it, and it was anticipated that thousands of men together with tonnes of their heavy military equipment and lorryloads of supplies would soon descend on the Chindwin Valley route. An emergency road-building project of epic proportions was set in hand and the India High Command insisted that troops and their equipment must take precedence over civilians.

Upgrading work was considered to be necessary on *three* relatively short but vital sections of the route on the Burma side of the border. The first of these routes linked Tamu and a large civilian evacuation camp at Korengei. It was decided that only European and Anglo-Burmese evacuees would be allowed to use this route. The second route was to be reserved for military vehicles, and the third route (known as the 'overflow' route) would be reserved for the exclusive use of Indian evacuees. This was euphemistic, for neither Europeans nor Anglo-Burmese evacuees had any desire to use the overflow route. It was not due to be surfaced and was longer, slower, rougher, more mountainous and more potholed than either of the other routes. At least 86 miles of the track was so narrow and steep that it was unsuitable for even the most primitive wheeled vehicles. There were also fewer camps along the overflow route and the camps were considered to be second-rate. It followed a tortuous track alongside the Surma River from Bishenpur to Jhirighat before linking up with the Assam–Bengal Railway terminus at Silchar.

The poor conditions on this overflow route prompted frequent complaints from Indian evacuees and politicians about racial segregation and discrimination. Furthermore, the Indian evacuees were detained in Burma for a very long time so that troops and equipment could get through first. Indeed, there was a six-week delay before the first civilian refugees started arriving along the 'overflow route' and it was not officially opened to traffic until 28 April 1942.

In March 1942, Japanese forward units were so close by that road works could not be carried out on the Burma side of the border. Consequently, the road-building gangs had to concentrate on the narrow, mountainous track linking Yuwa, Tamu, Palel, Imphal and Dimapur on the Indian side of the frontier. It was a heart-stopping journey, while construction on this stretch of the track was underway. Evacuees, soldiers and military equipment hurtled up the track in one direction, while thousands of road-workers and tons of building materials hurtled down in the other direction. The civilian evacuees who were prevented from using the road until the end of April 1942 at least had the consolation of being transported in army lorries along the 164-mile section of new metalled road between Palel and Dimapur. However, Europeans were always ushered into the army lorries first and Indians were always at the back of the queue. Many of them had to walk the whole way to Dimapur through the monsoon rains.

This road-building programme was the local section of a much bigger project. In the long term, it was intended that the military roads would be used in counter offensive operations. There were also ambitious plans to link India and China in order to transport supplies to Chiang-Kai-Shek and his Chinese nationalist forces in Kunming. The first phase of this road-building project (between Ledo and Shingbwiyang) did not begin until December 1942, by which time the civilian evacuation was over. The Ledo Road (or Stilwell Road) as a whole was not completed until *after* the Japanese had surrendered in 1945.[35]

The arrival of 600,000 retreating allied troops on the Chindwin Valley route between February and May 1942 hopelessly complicated an already chaotic situation. The troops had to be billeted in vast military camps that sprawled across 2,000 square miles in Manipur. Many buildings were requisitioned for 'barracks, hospitals, sanatoriums, water-plants, pipelines, and arsenals', and valuable resources such as bamboo, thatch, and timber were cut down to provide shelter and firewood. The troops consumed thousands of tons of imported food.[36] During this time the civilian evacuation became almost a sideshow to the more substantial military operation.

When Monywa fell, at the end of April 1942, evacuees using this route had to join it further north at Mawlaik. The track from Mawlaik to Tamu was only 106 miles long, but it was extremely rough and mountainous. After Tamu, it continued to Imphal. The rapid advance of Japanese units up the Chindwin Valley at the beginning of May forced the evacuees to move northeast to Myitkyina.

***

Only two overland evacuation routes led from Myitkyina to Assam. The most important of these ran through the Hukawng Valley and over the Pangsau Pass. The route ended 271 miles away in Margherita. It was almost impassable at the height of the monsoon season. Indeed, as we shall see, the wet weather caused very serious problems. The monsoon started unusually early in 1942 and was exceptionally severe. The evacuees squelched along the muddy jungle paths. A full account of the evacuation through the Hukawng Valley is provided in Chapters 3 and 4. Evacuees were warned *not* to take the Chaukan Pass route under any circumstances. It was approached by a rough track that started near Sumprabum before disappearing into dense, trackless jungle. The foolhardy souls who attempted this route had to contend with raging torrents, soaring mountains and dense jungles. In theory, the route ended 400 miles away in Margherita, but the trek had never been completed during the monsoon season – even in peacetime. It is not always easy to discover the precise nature of the travails presented on the journey. Minor exaggerations and dissimulations became de rigueur. Distances walked were never underestimated, and times taken to complete treks were rarely overestimated. Personal weight loss became the universal badge of suffering. The more pounds lost, the tougher the journey was considered to be.[37]

***

As conditions worsened the evacuees looked around for scapegoats. J. S. Vorley, Sir Reginald Dorman-Smith and Richard de Graaf Hunter were among the favourite targets, but vested shipping interests, the Government of India, senior army officers, so-called Burmese quislings and even miserable underpaid coolies also came in for their share of blame.[38]

Criticisms of British officials were not always fair. For example, in the early days, J. S. Vorley had only just taken up his post as Director of Civilian Evacuation three days *before* Pearl Harbor was bombed. The civil authorities followed the advice of military pundits, none of whom believed that Japan would invade Burma. Resources were tight, so Vorley, Dorman-Smith and Richard de Graaf Hunter had to scrap for every rupee and every team member. In many cases, they became competitors rather than colleagues. In view of these constraints, it was remarkable that Vorley managed to help thousands of evacuees to escape. His own evacuation organization crumbled at the end of April.[39]

Many evacuees complained about the number of British officers who had abandoned their posts. The number of absentees increased exponentially during March 1942 onwards, until 21 April when the Government collapsed. By then *almost* every post in Burma was unmanned.[40] By the beginning of May 1942, it seemed that only the Viceroy of India stood between the evacuees in northern Burma and disaster. The day was saved by the arrival of the ITA on the scene. Hundreds of ITA tea planters, estate managers, engineers and labourers poured into the remote frontier region of northern Burma and Assam to build camps, set up clinics, repair roads, provide porters and feed the evacuees.

It is estimated that between the end of February and the end of May 1942 approximately 250,000 evacuees crossed into Assam over the frontier routes from northern Burma.[41] On 25 February 1942, officials in Assam had received the first stark warning that this deluge was about to happen. During those months the civilian evacuation became the prism through which the collapse of the colonial project was viewed. Certainly, local tribesmen watched in disbelief as columns of dishevelled Europeans trudged through the torrential rain, while Burmese nationalists could hardly believe their luck. It was a monument to military defeat, colonial failure and official incompetence.

During the evacuation two persistent myths were put to rest. The first was that the administration would collapse as soon as senior British civil servants vacated their offices in Rangoon. It didn't happen, because a cohort of young, inexperienced – but idealistic – Burmese civil servants stepped into the breach.[42] The second myth was that over the decades an unbreakable bond of affection had been forged between colonial families and their Burmese house servants, and that they would hold together through thick and thin. Sadly, the bonds were often broken in the face of extreme danger.[43]

The evacuation was the *faux* beginning of the collapse of colonial Burma. It provided the clearest sign yet that irreversible change was on the way. It weakened the colonial regime in Burma, until it was no longer fit for the purpose. The evacuees were drawn almost exclusively from European, Indian and Anglo-Burmese communities with a smattering of Karen ayahs, Moslem house servants and senior Burmese politicians mixed in. The Burmese people had to stay put. They had little choice but to risk life under Japanese occupation.

The persistent rumours circulating about Burmese fifth columnists were rarely substantiated. Although there were violent episodes, on the whole the Burmese population demonstrated considerable restraint It would have been relatively easy to harass the evacuees when they were at their most vulnerable, but usually ordinary people looked on and learned. They saw that British forces were unable to defend the colony against the advances of a sophisticated and powerful Asiatic foe.

Several evacuation bundled together in a single operation all classes and ethnicities – from the poorest Indian sweeper to the loftiest British administrator. Such haphazard mixing had never happened before in colonial Burma. Races and classes had always been carefully stratified and segregated in the workplace, at home and in leisure.

***

It is not known how many evacuees died on the way out of Burma, but it fairly certain that about 350,000 civilians arrived in India in 1942. This is a relatively small number in the grand scheme of things. Seventy *million* people – many of them civilians – lost their lives during World War II, and forty *million* civilians were forced to leave their homes.[44] The scale of today's refugee problem is even more staggering. In 2015, it was estimated that 1 in 113 of the earth's population of 7.349 billion people was a refugee.[45] In 2017, nearly 1m Rohingyas fled from Burma. In numerical terms, the events of 1942 in Burma seem almost trivial.

Nevertheless, the implications were enormous. It is often the case that evacuees are drawn from the *least* powerful sections of society. A particular group of evacuees from northern Burma in May 1942 captured the world's attention. They were small in number, but they represented the *most* powerful and ostensibly least vulnerable members of colonial society. Moreover, by this time, they could not fly or sail out of the country. They had to walk vast distances in extremely degrading conditions. It was a moment of pure humiliation for the colonial upper-classes. The numbers of evacuees and the large proportion of them who died drew international attention to the Government of Burma's shortcomings. Churchill regarded it as a symptom of colonial failure and official incompetence. He singled out senior British officials (especially Dorman-Smith) as the chief culprits. An attempt was made to hide the consequences, but despite Churchill's efforts the debacle of the evacuation could not be brushed under the carpet. Public interest was too great and too many articulate (and opinionated) individuals were involved.

The local political ramifications were self-evident, as were the effects of the evacuation on subjugated Burmese peoples who witnessed the colonial top brass in headlong flight. British officials and their memsahibs were sans servants, sans status, and sans government protection. It was a major humiliation. There and then, most Burmans realized that the British would probably never return to power. At the same time, many evacuees lost faith in their own abilities, in the Governor, senior officials and the British Army. It shattered the myth that a few colonial administrators could impose their wills on the indigenous population by pretending to be more powerful than they really were. The spell was broken, and the genie could not be put back in the bottle.

The civilian evacuation from Burma was essentially an Indian evacuation. More than 90 per cent of the 350,00 evacuees were Indians.[46] Burmese nationalists regarded the Indians as British lackeys, and without British protection Indians who had lived and worked in Burma for decades knew that their days were now numbered.

The Indian community felt that it had been badly treated by Burmese people and by the British ruling class alike. Indeed, discriminatory practices continued on the trek out of Burma. It prompted the Indian National Congress to leap to the defence of the hundreds of thousands of Indian evacuees. On

28 April 1942 the Congress Party published a damning dossier that fuelled anti-British feelings in India. In Britain, interest focussed exclusively on the fortunes of no more than 3,000 British evacuees, and it was regarded as a British evacuation. The view was reinforced because it was the Europeans, not Indians, who wrote letters describing their experiences to friends and families at home. British newspapers took up the story, presenting it as a sort of oriental British Dunkirk.

Two things had a devastating effect on the evacuees trapped in northern Burma. General Goddard announced on 28 April 1942 that *all* British military forces in Burma would immediately retreat to India, followed by the news that Sir Reginald Dorman-Smith had escaped from Myitkyina to India in a specially chartered plane. It appeared that Burma was completely unprotected and totally ungoverned. It raised questions about the probity of the colonial regime.

The intervention of the Viceroy of India and the ITA underlined the fact that the Governor of Burma and his officials had relinquished control of the colony, and it reinforced the view that May1942 was the de facto end of colonial rule in Burma, even if January 1948 was the de jure end.

In some ways, the civilian evacuation was a metaphor for colonial society. It yoked together dysfunctional groups of people in a bond of total disunity. It provoked simmering dissatisfactions and deep distrust. Indians were suspicious of Burmans, Europeans of Indians, while Eurasians trusted no one at all. Many evacuees lost faith in the colonial project and believed that things would never again be normal, after the war was over.

Now the scene is set. Next will follow a more detailed examination of the evacuation through northern Burma during May 1942. Chapter 2 will focus on the Chindwin Valley route.

2

The Chindwin Valley–Manipur Evacuation Route

Let us make an honourable retreat, though not with bag and baggage
Shakespeare, *As You Like It*, Act 3. Scene 2

By April 1942, most of the escape options from Burma had either been closed down or were too dangerous to attempt.[1] Evacuees still trying to leave the country – and there were thousands of them – were pushed further and further north. By this time the Chindwin Valley escape route offered by far the quickest, easiest, safest and most accessible of the northern overland evacuation routes to Assam, and it was certainly the most heavily used. However, its dangers should not be underestimated. It was a death trap, and an unknown number of evacuees died on the way. For most Europeans and wealthier Indians the plan was to sail up the Chindwin to Mawlaik, then to walk a relatively short distance over the Chin Hills, before being driven in army lorries all the way to Dimapur.

The Chindwin Valley route appealed to three very different types of evacuees. The first group consisted of youngish, reasonably fit European and Eurasian professionals – accountants, lawyers and government officials – many of whom lived in Rangoon and were now in a great hurry to leave.[2] Many of them had made no plans to evacuate until it was almost too late. A few of them drove their own cars up to Mandalay – a distance of 708 miles – but the majority travelled to Upper Burma by train or by Irrawaddy Flotilla Company (IFC) steamer. Once in Mandalay their usual course of action was to catch a slow train to Monywa, where they boarded one of the few IFC steamers still plying up the Chindwin River. From February onwards, these vessels were always dangerously overcrowded. Most of the evacuees in this first category had plenty of cash in their pockets, so they were able to push their way to the front of most queues.[3]

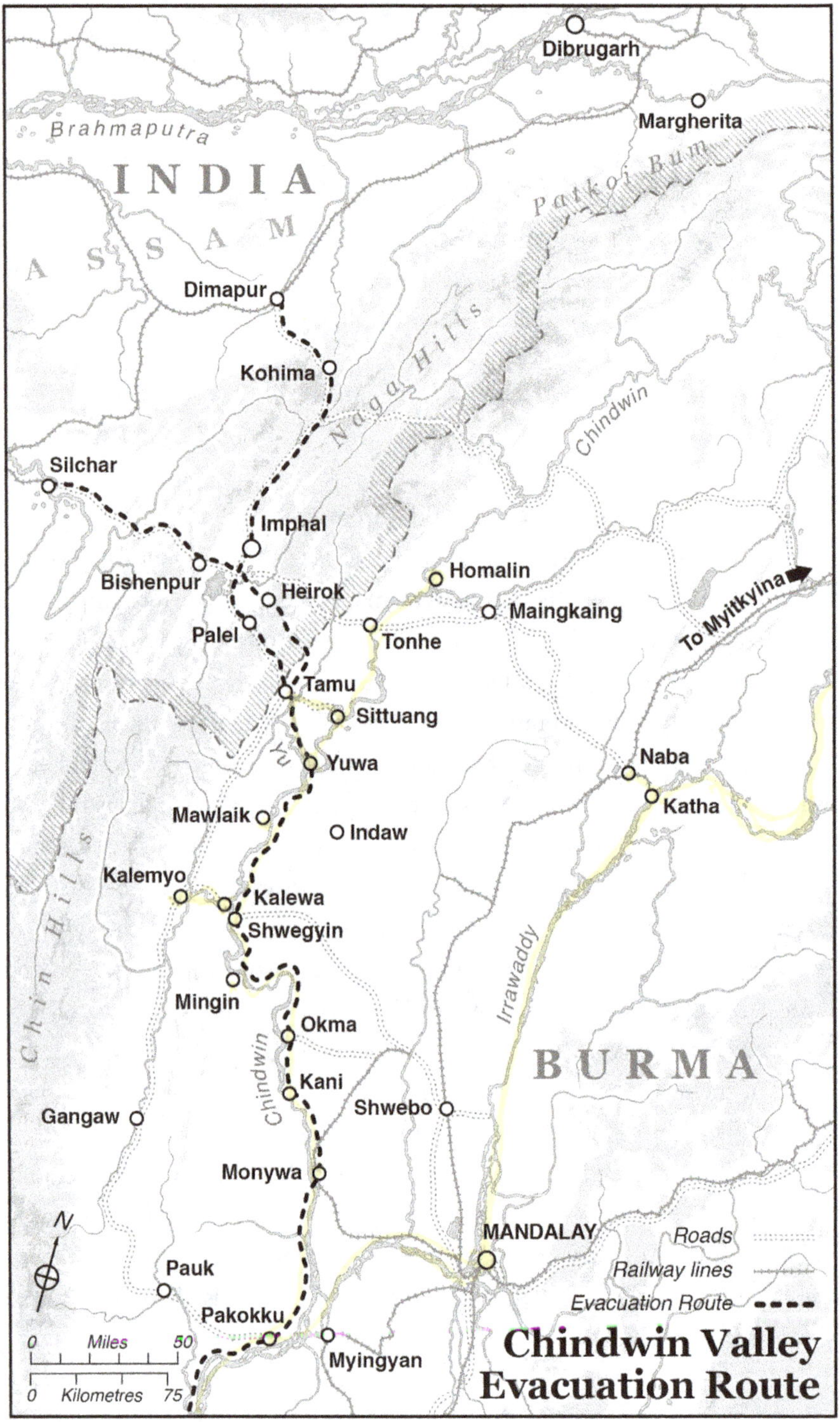

Map 2.1 Chindwin Valley evacuation route

At first, the more gung-ho of the European evacuees happily embraced the spirit of adventure – it was like a rather dangerous game. Many of them worked for one or other of the great trading companies, so benefited from the companies' ample resources and enjoyed the camaraderie of colleagues. A very interesting example of this phenomenon was a group of twenty-two wives of Bombay Burmah Trading Company (BBTC) managers. They and their fifteen children set off from Mawlaik on 23 February 1942. Fifty-six elephants carried their kit and stores. Gangs of coolies had been provided to carry in *doolies* the younger children and four of the mothers who were in the later stages of pregnancy. The party had been issued with tents and camp beds. However, as the mountains became steeper and the track became narrower the number of elephants had to be reduced. Some of the tents had to be jettisoned and the women were forced to abandon some of their luxury items. Each of them was permitted to keep one suitcase and a bedroll.

Cholera struck and the coolies started dying like flies. The women and children had all been inoculated, so they were safe. The company had sent two BBTC forest managers and 'a dentist-doctor chap' to accompany the women. The party spent most nights in roomy but completely unfinished refugee camps. Although the hills were very steep, the scenery was magnificent – so generally, it was a case of 'so far, so good'. The women had to jolly their children along and to feed them and themselves under mosquito nets. Washing was sometimes difficult because it was still the dry season and most of the water had to go to the elephants. All the drinking water had to be boiled, filtered and medicated too. The BBTC looked after the party extremely well – at least, as far as food was concerned. The coolies carried 400 live ducks and 200 chickens and enough vegetables to last them comfortably as far as Palel. They also had quantities of tinned stores and the services of a first-class cook and a baker They had two full meals a day, but they were always hungry because of the open air and exercise.

The daily routine was as follows. They were woken at 5.30 am and got ready at about 6.30 am. They consumed a hasty cup of tea and bowl of porridge in the midst of rolling up bedrolls, screaming children, trumpeting elephants, cursing men and yelling coolies. Then they marched for an hour or so until they reached the next campsite, usually at about 11.30 am or 12.00 noon. They washed, did their hair and brushed teeth, then waited until the elephants arrived with their kit. By this time the children were fractious, so at about 2.00 pm they were all served a jolly good stew and cheese. After that they retired to their straw beds and slept all afternoon until about 5.00 pm. A cup of tea and two slices of bread and jam followed, after which there was time for a gossip and a drink. By the light of candles and one lamp the children were served supper at 6.30 pm, and the women ate theirs directly afterwards. The evening meal usually consisted of soup, duck or chicken and pudding. Then they went to bed and slept like tops.

All went well until they reached Palel. Then their troubles began. They had to leave the elephants and transfer themselves and their belongings onto lorries for a 28-mile ride to Imphal. There they had to sleep in a most unpleasant refugee camp – it was the first camp they had encountered which was not solely for Europeans. They slept on hard bamboo beds in huts that were full of Eurasians and better-class Indians. They only managed to stick the squalor for two days before they 'jumped' on a convoy of army lorries, and set off for the railhead at Dimapur 132 miles away.

By the time they arrived, Dimapur was in such a state of chaos that the BBTC sent up two private railway coaches and lots of stores for them. They had to wait two days until it was possible to attach the coaches to the Calcutta train. Five minutes before the train was due to leave they were told to get out of their coach and find another place. No reason was given. They had to rush across the tracks and pile their belongings into any vacant corner of the train – any space had to do, '*third class or anything*'. There followed an uncomfortable 6-hour train journey.[4]

These women were part of the privileged few occupying the upper echelons of European society. The second category consisted of the poorer Indian manual workers and their families. Their experience was very different. Unlike the British and Anglo-Indian evacuees, they were often grindingly poor, so they had to go through the Chindwin Valley by the cheapest option available. Train, plane, steamer and lorry fares were beyond their means so, in most cases, they had to walk vast distances from Lower Burma to Monywa, where they drew their breath briefly before setting off again.

The third group of evacuees was much smaller in number. It consisted in the main of elderly, sick and infirm Indians. They could not afford to fly to India, so they had to depend on their able-bodied relatives and friends to carry, push and pull them up to northern Burma. The route presented major logistical difficulties, and they were about to encounter their greatest challenge of their lives on the rough, uneven and narrow track over the mountainous section between Tamu and Silchar.

***

The Chindwin Valley route worked tolerably as long as there were relatively few people using the track. Even then it was an extraordinarily complex situation, not least because Japanese forces were never far away. Apart from the river, transport links were non-existent. River launches were limited in size and, by April, the river had fallen to dangerously low levels at the end of the dry season. Moving hundreds of people at a time was out of the question. Difficulties arose when the number of evacuees using the route grew dramatically. Matters came to a head at the end of April and May when large numbers of troops joined the civilian evacuees crowding the escape route.

David Brown was right on the front line while all this was happening He was a senior manager in the BBTC and, between 1 February and 12 May 1942, he was given the rank of Deputy Commissioner and put in charge of the crucial part of the evacuation route between Sittang and Tamu. It was a huge responsibility.

Several boatloads of evacuees arrived in Sittang each day, and the camp was full to capacity day and night. In theory, Brown could accommodate a maximum of 300 people. In practice, many more stayed there and the space was always fully occupied. He faced two main challenges. The first was how to feed such a large number of people, and the second was how to transport them. It was complicated because vast amounts of kit and stores had to be moved around every day, and at the same time he had to provide special transport for non-walkers – that is, the elderly and infirm evacuees and expectant mothers and babies.

Brown had acquired a labour force of 800 coolies together with 200 elephants and 120 mules. In addition to the Sittang Camp, which he managed directly, David Brown was responsible for four other evacuation camps. These were situated at intervals between Sittang and Tamu. To assist him he appointed four Anglo-Indians, each of whom took charge of one of these camps. They were, he said, 'Corporation lads who were absolutely first class and who stayed to the bitter end' (see note 5).

Brown had to keep a close eye on the health situation, as cholera and smallpox were rampant the whole time. To make matters worse, at one point three cases of measles occurred in a boatload of evacuees, so Brown had to segregate sixty women and children from the rest of the evacuees for a period of ten days.

Another of Brown's worries was that Japanese troops were never far away. Indeed, shipping on the river became extremely unreliable towards the end of April, as Japanese troops got closer and closer. There was always a possibility that hundreds of Indian evacuees or British troops might suddenly descend on him at any hour of day or night – and indeed they did. For example, one night Brown had to put up 28 Europeans (including a general and his staff) in his small bungalow as well as 495 Europeans and 1200 Indians in a camp that was designed to accommodate 280. Fortunately, all his 'guests' got away by 8.30 am the following morning, so Brown and his staff had just enough time to clean the place up before 'the next avalanche of people arrived'.[5]

One evening, at the end of April, Brown received a note informing him that the final wave of evacuees would arrive that night and that the very last group of Burmese Government officials would pass through soon afterwards. Brown was instructed to get ready to leave as soon as the officials had moved on. He had to set in hand the final act of 'denial' designed to prevent valuable items from falling into enemy hands. This involved destroying forty-eight steamers and river launches, burning seventy-five bags of paper money and throwing several bags of silver into the river.

After spending four and a half months in Sittang, Brown finally left with the commissioner, his native crew and a group of nine Royal Marines. Brown described them as 'excellent lads'. He learned that the Japanese were only twelve and a half hours behind them. They sailed off on the very last launch on the Chindwin and continued via the Naga Hills. It took them three and a half weeks to reach Assam.

David Brown was an outstanding example of a young man who was unexpectedly thrust into a position of responsibility under extraordinarily difficult circumstances. He took the whole thing in his stride. His account provides an insight into his heavy responsibilities and his personal resilience. People often asked him about his chief impressions of the evacuation. He always answered that it was 'the marvellous spirit and courage of the women folk – European and Anglo-Indian alike. Having left their homes, belongings and husbands behind, with cholera raging in the camps, with the Japs getting ever nearer, they were facing a 120-mile march over terrible country (and most of them with children) with cheerful faces and brave determination'.[6] David Brown was unfailingly positive in the face of awful difficulties, and he always looked for the best in people.

David Brown's story illustrates some of the threats that were omnipresent on the Chindwin route. The first was self-evident – Japanese forces were advancing rapidly towards Pakokku and Monywa. Second, was the fact that at the end of the dry season the river was shallow so navigation was hazardous. The third was that cholera was endemic and at times it threatened to close the Chindwin route completely. A fourth threat was that the rough tracks began to crumble under the increased volumes of traffic. Another threat loomed just around the corner. A massive bottleneck was beginning to develop in Dimapur.

***

The experience of W. I. J. Wallace, ICS, well illustrates the dangers posed by advancing Japanese forces. Wallace was not a typical European evacuee in that he was not particularly young and did not come from Rangoon. However, he followed the same route that most Europeans took up the Chindwin. In that sense, he was archetypical. Indeed, he was a member of that last group of British officials to *sail* up the Chindwin, so he experienced the frenzy at first hand.

Wallace had been the District Commissioner in Moulmein. He had escaped by the skin of his teeth in January 1942 when Japanese troops arrived. As he retreated, he first took over the administration of Thaton and, when the Japanese arrived in Thaton, he took over the Pegu District.[7] He was a steely disciplinarian and severely reprimanded any subordinate officer who was caught trying to run away.[8] He led by example and stayed on duty until it was palpably unsafe to do so. At the last moment, he made his way up to Monywa. In fact, he was one of the very last to arrive at the jetty and was just in time to join a group of British officials who were about to sail up the Chindwin.[9] They were all painfully aware that Japanese units were approaching very rapidly.

Wallace and his colleagues boarded a small launch called the *Zobeda* on 30 April 1942 and they slipped away from Monywa in the middle of a very

Figure 2.1 The *Zobeda* on a sandbank, 4 May 1942. Credit: The British Library Board. The *Zobeda* was a small government launch. It left Monywa at midnight on 30 April as the town was being bombarded. It had a small country boat in tow (also packed with evacuees, so its progress was slow. Both vessels got stuck on a sandbank on 3 May and did not get off until after dawn the next day. The man with folded arms facing the camera is S. R. Rippon, Director of Veterinary Services in Burma.

heavy Japanese mortar bombardment. The *Zobeda* made excruciatingly slow progress, mainly because it was towing a small country boat. Both vessels were packed with evacuees.[10] During the night, the *Zobeda* and its tow went aground on a sandbank. Wallace and his companions spent an anxious 24 hours stuck in the middle of the river.[11] Several times Japanese planes flew low over the *Zobeda*. They were clearly keen to discover the nationality of the passengers.[12]

Figure 2.2 Indian evacuees on River Steamer Constructor. Credit: The British Library Board. The Chindwin river-steamer *Constructor* crowded with Indian refugees. Most evacuees escaping by the Chindwin Valley route were Indians. One can assume that this group were fairly prosperous, for most could not afford the steamer fare.

On 1 May the boats managed to float free on the morning tide and the *Zobeda* continued its painfully slow progress upstream. Advancing Japanese units were still in hot pursuit not far behind. On 3 May, the IFC Steamer *Sind* took the *Zobeda* and the country vessel in tow so that they could make faster progress. The little flotilla moored near Kalewa on 4 May and continued to Mawlaik the next day. Five days later the passengers transferred to a smaller river steamer, the *Constructor*, which took them up the Yu River, where they disembarked and began the 67-mile slog over the Chin Hills. They overtook several groups of elderly and disabled evacuees who were struggling along. They reached Palel on 12 May.

While they were in Palel, the monsoon broke with a vengeance. In the middle of a ferocious downpour they clambered into a fleet of waiting army lorries. They set out along the recently metalled road on the 164-mile drive to Dimapur. The convoy drove non-stop through the torrential rain (something that would not have been possible if they had left at an earlier date). They reached the Dimapur railhead on 14 May.

Wallace's party was extremely fortunate. Large numbers of Indians had no alternative but to walk along this stretch of road, a trek that often took them several weeks to complete. In contrast, it had taken Wallace's convoy just two days.

***

Mention has already been made of cholera. It was a massive threat to the evacuees in the Chindwin Valley. It could very easily have taken more lives than were taken by Japanese action, starvation and exhaustion put together. It is important to bear in mind that cholera had recently closed the Taungup Pass route completely. Now it threatened to close the Chindwin Valley route too. The disease had swept through Prome and had become a major problem in Mandalay and on the refugee routes to the north of the city. Cholera also threatened to wreak havoc in the Hukawng Valley. It was a major hazard.

A major cholera epidemic in the Chindwin Valley would have been trebly disastrous. It would have decimated thousands of evacuees, laid low troops and have caused havoc to the essential labour force. The medical battle waged against cholera was of strategic importance. A huge cholera epidemic was avoided, but only because of the heroic work of two men and their colleagues – Major William McAdam IMS, OBE, his predecessor Lieutenant Colonel E. T. N. Taylor, IMS, OBE and their staff of medical officers, doctors, assistant surgeons, and sub-assistant Surgeons.

Dr McAdam had served as a civil surgeon in Burma before the war. He was commissioned into the Army on 9 December 1941, and posted to Rangoon at the beginning of the Japanese bombing campaign.[13] On 5 January, he took up a senior post at the Dufferin and St Philomena hospitals. His responsibilities included making the necessary preparations for the evacuation of all medical staff, patients and equipment from Rangoon. This was an enormous, complex

Figure 2.3 Major William McAdam, IMS, OBE. Credit: Dr Archie McAdam. Major McAdam was in charge of medical arrangements in the Chindwin Valley in 1942. He did valiant work in keeping disease to a minimum, and was said to have shown calm devotion to duty in all emergencies.

and sensitive task, and it spoke volumes for McAdam's organizational skills that he was entrusted to carry it out. On 20 February, he despatched the first batch of 500 staff together with crates of surgical equipment by train to Mandalay. Three days later, a long convoy of lorries and ambulances set out with the remaining members of staff and large numbers of seriously injured patients, many of whom were stretcher cases.

McAdam followed the convoy by car and he arrived in Mandalay on 7 March. No sooner had he arrived there than he was posted to Monywa. The trains between Mandalay and Monywa had stopped running, so McAdam had to travel by car. The road was very congested, so it took him several days to get to Monywa. His instructions were to relieve Lieutenant Colonel E. T. N. Taylor (Senior Medical Officer in the Chindwin Valley), who was going on leave.

In fact, Taylor had been based further upstream in the Tamu–Kalewa area. He had already dealt effectively with a limited cholera epidemic that had broken out there on 12 March 1942. The most important measures he introduced were the establishment of isolation camps and the inspections of boats and steamers. He had also started a programme of mass inoculation of travellers 'including those who held doubtful certificates of immunity'.[14] These procedures laid the foundation for future action. At that stage, the military authorities decided to take over the Kalewa–Tamu section of the Manipur Road to enable them to deal with future cholera outbreaks.

Taylor had already gone on leave, so it was left to McAdam to deal with any fresh incidents of cholera in the more populous southern section of the valley. McAdam did not have to wait long. The first signs of the disease appeared at the beginning of March, and it began to spread very rapidly. Between 7 and 22 March 1942, a chilling 221 cases were reported and 91 deaths were recorded. The numbers grew each day. There were unexpected side effects. For example, road-building activities had to be suspended because labourers refused to enter infected areas.

McAdam acted with great energy. He inspected each of the refugee camps on the route in turn. The three largest ones each accommodated upwards of 10,000 evacuees. McAdam quickly identified contaminated water supplies, poor sanitary arrangements and foul ground conditions as the principal sources of infection. Furthermore, he was astonished to discover that thousands of unvaccinated evacuees had been allowed to enter Monywa each week.

McAdam immediately embarked on an awareness-raising programme. All members of camp staff were required to 'buy into' three objectives – the elimination of all sources of infection; the prevention of the spread of cholera; and a determination to save lives. To further these aims, McAdam made sure that there were supplies of Phenyle in every camp and that the staff knew how to use it. He set up training courses in preventative medicine and severely reprimanded any official who allowed contaminated clothing to pile up next to drinking-water taps. McAdam visited the District Commissioner and the District Superintendent of Police. He explained the gravity of the situation to them and reminded them that they were duty bound to impose appropriate regulations. For instance, he instructed the District Commissioner to inspect and chlorinate each and every water well in the area, and the Superintendent of Police was required to exclude *unauthorized* (i.e. un-inoculated) evacuees from the centres of all towns.[15] He also tried (unsuccessfully) to relocate all refugee camps from the centres of towns to the outskirts.

McAdam made a point of setting up vaccination centres in every camp, railway station and dispensary, and he regularly inspected each of them. He *personally* inoculated thousands of evacuees. One of the common scenes in the Chindwin Valley was the sight of the Senior Medical Officer inoculating long lines of evacuees, troops, coolies, members of the public, and even his own colleagues.

This 'hands-on' philosophy inspired McAdam's colleagues, who were aware that he performed a great number of operations on seriously wounded troops – often with little equipment and in bomb-damaged hospitals. He was constantly on the go – sailing up and down the Chindwin River or driving back and forth between Mandalay and Monywa. From 18 February to 12 May he was either on the road or on the river for 34 out of 91 days (see Table 2.1). In that time, he covered 380 miles by boat and 1483 miles by car and spent only seven consecutive days in any one place.

He distributed dressings, syringes, needles and vaccines to clinics and floating dispensaries. In the evenings, he kept meticulous records of the number of cholera cases diagnosed, the number of deaths and the number of corpses seen floating in the river.[16] He also found time to head campaigns against smallpox, typhoid and dysentery. McAdam despised slackness and sloppiness in any form. Nothing infuriated him more than the sight of unburied corpses, or the knowledge that a colleague had absented himself from a training session.

It must be emphasized that during the course of all this activity, Japanese warplanes roared overhead and Japanese troops advanced up northwest Burma. McAdam was in constant danger. Indeed, he was in Mandalay and Maymyo during the devastating bombing raids of 3 and 8 April and frequently had to chase off armed dacoits from his clinics.[17] To make matters worse, McAdam was suffering from a pernicious form of malaria that sapped his energy. He once confessed that he was '*deaf* with quinine', but although he was in constant pain he allowed himself no self-pity. Even at his lowest ebb, he admitted only to 'not feeling too good'.[18]

Table 2.1 Major McAdam's travel schedule, 13 February–12 May 1942

Date	From	To	Mode	Distance
13 February 42	Rangoon	Mmawbi	Road	31 miles
24 February 42	Hmawbi	Gyobingauk	Road	98 miles
25 February 42	Gyobingauk	Prome	Road	51 miles
5 March 42	Prome	Yanangyaung	Road	184 miles
6 March 42	Yanangyaung	Myingyan	Road	93 miles
7 March 42	Myingyan	Mandalay	Road	96 miles
8 March 42	Mandalay	Maymyo	Road	43 miles
19 March 42	Mandalay	Monywa	Road	85 miles
23 March 42	Monywa	Okma	River	
24 March 42	Okma	Pindin	River	
25 March 42	Pindin	Myingyan	River	
26 March 42	Myingyan	Kalewa	River	
31 March 42	Kalewa	Okma	River	
1 April 42	Okma	Monywa	River	
2 April 42	Monywa	Mandalay	Road	85 miles
4 April 42	Mandalay	Maymyo	Road	42 miles
8 April 42	Maymyo	Mandalay	Road	42 miles
10 April 42	Mandalay	Monywa	Road	85 miles
14 April 42	Monywa	Aindaing	River	
15 April 42	Aindaing	Mawkadaw	River	
16 April 42	Mawkadaw	Yabaw	River	
17 April 42	Yabaw	Kalewa	River	
20 April 42	Kalewa	Indainggyi	Road	24 miles
22 April 42	Indainggyi	Kontha	Road	22 miles
23 April 42	Kontha	Tamu	Road	60 miles
28 April 42	Tamu	Htinzin	Road	30 miles
30 April 42	Htinzin	Kontha	Road	34 miles
1 May 42	Kontha	Indainggyi	Road	22 miles
2 May 42	Indainggyi	Kalewa	Road	22 miles
3 May 42	Kalewa	Indainggyi	Road	24 miles
4 May 42	Htinzin	Tamu	Road	30 miles
11 May 42	Tamu	Imphal	Road	74 miles
12 May 42	Imphal	Dimapur	Road	148 miles

Source: Major William McAdam's Diary, 1942 (eds. Dr Archie and Dr Helen McAdam).

Although McAdam never boasted about his own achievements, he was unfailingly generous in his praise of others. For example, it was McAdam who wrote the glowing citation for Taylor in 1943.[19] He spoke of Taylor's 'drive and initiative' and insisted that he 'deserved as high an award as anyone in the show'.[20] The truth was that it was McAdam, no less than Taylor, who kept cholera in check. But for the monumental efforts of both men, catastrophe would surely have followed.[21] William McAdam was certainly one of *the* unsung heroes of the evacuation.

***

The very poor road system in the Chindwin Valley could so easily have rendered the evacuation inoperable. The main problems were the mountainous tracks linking the Chindwin Valley and Palel, and the long, tedious track from Palel to Imphal and Dimapur. It was crystal clear that these tracks would be unable to cope, if the numbers of evacuees and troops increased significantly.

This is precisely what happened. Between March and May 1942 approximately 250,000 civilian evacuees and 600,000 Allied troops tried to cross the border into Assam. Of this number, almost all the troops and about 187,500 evacuees followed the Chindwin Valley route to Assam. The track divided into three branches after Tamu – two of the branches continued via Palel to Imphal and Dimapur, and one branch struck off to Bishenpur and Silchar.[22] Otherwise, 22,000–45,000 evacuees trekked from Myitkyina to Margherita in Assam, following *either* the Hukawng Valley route *or* the Chaukan Pass route.

As the troops and evacuees jostled for precedence on the narrow tracks, the Chindwin Valley route almost collapsed. For a few weeks, senior army officers prohibited civilians from using the Chindwin Valley route. Although the embargo enabled retreating troops to get through to India, it created huge problems for the civilian evacuees. However, it was also essential to enable construction workers to get on with major improvements to the road system.

The ITA's first task was to upgrade the 125-mile stretch of road between Imphal and Dimapur. The Army High Command demanded that improvements should be carried out without delay. The existing track was narrow and unsurfaced, and it became impassable during the monsoon season. In order to bring it up to acceptable military standards the road had to be motorable in all weathers and wide enough to allow two 25-ton trucks to pass each other in opposite directions. The War Office pointed out that until the whole project was completed, the Burma Army (together with its heavy equipment) would be unable to retreat to India

Of equal importance was the need to upgrade the track between the Chindwin Valley and the so-called Manipur Road. It consisted of *three* short sections of track on the Burmese side of the border.[23] The plan was to reserve the first section (the 'main evacuation route') exclusively for European and Anglo-Burmese civilians. It would link Tamu with a large dispersal camp at Korengei before joining the Palel–Dimapur Road. The second section would run parallel to the main route from Tamu via Lamlong to Heirok. It would be reserved for

Table 2.2 The Chindwin Valley–Manipur routes to Assam

Route 1 (main evacuee route)	**24 miles**	**Route 2**	**Route 3 (overflow route)**	**90 miles**
Tamu to Mile 57	5 miles	Tamu to Woksu	Bishenpur to Lamatok	12 miles
Mile 57 to Lokchao River	7 miles	Woksu to Lamlong	Lamatok to Kopum	13 miles
Lokchao River to Tengnoupal	5 miles	Lamlong to Sita	Kopum to Lenvoluk	12 miles
Tengnoupal to Palel	7 Miles	Sita to Nangtok	Lenvoluk to Barak	15 miles
		Nangtok to Heirok	Barak to Makru	13 miles
			Makru to Jirighat	14 miles
			Jirighat to Fullertol	11 miles
Palel to Imphal/ Korengei camps by lorry		**Heirok to Imphal/ Koreingei Camps by lorry**	**From Fullertol to Silchar by steamer**	

Source: Geoffrey Tyson, *Forgotten Frontier*, p. 33.

troops and military vehicles and of course, had to be an all-weather metalled road. The third section (the so-called overflow road) was to be reserved for the exclusive use of Indian evacuees. It ran north of the main Tamu–Korengei road at an angle, and was the most difficult of the three sections – It was almost impossible to up-grade the track and it was equally difficult to walk along it. The existing track ran parallel to the Surma River between Bishenpur and Jirighat before it crossed the river and continued to the Assam–Bengal railway terminus at Silchar. The main problem was that everyone and everything passing along the track – be they able-bodied or injured and exhausted evacuees, labourers, building materials, food and medical supplies – either had to walk along the narrow track, or be carried along it by porters (see Table 2.2).

***

The political agent (Manipur) was Mr Christopher Gimson.[24] He was charged with the task of overseeing the movement of thousands of civilian refugees to the railhead at Dimapur, assembling an enormous labour force, supervising a number of road-building projects, and acquiring vast quantities of food for the retreating Army. Gimson was in his late fifties at the time. It was a task beyond his limited resources, and he wisely decided to call on the services of the ITA. For several months, therefore, the Chindwin Valley–Manipur Road evacuation route was under the exclusive control of the ITA.

At the end of January 1942 an ITA quartermaster arrived in Imphal and immediately set about procuring stores, elephants, ponies, bullocks, equipment and building materials. He also erected huts and organized transport for the labourers. A few days later a party of twelve ITA planters arrived in Dimapur to survey the tracks to be upgraded. In no time at all they had completed their work and reported that 75,000 labourers and scores of ITA managers were required on the Chindwin Valley–Manipur Road project. There was a great sense of urgency and the ITA immediately began recruiting labourers and managers.[25] The whole project required a colossal investment since transport, accommodation, equipment, food, doctors, pay clerks, and supervisors also had to be factored into the cost.

During the course of the next few weeks hundreds of coolies were taken by train to Dimapur station, from where they were shuttled in lorries to various construction sites along the route. By the end of February, work began on the Imphal–Dimapur section of the Manipur Road. It was completed within five weeks – an astonishing feat in the circumstances. Vehicles were rolling along the new road by the beginning of April 1942.

At the same time, work got underway on the three sections of track north of Tamu in the Chindwin Valley. The Administrator General, Major General Wood decided that the races should be separated – that Europeans and Anglo-Burman evacuees should be confined to the main evacuation route and Indians to the 'overflow route'. He argued that the overflow route was suitable only for the fittest evacuees (implying that they were Indians), and that by dividing the races the authorities would be able to provide European food on one route, and Indian food on the other. He set up elaborate segregation procedures at Thobal (between Imphal and Palel). Those deemed fit enough to walk along the overflow route were taken by lorry to Bishenpur, where they set off on the 86-mile march to Silchar. Wood felt vindicated when the evacuees who completed the overflow-route emerged exhausted and suffering from malaria. The Indian National Congress was not convinced by his arguments, and his decision subsequently gave rise to bitter complaints about racial discrimination.

Indeed, the Bishenpur–Silchar overflow-route provides an interesting case study. It was only 86 miles long, and little more than a bridle path. It was completely unsuitable for vehicles of any sort – even packhorses were unable to use it. It was difficult to trek along, but even more difficult to construct. Upgrading work on this road began on 6 March 1942, just nine days after the signing of contracts. However, after weeks of hard work the ITA labour force managed to achieve only minor 'cosmetic' adjustments. It remained an unsurfaced, mountainous and slow track, completely unsuitable for vehicles. It was vastly inferior to the metalled roads along the other main evacuation routes, and at least four porters were required to carry one infirm evacuee.

Because there was little suitable accommodation along the route, tea planters and ITA labourers were rushed there in an attempt to remedy the situation. They constructed the first camps at Jiribam, near Jirighat, and at the Makru and Barak river crossings. On 5 and 6 March, long before construction work on the camps was completed, twelve teams of ITA planters and labourers were drafted in to prepare for the imminent influx of evacuees. One team was allocated to each camp on the route and a senior tea planter was designated as 'camp commandant'. This was a key appointment, for each commandant was responsible for recruiting porters to carry in supplies and eventually to help elderly and infirm evacuees along the track. The commandants also had to pay, feed, equip and supervise the labourers and porters, and to ensure that there was enough food and medicines in their camps for the anticipated influx of evacuees. When the evacuees started arriving, the standard drill was that each commandant was responsible for emptying and cleaning their camps once every 24 hours and for making all necessary sanitary arrangements. In some cases, the commandants also constructed or extended their camps. They had to work around the clock in order to meet their deadlines.

Work on the Bishenpur–Silchar track was completed by mid-March 1942, and soon afterward the camps were fully stocked in readiness for the arrival of the evacuees. Frustratingly, however, the first refugees did not arrive on the overflow-road until 28 April 1942. The ITA officials were extremely disappointed. The reason was that senior army officers had been unwilling to allow civilian evacuees to pass along the track until all the troops had got through. On the other hand, European and Anglo-Burmese evacuees continued to use the main route – and at Palel they received a double benefit, because they were also transported non-stop in army lorries along 164 miles of new, metalled road to Dimapur. Meanwhile, Indian evacuees faced two unpalatable choices – they could either struggle to the railhead at Silchar, or walk through the rain to Dimapur.

Ironically the Bishenpur–Silchar route was in use for less than three weeks. Huge sums of money and lots of effort had been invested in it. At one time

30,000 tea garden labourers had been employed on the stretch between Palel and Heirok alone (in addition to the 45,000 garden labourers already employed on other road projects).

They were all housed in camps intended to accommodate troops and refugees. The route was eventually closed when Kalewa was abandoned on 12 May, and two weeks later the last of General Alexander's retreating troops reached India. The other two branches of the Manipur Road were closed soon afterwards.

There was now no real *military* justification for keeping the route open, particularly as Japanese units were not far behind. Major General Wood made it clear that he could neither guarantee the safety of evacuees nor of the camp staff. For this reason, he announced the closure of all the forward camps on the Tamu–Palel and Tamu–Heirok evacuation routes. The ITA camp commandants were released from duty. As they made their way to Dimapur many of them were suffering from exhaustion and dysentery. The remaining refugees feared that they would be overtaken by Japanese troops. Many of them struck off towards Homalin (60 miles north of Tamu) and entered India at obscure frontier posts such as Yarapok, Thobal, Mao and Ukrul. It is estimated that about 37,500 evacuees reached safety in this way.

***

The closure of the Chindwin Valley–Manipur Road evacuation routes highlighted the situation in Dimapur. Since the end of February 1942, the focal point of the evacuation had moved rapidly northwards. One after the other, successive waves of refugees, troops and road-workers swamped Dimapur. The unenviable task of creating order out of chaos had landed in the lap of Major General A. E. Wood (Administrator General Eastern Frontier Projects).

Wood had established his headquarters in a small, unprepossessing, five-roomed dak bungalow in the centre of Dimapur.[26] The dining room acted as a mess and meeting room, and through it traipsed a never-ending stream of high-ranking army officers, ITA agents and government officials. Wood's office was located in one of the two bedrooms and an ITA director was based in the other. It was a surprise to discover that decisions affecting the lives of thousands of men and women were being taken in two rather dingy bedrooms in Dimapur.

Every day between 1 February 1942 and 15 March 1942 about 600 labourers had poured into Dimapur station from one direction, and in the same period, about 350 evacuees per day (making a total of 15,400) had arrived from the opposite direction. By the end of March, the number of labourers passing through each day had risen to 2,500, and during the whole of April about 32,000 refugees passed through Dimapur.[27] The number of evacuees increased day by day during May, and they reached a peak at the beginning of June when 25,000 arrived during the first two weeks.

Against all odds the arrangements had run like clockwork until the middle of April 1942. The procedure was that newly arrived evacuees reported to the refugee camp in Dimapur, where all that day's arrivals were issued with railway tickets, given hot meals and taken by lorry to the station in time to catch the night train to Calcutta. At 10.00 pm each night, as the Calcutta train steamed out of Dimapur Station, the camp commandant and his officials returned to the camp to clear up any mess in readiness for the next day's influx.[28] At this stage, most evacuees were young and fit so it was possible to keep the 'conveyor belt' moving without too much difficulty.

The situation deteriorated in the second half of April 1942. Both the Dimapur Evacuation Camp and Dimapur Railway Station experienced considerable difficulties. Many of the evacuees were in a bad state when they arrived. A considerable proportion of them were injured, sick, infirm or just plain exhausted. A large number of unaccompanied orphans and women with very young children also began to arrive. The turnaround slowed down appreciably. The evacuation camp officials had to provide sickbays and rudimentary crèches for these new sorts of evacuees.[29] At the same time, thousands of troops began to arrive in Dimapur. A large number of them were seriously wounded. The camp hospital was swamped and the more seriously sick patients had to be transferred to the local Tea Labour Hospital or the American Baptist Mission Hospital at Gauhati.

Such was the pressure that, by the beginning of May, the Calcutta trains rarely left Dimapur Station on time. Every train was grossly overcrowded and sick evacuees dreaded the long journey that lay ahead of them. Various volunteer groups stepped into the breach – for example, the Ramakrishna Mission set up clinics on the trains, Lady Reid (wife of the Governor of Assam) opened a Women's Volunteer Service Camp at the Pandu River crossing, and groups of planters' wives provided 24-hour canteens at several stations along the route.[30]

As the volume of traffic reached its height in May and June, railway officials struggled to shift people quickly enough. One narrow gauge railway line ran in and out of Dimapur Station. There was only one platform so no more than twelve trains per day could enter or leave the station. The stationmaster and his assistant refused to give up and they kept the operation moving as best they could.[31]

A further complication was that vast quantities of food and hundreds of crates of heavy equipment also arrived at the station. These were needed for the swollen migrant population and for the ongoing road-building projects. Distributing all this freight was no easy matter. All of it had to be unloaded from railway wagons, divided up, loaded onto trucks and dispatched to scores of different locations – camps, stores, construction sites, bazaars and the like. The existing station goods yard was tiny and it seized up completely. A new goods yard had to be found and, very quickly, everything had to be decanted from one yard to another. At the same time there was an acute shortage of lorries, so urgently needed stores and equipment were often stacked up in the yard for days on end. Road builders, refugees, contractors and soldiers all competed for the available lorries. Major General Wood was left tearing out his hair as he tried to sort out the claims of rival parties. In the end, he tried to requisition 120 tea estate lorries. The ITA responded by creating its own transport organization, complete with repair shops, mechanics, drivers and labourers. It quickly established itself as a reliable service because each ITA convoy of twenty-five lorries was under the firm control of a European planter.

However, the cumulative chaos had dire consequences. The railway system came close to total collapse and the local porters were completely overwhelmed. To sort out the mess, teams of specially selected labourers had to be brought in from the tea garden estates.[32]

The Dimapur Evacuation Camp was in the eye of this storm. Thousands of evacuees queued up to register at the camp. It had been squeezed into a primary school playground next to the railway line and was certainly not the 'place of superior comfort' the authorities claimed it to be. Apart from anything else, during the monsoon the evacuees had to approach it through a sea of thick mud and the death rate rose alarmingly. The camp had one tiny water tank that frequently ran dry even in the rainy season. The sound of engine whistles and clanking railway trucks meant that it was extremely noisy. Moreover, it was intended to be no more than an overnight hostel, so its viability depended on a rapid turnover.[33]

Alexander Beattie was Commandant of the Dimapur Evacuation Camp. He had been the manager of the Woka Tea Estate, where he had a beautiful house and a job he loved. At the beginning of 1942 he accepted the enormous challenge in Dimapur. For the next six months he worked tirelessly to make the Dimapur Evacuation Camp the best it could be.[34] The quality of the meals was very poor when he took over, mainly because food was in short supply in Dimapur. He managed to persuade his colleagues in the tea garden estates to deliver supplies of fresh vegetables and fruit daily to the camp and dispatched his men to scour the local area for good quality rice. Then he hired a small team of renowned Hindu and Moslem chefs.

Beattie refused to be bogged down by red tape. He bypassed regulations and at his own expense brought in seventy skilled tradesmen from the Woka Tea Estate. First, they replaced the old water tank with a brand new 400-gallon tank and installed state-of-the-art plumbing. They constructed a new entrance to the camp, avoiding the thick mud that lay all around. His workmen improved the camp's inadequate sanitation system and built innovative bamboo platforms in the sleeping accommodation. Under Beattie's direction a new camp hospital, dispensaries, isolation wards, kitchens and offices were constructed between February and May 1942.

It was estimated that 30,000 refugees passed through the Dimapur Camp between 27 May and 17 June – 3,200 on 30 May alone. The camp was always full to overflowing. The main reason for this was the chronic congestion on the railway track. The evacuees often had to stay in Dimapur longer than they wished or intended. Others were too ill to move, and several large family groups were unable to move aged dependents.

There were other reasons for the increased numbers. For example, on 10 and 16 May1942 Japanese planes bombed Imphal. It was a terrible shock – the first direct Japanese attack on India. The European Evacuation Camp in Imphal received a direct hit.[35] Ten thousand civilian evacuees were passing through the town. They panicked and made their way along the road to Dimapur. Terrified locals – menials, postal workers, clerks, railway workers and the like – joined them. The ITA camp at Korengei – the so-called Indian Camp – was not bombed, but nevertheless the inmates feared the worst and joined the throng. Imphal ground to a halt. Civilian lorry drivers fled along with everyone else causing acute shortages of food or drink. ITA managers did what they could to pick up the pieces. Lorryloads of supplies were dispatched to Imphal and food and water was dispensed to refugees along the road.

The effect on the Dimapur Camp was devastating. Over several weeks, refugees from Imphal turned up day after day and occupied every bed and every inch of floor space. Most nights the camp accommodated up to 5,000 refugees, many of whom suffered from dysentery, malaria, smallpox and fractured limbs. Beattie and his assistants had to work around the clock and were only saved from complete disaster by two strokes of luck – it only rained twice between 10 and 17 May and there were very few cases of cholera.[36]

During the first two weeks of June an estimated 25,000 evacuees descended on the Dimapur Camp. This was surprising, for by this time all the routes up the northwest flank of Burma were officially closed. Yet stragglers continued to arrive – many of them were walking wounded and stretcher cases. At last the numbers declined sharply from mid-June onwards, and by the beginning of July the Dimapur Camp was almost empty. Only 1,000 refugees passed through the camp during the whole of July (see Table 2.3).

Unfortunately for Beattie the story did not end happily. On 27 June 1942, he contracted typhoid and became seriously ill. He took his first day off work since February when he had started at Dimapur. Since then 150,000 evacuees had passed through his hands. They all owed their lives to Beattie. He died on 12 July. Mr Justice Braund wrote a heartfelt eulogy in which he spoke of Alexander Beattie's 'wonderful work', his 'utter steadiness' and how he had done everything 'humanly possible … always with a kindly word for the distressed'. Indeed, Beattie had given 'his life for the refugees he served'.[37]

***

So far, this chapter has concentrated on the activities after April 1942 and on the people who organized the Chindwin Valley–Manipur Road evacuation route. Little has been said about the evacuees who escaped along it. Surprisingly few of their memoirs, diaries or accounts have survived. Letters written home after the trek make frequent reference to the *effects* of the evacuation including dramatic weight loss, illness, physical suffering and mental trauma. However, the accounts tend to be incidental and retrospective. Perhaps the

Table 2.3 Numbers of refugees passing through the Dimapur camp, 1942

1942	Number
February	7,000
March	25,000
April	36,000
May	51,000
June	28,000
July	1,000
Total	**148,000**

Source: Geoffrey Tyson, *Forgotten Frontier*, p. 50.

memories were too painful, or perhaps the evacuees were too rushed, stressed or exhausted to put pen to paper. The gap is filled by the accounts of two senior European officials. Between them they provide glimpses of conditions on the trek. Unusually neither of them had approached the Chindwin Valley–Manipur Road from the southwest.

At the beginning of 1942 Colonel J. S. Vorley was the evacuation commissioner and he held the fate of thousands of refugees in his hands. At the end of April, he suddenly became an evacuee himself. Vorley's escape route zigzagged wildly from the northwest of Burma to the northeast and back again to the northwest, ending up in Dimapur.

Vorley and his colleague Dr Lusk had spent the night of 30 April in Shwebo, when Japanese aircraft finally destroyed the airstrip there. They squeezed into an open cattle truck full of wounded Chinese soldiers on a train bound for Naba, and arrived 64-hours later on 2 May. The tiny British garrison had abandoned Naba on 5 May. Later that day, Vorley assembled a party of about fifty people that included several of his former colleagues, a tobacco merchant, a missionary, two IFC captains and an old man from Hong Kong. They set off from Naba at dawn on 6 May in a convoy of requisitioned vehicles. Japanese reconnaissance planes flew overhead as they drove off. When they reached the Uyu River they abandoned the vehicles and piles of heavy items (including several heavy bags full of silver rupees). They were astonished when General Stilwell and a long column of troops, Indian coolies and tons of military equipment passed by in the opposite direction.

Two of Vorley's most trusted lieutenants, Bob Forrest and Andrewartha, fell ill on the way – one with dysentery and the other with phlebitis. Therefore, Vorley decided to divide his party into two. Lusk led a 'sick group', and Vorley led the 'fit group'. When the monsoon broke on 11 May, Vorley's 'fit' group constructed primitive rafts on which they careened dangerously down the river. They reached Homalin on 14 May to find notices warning evacuees that the town was 'closed to visitors' because of threatening behaviour of armed Chinese soldiers. Kalewa had fallen at about the same time, and Japanese units were advancing rapidly up the Chindwin. Vorley and his party moved on as quickly as possible along an overgrown path that went up and down a succession of steep ridges. They were hot, exhausted, hungry and dehydrated.[38] To make matters worse, they were frequently held up behind long processions of slow-moving Indian refugees. This part of the track was littered with dead and dying evacuees.[39]

Vorley's 'fit party' eventually crossed the Indian frontier at the remote Naga village of Kanpat, which was perched on a 5,000ft-high ridge. Groups of aggressive Manipuris demanded money as the party descended into Assam. On 21 May – after walking 240 miles in fourteen and a half days – they reached the village of Yarapok.[40] From here they were taken in bullock carts to the main Tamu–Imphal road where a fleet of army ambulances took them onto Imphal. Vorley was interrogated for several hours in Imphal by two Indian Army majors.[41] When he was released, a fleet of army lorries took the whole party all the way to Dimapur. They caught a train to Calcutta on 23 May and two days later Vorley reported to the Burma Secretariat in Simla.

Meanwhile Lusk's 'sick party' fared worse. They reached Calcutta a long time after Vorley. Two members of the party had died, and Major John R. Pughe was badly injured so was left behind in Burma. He was captured and executed as a spy. Another member of Lusk's party, Ricketts, had opted to stay behind in Burma. He led a party of ninety-two refugees by a back route to India. They arrived in Dimapur after a terrible journey. A number of them had died on the way and Ricketts himself developed severe lung problems from which he never recovered.[42] Subsequently, Vorley lost three other colleagues: John Richard Elton-Bott died in Assam and Stanley Booth-Russell and Robert Forrest died in India.

***

The story of Henry Seppings and his family's escape during May 1942 illustrates not only the extreme dangers, but also the way in which the northern evacuation routes criss-crossed one another. The Seppings family had lived in Shwebo for several years before the war.[43] Henry Lockyer Seppings was the superintending engineer in Shwebo. He left Shwebo with his family, when the town was bombed on the 30 April. They managed to catch the last train from Shewbo to Myitkyina. They arrived in Myitkyina on 5 May, and on 6 May 1942 they were among the thousands of evacuees hoping to board a plane at the airstrip. They saw the Japanese bombing raid at close quarters, and afterwards realized that they must leave Myitikyina as quickly as possible – not only because of the tragedy at the airstrip, but also because of the fast approaching monsoon.

The whole family squeezed into the black Ford Sedan, which was driven by Mrs Sepping's brother, Claude Blazey.[44] They drove out of Myitkyina past the airstrip and eventually skirted around Mogaung and Indaw to the north of Myitkyina. They then turned off the road onto an obscure traders' track. A group of forest officers had told Henry Seppings about this little-known cross-country route to the Kabaw Valley. The track was narrow, deeply rutted and strewn with huge boulders. It was also extremely hot so the engine overheated and the radiator burst. They were forced to abandon the car and continue on foot. They made very slow progress, but after several days they eventually reached the Kabaw Valley (known as the 'Valley of Death').[45]

Because it was at the end of the dry season the earth was bare and tinder dry. Most of the vegetation had died and only a few spiny shrubs had survived. Rocks and boulders were strewn everywhere. It was ferociously hot not just during the day, but also at night. When they set up camp each night Henry Seppings and his family had to construct a barrier of thorns around them for protection against prowling animals. They trudged through the Kabaw Valley for several days, and during the whole time they did not see another human being. At last they reached the Chindwin River. They stood and gazed at the Patkai and Chin hills, which rose steeply from the opposite bank. The river was at its narrowest, deepest and most turbulent at this point, but after protracted negotiations with local fishermen they were ferried across to the other side in return for Henry Seppings's Rolex watch.

The next day was extremely exhausting. The Seppings party hacked its way through dense jungle in sweltering heat. As they did so, they became uncomfortably aware that a group of Lulung tribesmen armed with spears and machetes was following them. Fortunately, the men took fright and turned back as soon as they reached the main Imphal–Dimapur road.

The traffic on the road was very light. A few bullock carts trundled by and large groups of Indian refugees shuffled along towards Tezpur, Dimapur and Dibrugarh. They pushed carts and carried enormous bundles on their heads. A lorry stopped to pick up Alwyn Seppings and his family. It took them to Dimapur where they spent the night in the Dimapur Evacuation Camp – in the care of Alexander Beattie. ITA officials interviewed them. They looked up the records and confirmed that some of Henry Seppings's relatives had already crossed into India and were now staying in Allahabad. Alwyn Seppings was required to hand over his precious colt revolver to the officials, who promised him that the gun would be returned, if he could produce a firearms certificate.[46] They were then issued with railway warrants to Allahabad, and left on the train to Calcutta soon afterwards.

***

The Chindwin Valley–Manipur route was immensely important because it provided a mass overland escape route for tens of thousands of civilians and military personnel. However, it was also beset with problems. There was racial distrust, roadwork disrupted the flow, and there were terrible health problems. Nevertheless, the courageous endeavours of individuals like David Brown, William McAdam and William Beattie, as well as cohorts of ITA planters and anonymous labourers and porters enabled thousands of evacuees to reach safety. It should not be forgotten that despite their efforts thousands of evacuees (many of them unknown) died along the way.

***

3

The Hukawng Valley to Margherita: Part One

The rain it raineth every day.

Shakespeare: *King Lear,* Act 3. Scene 2

Chapters 3 and 4 are part of a continuum. They cannot properly be separated, nor can the journey from Mogaung through the Hukawng Valley to Margherita be divided into two. Both chapters are concerned with the same set of events, so there is bound to be some overlap between them. Chapter 3 describes the experiences of groups of evacuees travelling along the route. It will also examine the extraordinary phenomenon of Shingbwiyang and its amazing young Commandant, Cornelius North. Chapter 4 will concentrate more on some of the underlying themes – the phenomena of death, and the Bishop Strachan Home, and the role of the Indian Tea Association (ITA), for example. It will also examine the final days of the Hukawng Valley route as the evacuation came to an end.

June and July are the wettest months in northern Burma. The average monthly rainfall is 30 mm and the temperature reaches 90°F on most days. It is unremittingly hot and sticky. In 1942, the rains began unusually early and fell with exceptional venom. In most parts of the frontier between Burma and Assam the monsoon began on 10 May and the rain continued to fall almost without ceasing for the next thirty days. It drenched the refugees wending their way through the Hukawng Valley and the Chaukan Pass and transformed gentle streams into raging torrents. The rain continued to fall with a vengeance throughout June and much of July. A situation that was already difficult became one of extreme peril, for the rain affected every minute of the evacuees' lives during that whole time.

Sir Reginald Dorman-Smith had flown from Myitkyina to India on 4 May 1942, just before the rains started. The colonial political infrastructure had

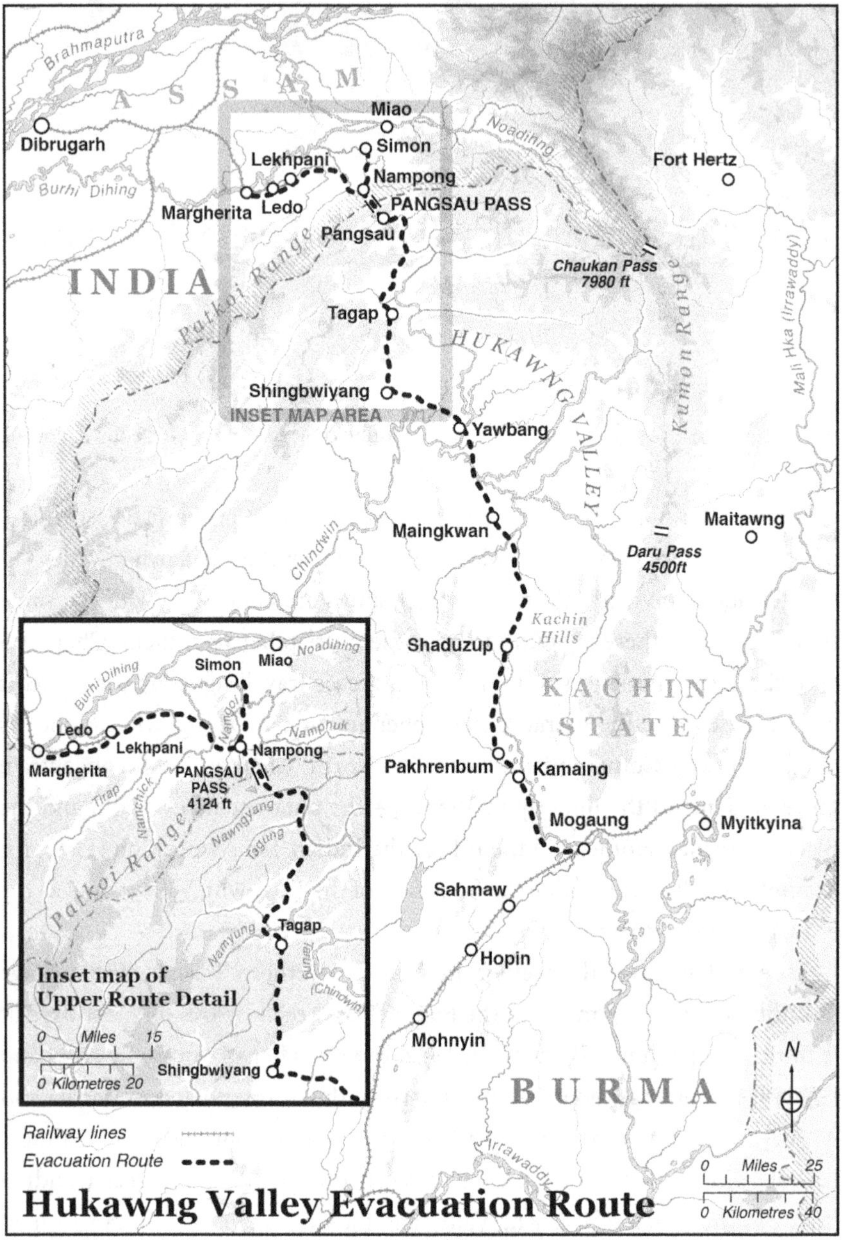

Map 3.1 Hukawng Valley evacuation route

collapsed and Japanese troops were advancing towards Myitkyina, which was the last British toehold in Burma.

Before he flew out, Dorman-Smith designated R. S. Wilkie ICS (Commissioner for the Sagaing Division) to be the 'Governor's Representative in Burma'. Wilkie was now the most senior official in the country. It was a poisoned chalice. He was a prime target as far as both Japanese invaders and Burmese nationalists were concerned. He was understandably nervous, for in those perilous times, it was perfectly possible that he would fall into enemy hands. If that were to happen he would become the 'poster-boy' of the British collapse.[1] The rain both helped and hindered. It caused the Japanese advance to grind to a halt but also reduced the evacuation to a snail's pace.

Japanese planes bombed the airstrip at Myitkyina on 6 May. It was a moment of unalloyed tragedy. Nowhere was now safe. Two Dakotas were destroyed on the runway. Both planes were full of women and children evacuees, who were killed in the conflagration. The moment of truth had arrived. Very soon Burma would have to be *formally* abandoned. On the evening of 6 May, Wilkie convened an emergency meeting in Government House. The few remaining civilian and military officials attended. Most officials had already left. Important decisions had to be made.[2] Brigadier Upton was the garrison commander. He announced that his British and Indian troops would march out of the town the following morning. Where they would go was unclear. Everything else followed: non-Burmese civilians were to be instructed to leave Myitkyina immediately. Many of them had already done so. Several hundred had left Myitkyina Railway Station for Mogaung that very morning. Wilkie's colleagues estimated that about 800 non-Burmese civilians still remained in the town. Not all of them were young or fit enough to travel. They were to be advised to stay put and hope for the best. A few civilians still loitered hopefully at Myitkyina airstrip. They refused to believe that the last flight had gone. They forlornly hoped that one more plane would land and take them to India. They were wrong. Otherwise all able-bodied civilians were encouraged to start walking to India at first light the next morning.[3]

Wilkie and his colleagues worked late into the night. They had to put in place their own escape plans. So they gathered together what food they could, and assembled a fleet of battered old vehicles. They intended to drive off towards Sumprabum the following day, and then walk to Margherita in Assam.

They still had not agreed on what route to take beyond Sumprabum. Those who favoured the Hukawng Valley route pointed out that the Burma Frontier Service had set up rice dumps at regular intervals along the way, and that the Government of India had promised to provide food and shelter in the camps beyond Shingbwiyang. Supporters of the Hukawng Valley route had also read the leaflets circulating in the town warning evacuees not to risk going by the Chaukan Pass, which was the only alternative route. Wilkie was in a minority of one. He favoured the Chaukan Pass route. He had heard reports of cholera and food shortages in the Hukawng Valley and he feared that Japanese units were about to cut off the road between Mogaung and Mainkwan. He also thought the Chaukan Valley route would give him a chance to say goodbye to isolated Kachin hill tribesmen in the north of the district.[4] It was pure romanticism. His colleagues protested that this was not the time for fine gestures. Nevertheless, they agreed to defer the final decision until they got to Sumprabum, where they would take local advice.[5]

Wilkie and his colleagues were about to drive off from Government House early in the morning of 7 May. Suddenly Japanese planes flew low over the town. The airstrip was bombed yet again. Wilkie and his party stood and watched from the Government House veranda as fires blazed across the town.[6] When the planes had flown off, the convoy drove through burning rubble along the road towards Sumprabum. There were nineteen people in Wilkie's party. The list was impressive. It read like a colonial *Who's Who* – the Controller of Finance, Arthur Potter, ICS and the Defence Secretary, Gordon Apedaile, ICS were both very senior members of the Governor's Secretariat. The Deputy Commissioner Myitkyina, R. E. McGuire, ICS, Secretary to the Financial Commission, R. R. Langham-Carter, ICS and the ADC to the Governor, Eric Battersby were also very high-ranking government officials. Edmunds and Sett Kaing were senior officials of Burma Railways; C. T. Bogg was a distinguished official in the Burma Forestry Service. He was Director of the Maymyo Botanical Gardens; L. O. Nell was a friend of the Dorman-Smiths and U Aye was an executive officer of the Rangoon Corporation. He was married to an Englishwoman.[7] Naik Sheriff, an Indian Army Lance Corporal, Wilkie's Indian cook, an Anglo-Indian electrician from Government House and two of his female relations and their Indian ayah also travelled in the party.[8]

A few miles down the road, Wilkie and his companions stopped for a moment. They looked back towards Myitkyina for the last time. Yet another air attack was underway. Alistair Rose had turned into the drive of Government House at just that moment.[9]

The road to Sumprabum was in a terrible state. There had been a cloudburst and many vehicles were stuck in thick mud. Others had been set on fire and left to burn. Wilkie and his colleagues progressed extremely slowly, but their convoy ground to a halt completely on 8 May at the village of Maihtaung. They abandoned the vehicles and asked local people about the relative merits of the Chaukan Pass and Hukawng Valley routes.[10] The advice was unanimous. The Chaukan route was impassable. At last, Wilkie had to accept that they had no alternative but to go via the Hukawng Valley.

A key date was 10 May. It marked the first of thirty days of continuous walking, and the first of thirty days of continuous drenching rain. It was a terrible combination, and the monsoon closed in for the remainder of the trek. At a junction, some thirty miles south of Sumprabum, the party turned off the road towards the Daru Pass. It led into the Hukawng Valley. Wilkie still feared that they might come up against Japanese patrols. However, his fears were unfounded and in the event, they did not see a single Japanese patrol all the way to India.

On the 10 and 11 May the party managed to cover only thirteen miles. They were weighed down by heavy loads and laboured up one steep, muddy hill after another. Porters – or lack of them – presented constant problems. On 10 May, Wilkie had dragooned nine reluctant Hmong coolies into service as porters, but they were hopelessly overburdened, unenthusiastic and deeply disgruntled.

On 12 May, one of the porters seized a gun and ran off into the jungle. His load had to be distributed between the remaining eight coolies, making them even more disgruntled than before. Thereafter, whenever Wilkie managed to persuade Kachins or Hmong hill tribesmen to act as porters, but they melted away one by one over the next few days. In desperation, Wilkie bought four bullocks and a cart to carry the kit. The bullocks were unbelievably slow, and the carts sank deeper and deeper into the mud. The party had to throw away all non-essential articles of clothing and equipment and to carry their own kit. By the time they reached India they had nothing but the clothes they stood in.

At night, Wilkie and his colleagues were forced to huddle together in filthy coolie camps that stank of human excrement. On 14 May they reached the settlement of Naiding. It was like many other villages on the route. Chinese soldiers had got there before them. As always, they had looted the livestock, ransacked the houses and driven the villagers away, leaving the place deserted and ruined. In fact, very few villages offered shelter of any sort, and Wilkie and his colleagues discovered that many of the flimsy bamboo huts contained the corpses of cholera victims. In these cases, the only recourse was to burn the huts over the corpses.[11]

One of the major problems the party encountered was that their shoes were constantly being dragged off in the glutinous mud. As a result, they all suffered from foot blisters. These often turned septic. Without medicines or bandages they could merely wipe their feet with filthy rags in the evening. Occasionally the RAF dropped crates of boots, but they rarely fitted and tended to do more harm than good. One Anglo-Indian man in Wilkie's party suffered from such severe foot blisters that he was unable to walk. At first, they slung him over a bullock and when this was too excruciating they put him into a bullock cart. Periodically the cart got stuck in deep mud and the man lagged further and further behind. He was last seen hobbling along by side of the track – presumably to die. Such were the brutal realities of life in the valley

Wilkie could not help noticing the complete absence of government officials in Maingkwan, which was an important regional headquarters. Indeed, very few British administrators had remained at their posts anywhere. Wilkie had one stroke of luck. The usually marauding Chinese troops had overlooked a small store of undamaged rice in Maingkwan, so he and his colleagues were able to enjoy a rare cooked meal.[12] When they left the town, Wilkie's party had to be ferried across several swift-flowing rivers, while the bullocks swam by their side.

By 20 May the evacuation through the Hukawng Valley was in full swing. A steady stream of hundreds of civilian refugees, many of them weak and hungry, came along the track. They were interspersed with soldiers, some of whom had been prematurely released from hospital and looked like skeletons clad in rags, and some of them had no boots. There were groups of Sikhs and Punjabis of the Burma Frontier Force (BFF) with tiny pack-ponies, a 150-strong detachment of the BFF and groups of Chin troops.

***

Percy Salkeld had just arrived in the Hukawng Valley. He was a senior manager at Steel Brothers & Co. Ltd. (Steels) and was in charge of the Steels rice office.[13] What Salkeld did not know about rice, its properties, its price and the rice market was not worth knowing. He was a remarkable man and well used to danger. He kept a very detailed diary of his journey. He had started from Shwebo, had slogged through the Hukawng Valley and paused briefly in Shingbwiyang, before going over the Pangsau Pass and on to Margherita.

Two things were unusual about P. G. G. Salkeld. First, he described his journey in vivid detail, analysed the dangers, commented on moral issues and described his travelling companions with compelling candour. Second, a string of twenty-two Steels elephants carried him and his party. The elephants were very well behaved, and they added a whole new gloss to the journey

Salkeld had been in Mandalay on 3 April when the town was bombed. He had stayed on in the city until the end of the month, but it was a grim place. It was 110°–117° F in the shade and there was no clean water, no electric light, no fresh food and no *punkah*. Like many prominent Europeans, he was 'militarized', elevated to the rank of lieutenant colonel and his unit was renamed the 'Rice Buying Section'. On 25 April, Lieutenant Colonel Salkeld moved on to Sagaing and the next day he moved on again to Shwebo, where he watched the area being bombed several times. On 28 April, his colleague, John Kennedy arrived in a Steels launch, and another colleague, Pani Waters (the Steels Bassein Manager) arrived on the same day. At this point the small group of Steels senior executives moved up to Katha where they met with two other Steels men by the name of Clark and Scales. The next morning they all set off for Myitkyina. They arrived in Bhamo on evening of 2 May, just before the Japanese arrived. Moving straight on, they reached Myitkyina on 4 May. Here they joined up with four more Steels engineers. P. G. G. Salkeld, who was a man of high moral principles, felt that these men had not been properly looked after. He blamed their misfortune on 'a lack of a sense of responsibility in the right quarters – one of the most tragic common failures both in senior Government and Civilian circles'[14] in Burma. They all decided to make their way to India via the Hukawng Valley as quickly as possible.

They went to the Myitkyina Railway Station early the next morning and in the midst of chaos they found an empty cattle truck. They piled their kit into it – and there they were – sundry Steels people (five Europeans and twenty Indians) in a train full of evacuees, most of whom were walking wounded. On the way to Mogaung, which was 40 miles back along a single railway track, they had to move two abandoned trains before their train could move on. On every incline, everyone had to get out of the train and push. It took nine hours to cover those forty miles.

At Mogaung, they met yet another Steels man. His name was Edmeades. He was an elephant expert who was working on the first section of the Ledo Road. Edmeades arranged for a lorry to take them to Shwedizup (64 miles away). Here they met Mitchell, who was a Steels rice engineer. He helped them buy ten bullock carts, which they then used to carry their kit, and off they set off for Maingkwan 55 miles away.

They had a stroke of luck at the remote village of Htinkawk. Kennedy came across an old elephant headman by the name of Maung Myo, whom he had known when he was a small boy. Maung Myo managed to persuade twenty-two elephant men to join Salkeld's party together with their elephants. The cavalcade moved forward. They covered 10 to 15 miles per day (elephants cannot do more than that) and reached the administrative HQ at Maingkwan on 9 May. Ferrier (an ex-Steels Forest Assistant) joined them here together with Slator, and Major Fuller of the Royal Signals.

Salkeld's party now consisted of John Kennedy, James Ferrier, G. B. Dent, H. P. West, J. H. Slator, P. Dewar, E. Soord, J. Smith, H. Mitchell, and P. G. G. Salkeld (all of Steels), plus J. Crawford and E. Taylor (Government Forests); J. Crawford (Royal Corps of Signals) and J. Blaquiere (Assistant, Government HQ, Maingkwan). There were also twenty-three Indians (mainly launch crews and personal servants). It was raining heavily and the track became difficult. It was 'just a path through dense jungle'.[15] Salkeld could thank his lucky stars that because he had twenty-two elephants and ten bullock carts, he was infinitely better off than most evacuees.

They left Maingkwan on 10 May. They paid off the bullock cart drivers and loaded all the kit onto the elephants. After three days of marching, they reached the village of Yubang on the Turung Hka. A ferry was still plying across the river, but it became very unsafe when panicky crowds overloaded the boat. Salkeld decided that his elephants were the safer option. Over the next few hours, the elephants carried scores of people across. Unfortunately, one elephant and a boy were swept away in the swollen river and drowned. It was a reminder of the lurking dangers. As the path became narrower, Salkeld and his colleagues 'passed a number of corpses both human and animal – the former were mostly Indians who had died from exhaustion or cholera'.

After a very long walk they eventually reached Shingbwiyang, which provided a natural break. The party lingered in the settlement for a full day to rest and dry out their kit. Half the elephant men refused to go any further, but fortunately the other eleven were willing to continue with them into Assam. In Shingbwiyang Crawford and Blaquiere also decided to leave Salkeld's party and to go off on their own. Salkeld chose not to stay in the evacuation camp, but for the moment we will pause and pick up Salkeld's story again later.

***

The Naga settlement of Shingbwiyang was situated at the head of Hukawng Valley. Although Salkeld and his party did not stay in the evacuation camp, thousands of other evacuees did. Indeed, it was calculated that from May to October 1942 about 45,000 civilian evacuees and Chinese soldiers passed through the camp in the space of five months.[16]

Shingbwiyang lay at the foot of the Naga Hills. Before the war it was regarded as one of the most remote, primitive, and most unremarkable outposts in the British Empire. Now it was bursting at the seams; it was the last evacuation camp on the Burmese side of the Indian frontier and the main refugee junction in the Hukawng Valley. It consisted of half a dozen dismal thatched bamboo huts. Shingbwiyang was devoid of local food supplies, sanitation, medical facilities and any other amenities.

Although the camp itself was uncompromisingly awful, almost everyone spoke glowingly about the efforts of the resolute and courageous young Burma Frontier Force (BFF) political officer – Cornelius North – who had been put in charge of the camp in Shingbwiyang. At the tender age of twenty-five, North was suddenly given responsibility for this hideously bloated operation.[17] It must be borne in mind that many of North's superiors had already 'jumped ship' and fled to India, so he was almost entirely on his own, assisted only by a handful of unreliable policemen. However, he stayed at his post in Shingbwiyang through thick and thin for months on end, and did not leave until the last evacuees had moved on in October 1942. He played a heroic part in the evacuation.

Geoffrey Tyson paid this tribute to Cornelius North. He confronted a situation that would have turned many a more experienced man's reason. But throughout the long monsoon months he stuck to his post in Shingbwiyang, and by his own personal example and the exercise of strict discipline and an iron will he prevented a tragedy from becoming a wholesale disaster. At one point with both Chinese troops and refugees on his hands, North's troubles were almost unsupportable. The death rate had risen to fifty a day, and North was having great difficulty in burying the corpses, while the Chinese, armed but hungry, were disposed to demand more than their fair share of the very limited quantities of the food available. But he carried manfully on, and for services to his fellow men, which rank with the great epics of siege warfare, a grateful government awarded him with the MBE.[18]

North had to deal with some very difficult issues. There were frequent outbreaks of malaria, dysentery and other diseases. He had no medicines (apart from those that were very occasionally dropped by air) with which to treat sick refugees. Nor did he have any way of communicating with the outside world until, very late in the day, a system of dak runners was established and he was given an unreliable wireless transmitter. For a long time therefore, no one outside Shingbwiyang – neither the ITA nor the Indian or military authorities – had any idea of the dire conditions in Shingbwiyang.

Shingbwiyang did have one great advantage. It was one of the very few places where RAF planes could drop supplies twice a day. However, even this was a mixed blessing. It meant that North had to prevent unsupervised and heavily armed Indian and Chinese soldiers from grabbing the packages as they hit the ground. They sold the airdropped items at exorbitant prices. They also left a trail of deserted villages in their wake, shooting anyone who got in their way. These men frequently managed to infiltrate the Shingbwiyang camp, and North had to post armed guards around the RAF drop zone. Unfortunately, the guards were also quite capable of stealing a bag or two. Lawless Shingbwiyang may have been, but at least it provided shelter, and the RAF airdrops ensured that stocks of rice and dahl were usually available. The unremitting monsoon rain often encouraged evacuees to linger in Shingbwiyang for weeks on end. This put pressure on North's dwindling food stocks. Most of the evacuees were already extremely weak by the time they arrived in Shingbwiyang and the death rate in the camp was very high.

Wilkie and his party stayed on in the camp for a few days in order to give Cornelius North a helping hand.[19] In return, North gave Wikie an RAF parachute, which proved to be invaluable as he continued over the Naga Hills, where there was no shelter of any kind. Suffice it to say that Wilkie was very impressed by North.

Herein lies a mystery. One family (but it seems, only one), was highly critical of the young BFF officer. Major Brookes was an elderly Anglo-Indian Army doctor. He was English and his wife was Burmese. Their three children, Maisie, George and Stephen (who was only eleven years old at the time) were a tight-knit, intelligent family. They had lived in Maymyo before the war and only narrowly had escaped disaster at the Myitkyina airstrip on 6 May 1942. Fifty years later Stephen Brookes was to describe the family's experiences in the Hukawng Valley.[20] He wrote an elegiac account of the monsoon, which broke on 12 May. It 'saturated the thick jungle and cascaded down the mountain slopes in a brown slurry', creating 'knee-deep quagmires of thick gooey mud … and 'barriers of deep swirling water'. But Stephen recalled that at night the family had to sleep on wet earth in dilapidated huts, covered in leeches, sandflies and mosquitoes, and observed that death was so common that it 'was briefly mourned by near relatives but ignored by the passing crowd'.[21]

Stephen Brookes described how on 16 June 1942, a group of armed Chinese troops attacked their family. They molested Stephen's older sister, Maisie, and stole their meagre possessions. It was humiliating, for they were powerless to resist, and no one helped them.[22] A few days later, the same thing happened again. On this occasion their assailants stole their last few coins and a precious gold watch. Major Brookes suffered a serious breakdown. He felt angry, ashamed, frustrated and impotent. Mrs Brookes became more and more dispirited, Maisie contracted cerebral malaria, and even the eleven-year-old Stephen Brookes began to feel that the 'struggle was pointless'.[23]

As luck would have it, the Brookes family arrived at Shingbwiyang on exactly the same day that Wilkie's party arrived. Stephen Brookes published his memoirs, *Through the Jungle of Death* in 2000, nearly sixty years after these events. He claimed that Wilkie's party and his family were treated very differently – that Cornelius North invited Wilkie and his colleagues to a meal in his 'big house' on the hill and provided them with food from the godown. They were allowed to leave the camp at any time. By contrast, he claimed that the Brookes family was ignored. The reasons were understandable. Wilkie was the Acting Governor of Burma. His presence in the camp created security problems. Cornelius North was a very young BFF officer at the time and he felt duty-bound to offer Wilkie a modicum of privacy. It cut no ice with Major Brookes. He muttered that only money, status and race talked in colonial Burma, which operated on an, 'old boys' network', and accused Wilkie and his colleagues of enjoying too cosy a relationship with Cornelius North. Furthermore, Major Brookes suggested that he had known Cornelius North before the war and had once given him a meal in his house in Maymyo. He implied that North owed him a favour.[24] There is no external evidence to corroborate these claims, and it is probable that Cornelius North was well used to receiving demands from evacuees expecting preferential treatment.

Of course, Major Brookes is to be admired for wanting to do the best for his family. He was an Englishman, but his wife was Burmese. His family had been discriminated against in the past. Therefore he took exception when his family was lumped together with all the other evacuees. They were 'incarcerated' in a grossly overcrowded Naga longhouse with a hundred or so Indian and Anglo-Indian evacuees. It was not pleasant. Stephen Brookes described how each inmate was issued with a 'bed' that consisted of a small square of grubby hessian sacking. Some of the evacuees had lit fires on the earthen floor, so the longhouse was gloomy, smoke-filled and suffocating. It stank of human excreta, rotting bodies, infected sores and putrid food waste and was swarming with flies. Men, women and children had to lie in their own dirt and were treated like cows. The atmosphere was undoubtedly oppressive. Stephen Brookes said that they lacked all human dignity and that he had 'never felt so low or so despairing'.[25]

The Brookes family put down their pieces of sacking on the only vacant space in the room. They later learned that the previous occupants had just died. The cries and moans of sick people echoed around. A gaunt and listless Indian family occupying the space next to them died one by one, until only a little boy of six remained. Many people were delirious, and at night a deranged Indian woman wandered around bumping into the sleeping evacuees. The Indian and Eurasian inmates (including the Brookes) were told that they had to stay in Shingbwiyang until the rains stopped, which meant they might be stuck in 'this appalling asylum' for many weeks. In fact, they did *not* leave until 1 October 1942.

Major Brookes bore a grudge against Cornelius North, and all these years later Stephen Brookes took up the cudgels on his late father's behalf. He accused North of failing to visit them in the hut and claimed that the camp food was poor. He said that there was a great deal of violence in the camp, and that the bodies of cholera and malaria victims were often not moved for some time. A tragedy occurred, for Major Brookes died from black water fever while they were in Shingbwiyang. Stephen Brookes claimed that his father was not buried for several days afterwards and that North did not visit them in their hour of need. Certainly the whole experience was horribly sad and traumatic.

But spare a thought for Cornelius North. He was rushed off his feet. He was responsible for a shifting population of several hundred evacuees. They arrived and left at all hours of day and night. North had very few porters and at the same time he was struggling to deal with a major cholera epidemic. It must be pointed out too, that Stephen Brookes levelled the charges in public after Cornelius North had died. So no 'defence' was possible. Here is the strange thing. Evacuees of all races spoke highly of Cornelius North, and no one else had a bad word to say against him.

No one knows where the truth lies. One surmises that Major Brookes (like many other elderly British Indian Army officers at the time) probably tried to 'pull rank' on the young BFF officer. Possibly the two men had a heated argument. After all, Major Brookes had something of a reputation for throwing his weight around. It is also quite possible that Major Brookes had fabricated the claim that he had provided hospitality to Cornelius North before the war.[26] Suffice it to say that all those who knew Cornelius North in Shingbwiyang and elsewhere spoke of his tolerance, fairness and generosity to people of all races. It suggests that Stephen Brookes chose the wrong target for his criticisms. The fact was that Cornelius North struggled on against all odds for month after month. He heroically stuck to his thankless task long after most of his seniors and colleagues had fled.

There is another mystery, too. Long after the event, Stephen Brookes complained bitterly about their 'disintegrating charnel house' in Shingbwiyang. Yet he, George, Maisie and Mrs Brookes did *not* leave until 1 October 1942 – more than three months after they had first arrived, and long after most of the other evacuees had left. They willingly accepted the security and sustenance that Cornelius North provided. Moreover, North went out of his way to help them on their journey to India.

Stephen Brookes's account serves to illustrate a more general point. Bitter emotions and profound senses of wrong festered and erupted during the terrible days of the evacuation. They did so especially in remote godforsaken places like Shingbwiyang. Indian and Anglo-Indian families were more vulnerable to abuse than Europeans. It is almost certain that Stephen Brookes encountered discrimination in the murky underworld of the evacuation trail, and it is also perfectly possible that he was extraneously influenced by discrimination later in life. What *actually* happened to the Brookes family in this obscure outpost of Empire in northern Burma in 1942 will forever remain a mystery, but it can be assumed that Cornelius North was much more of a saint than a sinner.

Stephen, Maisie and George Brookes reached Margherita on 24 October after walking 421 miles.[27] There was a sad postscript to the story. Stephen, Maisie, George and their mother split up in Margherita and never met again. Clearly their horrific experiences in Shingbwiyang left deep psychological scars. George died in 1969 aged forty-two and Mrs Brookes died in 1971. About 45,000 evacuees, mainly Indians and Anglo-Indians, passed through Shingbwiyang during the second half of 1942. How many of them died in the camp will never be known, but in these unremittingly terrible circumstances, Cornelius North was undoubtedly a hero.

***

We must pick up the saga of P. G. G. Salkeld where we left off. Two days after his party left Shingbwiyang Salkeld came across Blaquiere again. He was 'sitting dejectedly by the track with his sister (Mrs Denner) and her two small girls'.[28] Salkeld was surprised that Blaquiere had not bothered to get them out on an evacuation flight. He wondered if it was perhaps because she incapable of looking after herself. As it was, Salkeld's colleagues rallied around to take her with them. Everyone in the party discarded one or another of their precious possessions, and they managed to fit the rather amply proportioned Mrs Denner and her daughters into one of the elephant baskets. Unfortunately, Mrs Denner died later in the journey.

There was a violent thunderstorm as they approached the Namyang Hka. Cholera had broken out and the temporary shelters stank. Moreover, the ferry was out of action because a steel rope had snapped. Salkeld organized his elephants. They went back and forth across the river and carried 60–100 refugees to safety. They were also pleased to pick up the wife of a Punjabi subedar major who had given birth to a child the day before. However, Salkeld noticed that there was 'very real distress on the road'. The trouble was that 'those who had crossed the river had no rations'.[29] Salkeld feared there would be dreadful scenes at Namyang unless something was done to get the people across. He managed to get a message through to an RAF commander, who arranged for a plane to drop a hawser, which was duly fitted. Many lives were saved when the ferry resumed operations again a couple of days later.

The next five days were the worst part of the whole trip. They came across many corpses and everywhere refugees begged for food. Salkeld was deeply moved. These people were *actually* starving, he said. On one occasion too, he came across two Europeans lying by the side of the path in a bamboo hovel. Both of them were completely exhausted and on the point of death. One was a King's Own Yorkshire Light Infantry (KOYLI) sergeant who had had cholera and the other was a Rangoon customs officer, who had a high fever and was suffering from malaria. Salkeld gave each of them a blanket, some warm Horlicks and a little brandy before putting them on one of the elephants. He noted wryly that by this time the elephants had become like walking hospitals because they had picked up so many invalids. One of the more recent invalids was a man called Peachey, who was manager of Coombes & Co. He was completely paralysed and had lost a lot of weight.

In due course they reached the ITA camps. Salkeld recalled how at one of the camps two planters and a young police officer named Walker had welcomed them with strong hot tea, an army biscuit and two tins of 'Australian camp pie'. At another ITA camp, the tea planters and a Burma PWD engineer called Clarke gave them enough biscuits, tea and rations to sustain the whole party for two days. At yet another camp a European doctor examined all the sick evacuees in the party.

They climbed the Pangsau Pass and, on the other side, the elephants slid down an almost perpendicular descent. Eventually they reached the base camp at Namphong, where there were plenty of dormitories, a small hospital, and a European doctor. They unloaded their patients and senior planter served them all hot meals.

The march became increasingly difficult after Namphong. There were steep ups and downs, and eventually they came to the golden staircase, which was extremely slippery. At the Namgai Camp, Salkeld met the illustrious Gyles Mackrell for the first time. Mackrell, about whom much more will be said in due course, put the able-bodied members of the party in a large canoe and provided them with four boatmen. On the way, they stopped at Simon where Salkeld had a hot bath – his first for many a long day. The next morning, they set off again in the boat. The river was very turbulent and they ran aground on a sandbank, but eventually arrived at the Refugee Camp at Margherita. The journey had taken them twenty-seven days. P. G. G. Salkeld was told that about 17,500 refugees had taken this route and that 7–10 per cent of them had died on the way.[30]

***

Soon after Wilkie left Shingbwiyang, his party came to a halt on the bank of a large swollen river. Crowds of evacuees had gathered there. They were all soaking wet, cold, had very little food, and had been stranded there for several weeks. Luckily there was a brief spell of dry weather shortly before Wilkie and his colleagues arrived. Consequently, the water level began to fall and they were able to wade across with the water up to their chests.

On 2 June Wilkie had his first experience of ITA hospitality. He arrived at a rest camp, which Langham-Carter had described as 'the most blessed sight' of his life. A Union Jack waved above a group of small bamboo huts and four clean-cut young English officers dispensed biscuits and cups of tea. Thereafter there were ITA camps every ten miles to the Indian frontier and beyond. Each camp had a doctor, and most had a small hospital where medical staff could treat blisters, dysentery, leech bites and fevers.

Wilkie and his colleagues began to feel more relaxed. They marched for shorter periods each day and started later in the morning. The ITA provided them with porters to carry sick members of their party. On 9 June Wilkie's party crossed the Indian border at Tai-Pong where a railcar was waiting to take them to Lakhpani and on to Margherita.[31]

***

Alistair Rose made his escape through the Hukawng Valley at about the same time as Wilkie and his party.[32] It took Rose five months to complete his journey. It had begun in Moulmein on 23 January 1942 and ended in northeast Assam on 16 June. During that time Rose had driven his Hillman car 800 miles up through war-torn Burma. He had been in Mandalay during the air raid of 3

April and eventually abandoned his car near Myitkyina after a series of hair-raising adventures. He then *walked* the last 280 miles in twenty-three days.[33]

Rose had arrived in Myitkyina on 6 May 1942, the night *before* the bombing raid. He watched as hundreds of dazed people who were standing 'knee-deep in stuff' shoved their scanty possessions into boxes. The sky glowed red as bungalows and houses were set on fire. It felt like the end of the world. On 7 May, Rose paid a visit to Government House. It was completely deserted. Wilkie and his colleagues had left just a few hours before. The doors were wide open and clothing and documents were strewn across the floor. Rose's eye was caught by a telegram marked 'Top Secret' from Chiang Kai Shek to Churchill. It lay open for all to see. After a few minutes Rose stood on the veranda and watched as Japanese planes circled and bombed Myitkyina for the second time that day.[34]

At dawn on 8 May, Rose joined a small party of Europeans and Lushai troops. They drove out of Myitkyina along the road towards Sumprabum, intending to take the route through the Chaukan Pass. They were put off when Kachin porters hassled them, demanding Rs.7.00 to cover the shortest of distances. Rose and his party decided to double back to mile 109, where the track branched off to the Hukawng Valley.

The road junction was unbelievably chaotic. Brigadier Upton from the Myitkyina garrison stood in the middle of the road waving his arms in a desperate effort to restore order. Abandoned cars were pushed over the *khud*, armed Chinese soldiers demanded food and money and local Kachins squabbled with Putao Shans.

Rose and his companions dumped their vehicles and started walking. Rose took only a change of clothes, his passport and a signed affidavit stating the extent of T. D. Findlay's losses. However, not everyone travelled so lightly. One of Rose's travelling companions (a man called Anderson) was so heavily laden that he was 'seriously whacked'. The road was jam-packed with evacuees of all sorts – including Gurkha families bending under huge loads and a group of Bishop Strachan School pupils who skipped along in good spirits.[35] As Rose approached the township of Maingkwan he witnessed a bizarre sight. A Chinese infantry division was approaching from the opposite direction. There were long columns of armed infantrymen and behind them pranced two posses of troops, one carrying the general aloft in a plush sedan chair and the other carrying the general's lady friend in an even plusher sedan chair.

The track from Maingkwan to Shingbwiyang was extremely gruelling during the monsoon season. The evacuees had to hack their way through dense jungle and they often sank up to their thighs in thick, red, sticky mud. The strongest of men could cover only seven miles per day and many weaker evacuees collapsed, exhausted, by the side of the road and died. Those that made it to Shingbwiyang were already thoroughly demoralized and exhausted.

Rose and his party stopped only briefly in Shingbwiyang. They were so horrified by the conditions there, so quickly replenished their rice stocks and left as soon as they could. However, they spoke warmly about Cornelius North and the magnificent job he was doing.

After Shingbwiyang, Rose and his colleagues made very slow progress. They had to form human chains to get themselves across innumerable river gorges. At one river they waded across chest-deep and could feel decomposing bodies beneath their feet. They met a young BFF officer, Captain Stapleton, and a party of Chin labourers, who had the unenviable task of gathering and incinerating the corpses. Rose noticed that piles of bodies surrounded every rice dump along the way – posthumous evidence of desperate evacuees fighting tooth and nail to get at the food.

Rose's party still had to face the perilous and icy Namyang River. The footing was insecure and the river level could rise three feet in an hour during the monsoon season. It rained continuously from 12–28 May, from 3–10 June and from 14–21 June, after which there were several days of very heavy showers. The refugees had to choose between crossing the river (and either drowning or losing their kit) or staying on the Burma side of the river and starving.[36] The Nawngyang River was just as menacing. Rose was amazed to see more than 1000 refugees struggling to get to the edge of the river. Some of them had been waiting for four days. They had had no food, and had no protection from the pouring rain.[37] It was impossible to light a fire and desperate refugees paid up to Rs.10.00 for two pieces of dry stick. The only means of getting across the river was on a single small raft that was pulled from one bank to the other by a rattan cane rope. The bank on the India side of the river sloped steeply out of the water and was difficult to negotiate.

They had to follow the course of the river for the next few miles. This involved climbing over a jumble of huge boulders that were thrown around by the fast-flowing streams. In a number of cases precarious rope ladders had been slung from one boulder to another. Rose was told that hundreds of evacuees had been drowned as they tried to cross these treacherous boulders and swollen streams. Occasionally RAF planes dropped supplies to evacuees on the route, but Indian troops usually reached the drop zones first and made off with the spoils. The incessant rain and hundreds of feet churned up the track. It was impossible for the evacuees to walk more than a hundred paces at a time. Morale began to falter and bitter arguments broke out between members of Rose's party.

When all seemed lost, Rose's party reached the first of a series of ITA camps. The tea planters were extraordinarily hospitable. Every camp had a doctor and all evacuees were provided with a hot cooked meal. ITA coolies worked around the clock to bring in injured and exhausted evacuees. Rose had counted up to an average of six human corpses on every mile of the track since he had left Myitkyina. The smell of rotting human flesh had been all pervading. Rose noticed that as soon as the ITA took over responsibility for the track, the bodies were removed every day and burned immediately.

As he neared the frontier Rose suffered a very bad bout of dysentery and he was forced to stay behind to dose himself with 'bacteriophage'.[38] A few days later he set off on his own along a remote railway line. After walking many miles, he was on the point of giving up when a train bound for Margherita appeared out of the blue. He flagged it down and was hauled aboard. He spent many weeks in hospitals in Margherita and Panitola, but at the beginning of October was well enough to continue his journey. In Imphal he joined the Burma Intelligence Corps of the Indian Army 17th Division.

4

The Hukawng Valley to Margherita: Part Two

O the most piteous cry of the poor souls! Sometimes to see them and not to see them

Shakespeare: *The Winter's Tale*, Act 3. Scene 3

Shingbwiyang is situated about 65 miles from the Pangsau Pass. When the evacuees left the camp their first objective was the village of Tagap Ga, about 29 miles along the track towards the Taungup Pass. It was a very long, exhausting slog up steep hills and over an extremely rough track. Just beyond Tagap Ga was the formidable Namyang Hka, which posed one of the most dangerous obstacles on the whole evacuation trail. After crossing the Namyang Hka, the evacuees then faced a vicious scramble over the Patkoi Hills to the Pangsau Pass.

Few (if any) evacuees ventured beyond Shingbwiyang before 13 May 1942. There were good reasons for this inactivity. Many of them were exhausted after their trek through the Hukawng Valley. It was obvious that conditions would deteriorate when the monsoon broke, as it did on 12 May. Therefore General Wood insisted that the evacuees should be held back. Cornelius North was unable to restrain many of the evacuees who were desperate to make progress. He warned the camp commandant at Namlip that a small group of European businessmen and officials was likely to arrive on 17 May. In fact they arrived on 13 May, four days earlier than predicted. It was the beginning of a deluge. The following day, a huge party of 300 evacuees and Naga porters arrived at Namlip, among them were Mrs Cornelius North and twenty-three British troops.

The sudden influx caught the Namlip camp commandant off guard. He had run out of food and had no medicines. Luckily for him two ITA liaison officers, a doctor and a dresser turned up out of the blue on 15 May. They were on their way to Shingbwiyang but they agreed to stay for a time at Namlip.[1] From 15 May onwards evacuees continued to flood into Namlip every day right up

Figure 4.1 BCMS Evacuation Party in the Hukawng Valley. Credit: L. Knight, Darlington Collection. The party, which started out from Mohnyin included, Dorothy Darlington with Baby Anna, Mr Evan Darlington, Dr Farrant Russell and Rev. Wilfred Crittle, Rev. George Tidey, Rev. Rushton and Dr Pearson.

to 20 June. For a time, it looked likely that it would end in catastrophe The problem was that a cane bridge had been washed away at Nampong, which was preventing supplies from reaching the camp and evacuees from leaving it. By 21 May the evacuees were close to starvation. In the nick of time engineers of the Assam Rifles arrived to repair the bridge. It uncorked the bottleneck, which allowed porters from Kumlao to get through to Namlip. They brought in 300 headloads of food on the first day and the situation was saved. It also meant that the evacuees were able to continue on their journeys towards Margherita.

Russell and his colleagues were still in Shingbwiyang on 14 May. They were making preparations to leave Shingbwiyang the next day (15 May). They had a very pleasant surprise when 'Maggie' the mission elephant and her mahout turned up unexpectedly. It meant that they could load all their stores and kit onto the elephant. On 15 May they set off in high spirits. However a torrential downpour created 'cataracts of yellow water' and 'unspeakable sloughs' in the track. The evacuees' feet were quickly encased in heavy mud casts. Russell's party had to stop at every swift-flowing stream to wash the caked mud away.

Russell also stopped briefly at a series of supposedly 'Burma administered' camps that were located at Ngalang Ga, Taikham Zup and Yawngyang. He found that each of the camps was unmanned and was surrounded by stinking black mud, human excrement and decaying bodies. Usually a few rough shelters made from branches and leaves had been thrown together, but they offered no protection against the rain.[2]

Nevertheless, they continued to make good progress towards to Tagap Ga. Maggie made all the difference as she carried their kit all the way up the extremely long and energy-sapping gradient.[3] When they reached Tagap the mahout announced his intention to return home as soon as possible. Russell and Crittle had no idea how to handle an elephant, and although the mahout taught them a few basic words of command, Maggie completely ignored them.[4] Fortunately another mahout offered to go with them to Margherita.

On 23 May, Russell and his party reached the Namyang Hka. The river had burst its banks and was very fast flowing. Hundreds of Indian evacuees waited for the water level to fall. Most of them had run out of food, and some were close to starvation. Flimsy makeshift shelters sprawled for miles along the riverbank. By pure chance the rain stopped when Russell's party arrived, and gradually the water level subsided although it was still too deep to cross.

It was at the Namyang Hka on 24 May that Maggie achieved celebrity status. She crossed back and forth over the river, carrying evacuees to safety, each time she pushed her great bulk through the water and on one occasion acted as 'backwater' to rescue a group of women stranded in midstream. Long lines of evacuees queued up to 'board' Maggie as if she was a pleasure steamer. Russell turned down several huge wads of rupee notes that were offered as bribes. He explained that 'need' was the only qualification for a passage across the river.[5] Rev. Rushton and Rev. Tidey were fully occupied with rescuing evacuees in difficulty. Late in the day, Russell and his party took their place on Maggie and crossed to the other side of the Namyang Hka.

Wilkie and his colleagues arrived at the Namyang Hka several days after Russell's party had left. They had made slow progress because of the very long incline up to Tagap Ga. There had been no rain for a couple of days, so the water level had fallen slightly, although many disconsolate evacuees still waited on the riverbank. Wilkie found a reasonably shallow part of the river, and his party waded across. It was a risky operation because the water was still

Figure 4.2 The BCMS Mission Elephant 'Maggie' and her Jingpaw mahout. Credit: L. Knight, Darlington Collection. Maggie weighed 6,000 lbs and stood 7.5 feet high at the shoulder carried Dorothy Darlington and six-week old baby Anna from Maingkwan, and later performed heroic feats at the Namyang Hka.

shoulder-deep, the riverbed was uneven and the current was strong. One false move could have resulted in people being swept away. Once they reached the other side, they set off immediately towards the Pangsau Pass.

About a week after Wilkie had left, Rose and his party arrived at the Namyang Hka. By this time, it was raining.[6] Progress was slow because tiny streams had been transformed into raging torrents. The Namyang Hka was impassable because recent heavy rains had caused the water to rise three or four feet in an hour. Rose and his colleagues spent several days looking for an alternative crossing point. Fortunately the rain stopped, the water level fell, and they were able to cross the river.

After crossing the Namyang Hka, Russell's trek over the Patkoi Hills was far from easy. The track went up and down a series of hills between 3000 and 5000ft high. There was no food or shelter, and the rain poured down so the mud became increasingly thick and glutinous. Their progress slowed to a crawl and they began to run out of food. They had to ration themselves to two biscuits and a small piece of bully beef per person per day. Morale had hit rock bottom when, suddenly, out of the mists they saw the first ITA ration camp at Tagung Hka. More will be said about it later.

There was a featureless, 12-mile-long slog from the Tagung Hka camp up to the Pangsau Pass. A couple of miles below the summit, a short, lung-busting climb took Russell's party through overhanging jungle and on to a sinister plateau 2000ft above sea level. 'Silent and sinister' swamps, 'oily swirls' and deep, black streams pockmarked the landscape. Naga huts were dotted around *jhums* that had been cut into the hillsides. The huts were mysteriously uninhabited and there was no sign of either human or animal life.[7] Unexpectedly they emerged onto the bank of the deep, slow-moving Nawngyang Hka. Russell's party was pulled across it on unstable bamboo rafts.[8] It was only a short distance up to the Pangsau Pass and then the treacherous track descended into Assam. Torrential rain had transformed it into 'a rushing stream of liquid mud', while deep buffalo wallows and hundreds of boulders and rocks walking conditions very difficult.[9] Russell crossed over the Pangsau Pass on 28 May. The area was almost completely deserted. A few days later the situation would change spectacularly as 10,000 evacuees from Burma streamed over the pass during the first week of June.[10]

After the Pangsau Pass, the track went past a group of dismal porters' shelters at Pahari before it reached the ITA camp at Nampong (about which more will be said later). Immediately after Nampong there was an exhausting eight-mile trudge through glutinous mud to the camp at Namchik and then the route went on to Kumlao.

At Kumlao, most evacuees took a shortcut to North Tirap. This went down the notorious 'golden staircase' – a flight of 1000 steps cut into the hillside and strengthened with bamboo strips. It worked wonderfully in the dry season, but during the monsoon it was a treacherous quagmire of liquid mud through which the evacuees slipped, slithered and skidded. Many of them got completely stuck in the mud and ITA porters stood by to pull them out. The 'golden staircase' could be avoided by going the long way around. This was even heavier going. It involved a dangerous descent to Namgoi then a ten-mile hike to Namchik, over the Namchik suspension bridge followed by another ten-mile trek through mud to North Tirap.[11]

Russell reached the railhead at Tipong at 3.23 pm on 2 June. The moment was etched on his memory. A Dibru–Sadiya steam train took the evacuees to a reception camp known as 'the Teapot Pub' in Lekhapani. Then they continued to Margherita and spent a couple of nights in tented accommodation at a refugee camp on the golf course. After a hot bath and a cooked meal, they were issued with new clothing and clean bedding. On 4 June, they caught the 5.00 pm train to Calcutta.

Alistair Rose's story was rather different. It was a reminder that nothing could be taken for granted at any time. When his party was about fifty miles from Ledo, Rose had a serious bout of dysentery and he became very dehydrated. He was unable to continue the journey, but insisted that his colleagues went on without him. He lay down and dosed himself up with 'bacteriophage'.[12] When he felt slightly better he began to walk along a remote stretch of railway line until he became delirious. He was about to throw in the towel, when a train appeared out of the blue. He flagged it down and was hauled aboard. He spent many weeks in hospital in Margherita until he was well enough to catch a train to Imphal.[13]

Alistair Rose's predicament was by no means unique. By the end of June, the Indian authorities expressed concern about the state of the evacuees when they arrived in Margherita. Most of them were malnourished and several showed signs of starvation.

***

Two questions remain unanswered. The first concerned matters of life and death. Why was there such a high mortality rate in the Hukawng Valley and what were its consequences? The second question is why did the ITA become so deeply involved, and what effect did this have on this operation?

The journey from Mogaung to the Pangsau Pass was a catalogue of death and despair. The account so far has read like a sanitized travelogue, as if there were no victims. Nevertheless, there were deaths on a monumental scale. They cannot and should not be ignored. The evacuees were not *killed*. Death descended on them silently. There was no fighting, no bullets flew and no bombs were dropped. The evacuees died from exhaustion, exposure, hunger and disease in this, one of the unhealthiest areas in the world. They were engulfed in mud, swept away in rivers, infested with gangrene and bacteria, and plagued by insects and leeches. Cholera, cerebral malaria and black-water fever were endemic. In the Hukawng Valley, death was no respecter of persons. Europeans, Indians and Eurasians, children, old people, able-bodied, rich and poor, were all scythed down indiscriminately. Everyone lost someone, wives lost husbands, children lost parents, parents lost children, friends lost friends, and dead strangers lay around every corner. As Stephen Brookes put it, death 'was briefly mourned by near relatives but ignored by the passing crowd'.[14]

It is not known how many people actually died. The ITA claimed that 220,000 arrived safely in India and that 4,268 died on the way. Wilfred Crittle quotes from an unnamed 'official' source that 5,000 out of 10,000 evacuees died in the Hukawng Valley.[15] They are both random guesses. All that can be said is that the *actual* number of deaths was probably much higher than official figure suggests.

Reliable eyewitnesses claim to have seen hundreds of bodies. Russell reported seeing the corpses of hundreds of unidentified Indian evacuees on the track between Tagung Hka and Pahari. They had died of malnutrition, exhaustion and disease and their emaciated bodies were poorly clothed and often shoeless.[16] Near the Nawngyang River ITA officers discovered Naga huts filled with skeletons. In one hut alone, an officer counted fifty dead bodies.[17] Alistair Rose felt decomposing bodies beneath his feet as he waded across a river, and he counted at least six corpses per mile on the track between Myitkyina and Tagung Hka (a distance of 210 miles). The situation improved after Shamlung – not because fewer people died, but because ITA coolies removed and incinerated the corpses every day. Captain Stapleton of the BFF and a party of Chin labourers spent all day, every day clearing and incinerating corpses from the track and rivers in the Hukawng Valley. Stapleton reported that the corpses were piled high near rice dumps because of the fighting over food. Then there was Mr Jarman, a clerk working for Eric Lambert, the local political officer, who had gone up to the Pangsau Pass but found 'the stench of rotting corpses' was so strong that he could only keep going by stuffing his nostrils with cotton wool.[18]

There was a serious cholera epidemic in the Hukawng Valley. It is rarely mentioned in official reports. On 14 May Wilkie noticed that dead cholera victims occupied every bamboo hut in Naiding. Wilkie said that this was the case in every village in the Hukawng Valley.[19] Russell commented on the number of corpses of piled up in huts between Maingkwan and Shingbwiyang. Cornelius North estimated that he had to bury at least fifty cholera victims per day during May 1942. On 12 May Russell was alarmed to see cholera victims in the huts and godowns in Shingbwiyang displaying the classic symptoms of uncontrolled shivering and cramps. The camp had not 'even the simplest drugs' to treated the sufferers.[20]

The registration authorities in India only recorded the deaths of evacuees when they were told about them. It is highly unlikely that any of the aforementioned 'bodies', 'corpses' and 'skeletons' were registered anywhere. Moreover, Indian evacuees were suspicious of the authorities and refused to register the deaths of friends and relatives, so the total number of deaths was almost certainly much greater than the 'official' figures suggest.

According to the eyewitnesses most of the unidentified bodies were of Indian evacuees. However Anglo-Burmese evacuees also suffered heavy casualties. During April and May 1942 large numbers of them arrived by train at Myitkyina railway station. U Khin Aung Nyunt recalled seeing hundreds of them arriving every day when he was a boy. They were smartly dressed, as if they had come straight from offices.

At the end of April 1942 a Bible Churchmen's Missionary Society (BCMS) missionary, Rev. Wilfred Crittle was based in the town of Kamaing at the southeast end of the Hukawng Valley. Every day buses arrived from the Mogaung railhead. They were filled with Anglo-Indians evacuees. Crittle remembered the arrival of one bus in particular. It drew up in the centre of Kamaing and about forty young Anglo-Burmese women spilled out onto the road. They were uncertain about what to do next, until one of them – a very striking young woman dressed in a pretty frock, a crisp white blouse and dainty court shoes – walked over to Crittle. She asked where the buses left for India. Crittle told her there were no buses. She was surprised, but asked what was the best way of getting to Margherita. Crittle told her there was only one way – and that was to *walk* 286 miles. The young woman was visibly shaken. She went back to break the news to her friends and Crittle last saw them walking down the muddy track towards Shingbwiyang. They were *all* inappropriately dressed in smart dresses, lisle stockings and fashionable shoes. He wondered how many of them would survive. Many were likely to die as they grappled with the mud, jungles, rivers, swamps and mountains that lay ahead.[21]

A few days later Crittle had also become an evacuee. As he walked from Maingkwan to Shingbwiyang he came across a young Anglo-Burmese woman and her husband. They sat by the side of the track clutching their two-year-old child and a baby. It was pouring with rain. The young woman was hungry, thirsty and utterly exhausted. She muttered that she could go no further and asked Crittle what she should do. He felt helpless and mused, 'What *do* you say to such people'? He believed the young woman was close to death as were many others on this part of the track.[22]

European evacuees were generally better off than other refugees. However, even they had to face death. Just beyond Maingkwan, Crittle passed an English girl lying by the side of the track. She was spattered with mud and soaked by the rain. He recognized her as the sister of a BFF officer he knew. The young woman was in intense pain. She was covered in leech bites and her legs were gangrenous. Crittle tried to put her on a pony, but she kept rolling off. Eventually, he had to leave her by the side of the road – and he presumed she would die.[23] Such were the brutal realities of life and death in the Hukawng Valley.

A bizarre, but persistent, rumour circulated that primitive tribesmen had discovered a number of dead *European* women in a remote part of the Patkoi Hills. The women were all dressed in fine evening dresses and wore strings of pearls. The story seemed improbable, but it may have contained a grain of truth. Passengers on flights from Myitkyina to Dibrugarh could carry only 32pounds of luggage. Many of them stuffed their bags full of jewellery, silver and trinkets and wore layer upon layer of their most expensive clothes. It was a perfectly sensible way to bypass the regulations on short air flights. However, it made no sense whatsoever for long treks through mud. Passengers quite frequently had to leave a plane shortly before take-off, in which case they were in serious trouble

The closeness to death and suffering produced countless acts of heroism. Here are just three examples. A young Englishwoman by the name of Mrs

Wilby struggled through the Patkoi Hills at the end of May 1942. She was looking after two frail old men, a twelve-year-old boy, four very young girls and a tiny baby. Mrs Wilby stuck to her task courageously, but ran out of food. All nine members of her party died from exhaustion and starvation.[24] Anglo-Indians, who often travelled in large extended family groups that included the young and old were very vulnerable. They usually depended on youngish men and women to get them through. Norman Richardson was a fourteen-year-old Anglo-Indian boy who was left in charge of a large family group. He looked after all of them as well as carrying his baby brother all the way from Ngalang to Tagung Hka, and retracing his footsteps at regular intervals to help his aged grandmother along the track. Frank Sinclair Gomes was an elderly Anglo-Indian telegrapher from Maymyo. He saw a canoe capsize in a turbulent river and swam out three times to rescue some Madrassi woman and a child.[25] Many believed that 'refugees of rank and ample means' were the most selfish, but generally the evacuation brought out 'the best side of human nature'.[26]

Even Steels elephants seemed to show compassion. They reportedly trod delicately between the corpses that littered the track between Maingkwan and Shingbwiyang, and sick and dying women and children were often placed in their howdahs. On one occasion, the wife of a Punjabi subedar major gave birth to a baby in a howdah, and on another occasion a KOYLI sergeant died peacefully in a howdah at the Pangsau Pass.[27]

Mud was one of the main killers. Of Passchendaele it has been said that 'mud weighed down the living and swallowed the dead'.[28] It was the case in the Hukawng Valley too. Ill-fitting shoes caused terrible blisters and there were no disinfectants. An Anglo-Indian man in Wilkie's party was typical of many. His feet became so painful that he could no longer walk. He was slung over a bullock, which merely increased his pain. So he was put in a bullock cart and left him to his own devices. The cart got stuck in deep mud and lagged further and further behind. The man was last seen hobbling off the track and was never heard of again. Presumably he died. In May 1942, an anonymous Gurkha mother was reported to have fallen flat on her face in the mud. She was too exhausted to get back to her feet. Several weeks later her body was found – still face down in the mud, but on her back was strapped a dead baby.

Wild water was another killer. During the monsoon, rivers swelled, bridges collapsed, ferries capsized and boats sank. The Namyang Hka was one of the most serious barriers. Many evacuees drowned as they tried to cross it. Russell had been horrified when several men were swept to their deaths, and a few days later Alastair Rose watched helplessly as a party of twelve super-fit Gurkha soldiers tried to take a rope across to the other side of the river. Seven of them reached safety, but five were swept away and drowned.[29]

Death was often caused by minor medical problems. The complete lack of medicines and basic clinical skills could be fatal. In normal times routine abscesses, broken limbs, bad teeth, septic sores and stomach upsets were all perfectly treatable. In the Hukawng Valley they frequently led to death. One small incident illustrates the point. When Dr Russell made his way down to the Namyang Hka in the pouring rain he came across a desperate young woman. She was in the final stages labour and in great pain. She obviously needed surgery. There and then by the side of the track Dr Russell performed a delicate operation with the aid of a rusty penknife and a bit of parachute cord. He successfully delivered a healthy baby girl and continued on his way. It was pure luck, of course, that an experienced surgeon happened to be on hand, but it wasn't the case in ninety-nine cases out of a hundred and hundreds of personal tragedies went completely unnoticed.

Quite haphazardly unlikely incidents tugged at the heartstrings. The discovery of two tiny English girls in a flimsy makeshift shelter between Tagup Ga and Namlip struck a chord. They had died of starvation in each other's arms and were completely on their own, and miles away from anywhere.[30] The fate of a group of Bishop Strachan Home orphans should surely have excited much more interest than it did, but in 1942 it hardly got a mention.[31] J. S. Vorley described it as 'one of the worst tragedies of the evacuation'.[32] In many ways their plight was synonymous with the Hukawng Valley.

In January 1942 about forty pupils of the Bishop Strachan Home pupils had been evacuated first to Kyauktaga and then to Mogok. At the same time thirty pupils from St Matthew's Orphanage in Moulmein had been evacuated to Thadaung but their train had been bombed in Pyinmana. In April, it was decided to take the Bishop Strachan pupils to Myitkyina and then to fly them to India. An IFC steamer was detailed to pick them from Thabyetkyin and take them to Katha on the first stage of the journey. They would then be taken from Katha to Myitkyina. However there followed a chapter of accidents. On 23 April forty pupils and staff stood on the riverbank at Thabyetkyin waiting to board one of the last steamers bound for Katha. Unfortunately, the steamer was full to overflowing. It was decided that there was no room for even one extra passenger. Moreover, supplies of drinking water and food had run out.[33] Not one of the passengers volunteered to give up his/her place to the children – some of whom were as young as six years old.

Mrs Vorley was on board the steamer and when she arrived in Katha she arranged for the deputy commissioner to sail down to Thabyetkyin in his own launch to collect the Bishop Strachan party. They arrived back in Katha on 29 April, but it was too late because Myitkyina fell a few days later.[34] In the meantime, the younger pupils had been taken to Sumprabum, and some of them were later taken to Fort Hertz and then flown to India.[35]

The headmistress, Miss Lilian Bald, decided to take about forty of the older pupils with her through the Hukawng Valley to India. It was a fateful decision. She persuaded one of the teachers, Miss Dorothy Law, a British Army officer and an NCO, and two civilian officials to accompany her and the pupils. They started off from mile-109 on the Fort Hertz Road and then walked over the Daru Pass. Alistair Rose saw them at the pass on 27 May and he said they were in high spirits. A few days later Stephen Brookes and his family came across a group of about forty girls in a remote valley in the Kumon hills near the Hukawng Valley. They were astonished, and at the time they did not realize that they were the Bishop Strachan pupils. Brookes said that they were identically dressed in thin, white, cotton school uniforms and flitted barefoot up a slope like 'delicate white butterflies'. By the time they reached the Hukawng Valley a few days later the pupils and staff were beginning to run out of food. They were reduced to daily rations of a few grains of rice and a cup of weak tea. The Army officer who was accompanying them went off in search of food, but never returned. Shortly afterwards he died in Shingbwiyang.

Miss Bald and the rest of her party made desperately slow progress through the rain and mud. The NCO and both civilian officials died as soon as they reached the Tarung Hka at the beginning of August. Miss Bald and Miss Law and the pupils staggered on as best they could, but they were all so undernourished that several of them died. Thirteen-year-old Ruth Montgomery was the first to go followed a few days later by her best friend, Diana Doupe. Miss Law died at the village of Taihpa. Miss Bald and the remaining twelve pupils staggered on to Yawbang where they were so exhausted that they huddled together and died. The youngest of them was eleven-year-old Kenneth Morris, and the oldest, eighteen-year-old Zena Prosser.

When the bodies of the headmistress and her pupils were found some time later, Miss Bald still clutched in her hand the letter she had written shortly before her death. She described how they had all been living on 'one meal a day of watery rice'. They had had 'tummy troubles, bad colds and fevers and seven of the girls had malaria'. They had had to climb 'steep precipitous mountains in the pouring rain, [hack] through dense tropical jungle infested with wild animals and cross dangerous rapids.' Sometimes they had walked through 'paddy fields and ditches waist-deep in water and ploughed through jungle paths thigh-deep in mud'. At night they had slept 'in the jungle without shelter and with highly decayed corpses around us'. Miss Bald was afraid that they had reached a point when 'we cannot walk on any more as we are all on the verge of physical collapse'. She explained that 'most of the children are sans blanket, sans shoes, sans change of clothes' and she concluded by asking those who cared to, 'remember us in your prayers'.

Of the remaining Bishop Strachan Home pupils, five of the younger girls aged six, seven and eight respectively, died in Sumprabum. However, on 28 October 1942, a party of twelve pupils arrived in Margherita – the youngest of them was Annie Campbell, who was just six years old. Ten-year-old Elizabeth Doupe died soon after she arrived in Margherita.[36]

Miss Bald and Miss Law had started off with a group of thirty-eight pupils aged 6–18. Miss Bald, Miss Law, twenty pupils whose *average* age was twelve and the four accompanying adults all died in northern Burma. Eighteen of the Bishop Strachan orphans eventually reached India.

Death continued to haunt the Hukawng Valley route to the bitter end. Brigadier Whitworth was convinced that the premature closure of camps in July 1942 was responsible for the deaths of thousands of evacuees and that it reduced by 60 per cent the number of refugees arriving in Assam.[37] On 12 June it was reported that many evacuees in Namlip were extremely weak and that many more were dying on the road. An ITA official reported that he had counted 100 bodies on a short stretch of road, and that many more corpses had been dumped in the rivers or left to decompose in the jungle. Typhoid now became a real threat and a large number of Chinese troops arrived 'in a pitiable condition of starvation and sickness'. Although they were weak and emaciated, they were forced to haul heavy artillery pieces around and many of them died of exhaustion.[38]

Apologies are due if the foregoing section has teetered into mawkishness, but its main purpose is to explain why civilian death became the marque of the Hukawng Valley evacuation. The sheer scale, intensity and brutality of the fatalities and their intrusion into so many personal spaces profoundly affected the post-evacuation era. Survivors bore the scars of malnourishment, starvation, sickness, exhaustion and psychological disorder. But it was the ubiquity of death that provided the main legacy. There was also a lesser one. What really stuck in the collective craw was the administration's failure to prevent the disaster. Indeed, colonial credibility never recovered from the Hukawng Valley disaster and memories of it contributed to the regime's ultimate collapse.

***

Why did the ITA become so deeply involved in this operation, and to what effect? A deteriorating military situation, the monsoon, and the Japanese aerial attack on Imphal on 10 May galvanized the Government of India into action, and it ensured that the evacuees' experiences in Burma and in India were entirely different. It was as if chaos gave way to order, as a completely new set of dynamics developed from the Tagung Hka Camp onwards.

The scene must be set. Japanese forces closed the Burma Road to Kunming in March 1942. The British Army responded with its so-called two frontier road project linking India, Burma and China. The Army was utterly dependent on the ITA to construct the road. At the beginning of May, ITA labourers and supervisors arrived in Margherita to start work on the first phase of the project.[39] Severe monsoon conditions brought work on the Fort Hertz section of the road to a close, but with great difficulty the ITA workforce kept going on the Hukawng Valley section of the project.[40]

The closure of the Manipur Road in the latter part of April was a portent of things to come. It forced large numbers of civilian evacuees to look for alternative overland escape routes to India – the most obvious of which was the Hukawng Valley route. The trouble was that authorities had no idea whether the Hukawng Valley route could cope with a mass influx of evacuees.[41]

At the end of April, therefore, a group of Burma Government officers was sent to survey the Hukawng Valley route. They walked the whole distance from Shingbwiyang to Lekhpani. A few days later two ITA liaison officers and a Burma PWD engineer walked in the opposite direction from Lekhpani to Shingbwiyang. They produced a joint report indicating that the route was completely *unsuitable* for mass evacuation, warning that evacuees would be unable to 'get through unless the rain ceases'.[42] Particular concern was expressed about the state of 'the mule track' over the 4,000ft-high Pangsau Pass. It was already deep in liquid mud and extremely treacherous. Moreover, most of the rivers were now unfordable. The report pointed out that neither food nor natural building materials were available in the vicinity of the Pangsau Pass and that the few existing road-workers' camps were 'jerry-built'. Particular mention was made of the camps at Nampong and Shamlung. The former occupied a low-lying, muddy site and the latter was likely to collapse at any moment. Leaking roofs and non-existent sanitary arrangements were evident in every camp and the report concluded that as well as road-building work, extensive remedial work was necessary to make the camps fit for purpose. This was likely to take several weeks, but until it was completed the route was completely unsuitable for mass migration. There was a hint that the Hukawng Valley route would be a death trap.[43]

There was another reason for fearing a sudden influx of evacuees. The authorities believed it would interfere with the road works that had only just begun between the Pangsau Pass and the Namyang River as part of the 'two-frontier' military road-building programme. There was a last-minute proposal that a new road should be cut between Nampong and Simon to link the Jeep Road and Fort Hertz. A survey expedition was duly despatched to look at the feasibility of this plan. The survey party reported that the section between Yangman and Namgoi could only be constructed if a large team of skilled mahouts and working elephants was employed.

The bombing of the Myitkyina airstrip on 6 May altered the dynamics. It scotched any prospect of a period of preparation, and projected hundreds of evacuees towards the Hukawng Valley.[44]

On 12 May Major General Wood (Administrator General Eastern Frontier Projects and Refugee Administrator) summoned leading officials to a meeting in Margherita.[45]

Three major decisions were taken. The first concerned priorities. Two major military road-building projects in the Hukawng Valley were already in the very early stages of development. However, work on them would not be completed for several months so they were considered to be 'long-term' projects. On the other hand, the civilian evacuation from Burma was an extremely pressing concern – an emergency that required urgent (if short-term) action. The Director of Road Operations in Assam had been informed on 4 May that very large numbers of evacuees from Burma would soon be approaching the Pangsau Pass. They were expected to arrive within the next two or three weeks. It was decided to suspend the road-building activity and divert all the resources *to* the civilian evacuation. The ITA had already been appointed as the Government's contractor for the road-building projects and the ITA was now put in charge of all evacuation arrangements on the Indian side of the border.

Second, the authorities were keen to avoid the mayhem that had occurred on the Manipur Road when civilian evacuees were jumbled up with retreating troops. It was therefore agreed that civilians should have exclusive use of the main route between Shingbwiyang and Lekhpani, and that military units would have exclusive use of a new road that was being cut between Nampong and Simon, a project on which 1000 Abor coolies were employed.

The third decision was that Major General Wood would be in overall charge of the evacuation route and would issue '*directive orders*'. Under him a number of political officers would be responsible for procuring supplies, recruiting porters, setting up wireless communications and providing general security.

In preparation for the road-building project the ITA had already carried out a preliminary survey of the route between Lekhpani (its main base near Margherita) and Nampong (its main forward base near the Pangsau Pass). A two-man expedition had set out from Lekhpani on 6 May. It consisted of an ITA Liaison Officer, a Burma PWD Officer and a number of Naga porters. They went over the Pangsau Pass and got as far as Namlip by 13 May. It had taken them just seven days – an extraordinarily short time that was unlikely to be replicated at any time in the future. It reflected the fact that the monsoon had not arrived, the track was relatively 'unworn' and they did not meet any evacuees coming in the opposite direction. It must also be remembered that both men were extremely fit and were well supported by porters.

On the tail of the two-man survey party several ITA reconnaissance parties were dispatched from Lekhpani. Each party consisted of two liaison officers, a sub-assistant surgeon, a dresser, twelve menials and fifty Abor porters – riches and levels of support beyond Cornelius North's wildest imaginings. In fact, the task of the ITA reconnaissance parties was made easier because a series of camps had already been partially constructed between Lekhpani and Nampong. They were intended to accommodate road-workers, but could easily be adapted for evacuees. Within a matter of days, the ITA had completed the construction of twelve camps between Lekhpani and the Pangsau Pass. It had also provisioned them, provided medical facilities in each of them and deployed teams of porters who would be ready to assist any evacuees who needed help. It was an astonishing achievement in such a short space of time

The situation on the eastern (Burma) side of the Pangsau Pass was much more difficult. The ITA had originally planned to construct four camps, each capable of accommodating 500 refugees per night, between Shingbwiyang and the Pangsau Pass. It was unachievable because the Burma side of the Pangsau Pass was in hostile territory as Japanese attacks were quite possible. Moreover, the terrible weather and track conditions prevented porters from carrying supplies over the Pangsau Pass from India. The climatic conditions also made it impossible for the RAF to drop supplies at any point between Shingbwiyang and the Pangsau Pass. Consequently, General Wood proposed that the Burma authorities (whoever they might be) should be responsible for constructing, supplying and staffing four camps to be located at Taikham Zup, Yangman and Nawngyang Hka and Ngalang Ga on the Burma side of the border.

As Dr Farrant-Russell was to attest the plan was never realized. In the event the camps at Namlip and Tagung Hka were respectively redesignated 'temporary camp' and 'ration camp'. Namlip teetered on the brink of disaster for several days and Tagung Hka was the first of twelve camps that were solely managed by the ITA.[46] They were well organized, equipped and provisioned, and went some way to mitigate the effects of the challenging terrain and deteriorating physical condition of the evacuees. Nevertheless, despite the ITA's efforts, many evacuees died as they traversed Assam.

The ITA 'Ration Camp' at Tagung Hka astonished and delighted every evacuee. It was their first experience of ITA hospitality. Russell arrived on 30 May and the vision that greeted him was etched on his mind. A Union Jack fluttered over four clean-cut young English officers who dispensed biscuits, tea and sympathy, while a smartly attired Indian 'wound-dresser' tended to the evacuees' sore feet. When Langham-Carter arrived a few days later he described it as 'the most blessed sight of my life'.

The Nampong Camp was more substantial. It was located at the junction of the Yangman–Simon spur and had a fully equipped hospital. It was the ITA Road Commander's base and he had established the Jeep Club for evacuees who had come over the Pangsau Pass.[47] Wilkie and his colleagues arrived there on 2 June. A Canadian doctor gave them a thorough medical examination and treated any blisters, dysentery, leach-bites and fevers. They were all given a cooked meal and a warm shower before being shown to a dormitory in a large hut that was full of sick Indians. They looked like mummies 'muffled in their blankets'. However, Wilkie's bed was comfortable and he enjoyed his first sound sleep for a very long time. It came at a price, however, for his money and documents were stolen during the night.[48] Generous portions of rice and bullock meat were served for breakfast. It kept the evacuees going all day.[49] Wilkie was encouraged to hear that there were ITA camps at ten-mile intervals all the way to Margherita, and that ITA porters were on hand, if evacuees ran into difficulties between camps. For the first time they felt protected and relaxed. As a result, they started out later each morning and marched for shorter periods each day. Rose was similarly reassured when he stayed at Nampong a few days later.

***

The ITA set to work immediately. It exposed the wide gulf in perception that always existed between evacuees and organizers. Evacuees perceived that salvation is gained as a result of their own heroic deeds. Organizers believed that salvation depends on their preparatory work. Both were correct in their way. Most evacuees had no idea that ITA liaison officers, engineers, labourers and porters had sweated blood in constructing bridges, building camps, cutting tracks through virgin jungle, setting up clinics and importing supplies.[50]

This vast logistical exercise demanded careful planning, skilled management and imaginative innovation, which it applied in abundance. The ITA was aided and abetted by enterprising young army officers like Captain Alasdair Ramsay Tainsh, who established the wireless communication between Nampong and Ledo, and inaugurated regular armed patrols along the road to reduce the incidence of looting. His men disarmed many dacoits and 'rogue' troops and seized quantities of stolen food. He pioneered the technique of dabbing gentian violet on evacuees' wrists when they had been served food in the camp canteens to prevent them obtaining double rations.[51] Eric Lambert the local political officer' was also instrumental in laying out the camps up to and beyond the Pangsau Pass.[52]

Five aspects of the ITA's work – camp-building operations; medical provision; the management of porters; co-ordination with the RAF; and the construction of new roads – illustrate the point.

First, the camp-building operations. The ITA acknowledged that it was problematic. In places like Shamlung, the evacuees were housed in lean-to shacks. At first even the Nampong Camp (that had so impressed Dr Farrant-Russell) was surrounded by deep liquid mud. Duckboards had to be laid to make the sleeping quarters inhabitable. None of the camps between Shingbwiyang and Nampong had sewage disposal systems, so they were awash with human excrement. The conditions were sometimes so bad that evacuees refused to stay in the camps. There were also complaints of racial discrimination.

Second (and by contrast), the standard of medical care was universally excellent. The monsoon conditions caused sickness rates to increase and malaria reached epidemic proportions and healthcare could not be left to chance. The Principal ITA Medical Officer directed operations from his mobile headquarters, which could be moved along the route. He stipulated that every evacuee must be inoculated against cholera when he or she arrived at the Tagung Hka Camp. Five fully qualified European doctors and one Indian doctor were on duty at all times. On average, there was one doctor for every fifteen miles of road.

Basic clinics were provided in every camp on the Jeep Road between Namlip and Tipong, and resident assistant medical officers, compounders and antimalarial babus were stationed in each of them.[53] Most new arrivals were given medical examinations and pedicures, and first-aid sheds were set up *between* camps along many sections of the track. The Nampong Camp had a well-equipped and fully staffed hospital and it was linked by radio to the hospital in Ledo. Therefore, doctors could share their expertise. There were also major refugee hospitals in Margherita, at Dinjan Aerodrome and at the Tipong Military Camp.[54]

In due course it was decided to limit treatment in most camps to dispensing prophylactics and basic 'patching up' procedures. This was for clinical reasons. More seriously sick or wounded evacuees were moved to Margherita as quickly as possible. One health hazard was caused by the porters' refusal (for moral reasons) to bury or burn dead bodies, so corpses were often left to decompose where they lay.

Third, porters were absolutely vital to the success of the ITA's operations on the Hukawng Valley route. Managing them effectively was a colossal task. At its peak 5,750 porters and 400 mules were employed along the route. There were never enough porters, and they always seemed to be in the wrong place at the wrong time.[55] It was an uphill struggle to persuade porters to return to their base camps immediately after delivering a load. Ideally, the porters had to be tough, muscular, wiry and able to work hard in heavy rain and knee-deep mud. Locally recruited porters became less reliable as time went on. Many were not strong enough to carry full loads and others 'deserted' to work privately for evacuees who paid more money for less work. At one point 400 Garos were reported to be off sick at the same time, and between 29 May and 7 June all the Pnar porters had to be quarantined following their exposure to smallpox. Khasi porters (known troublemakers) went on strike for better living conditions between 10 and 15 June. Abor, Rangpur and Naga porters were more timid, and they often fled if fighting was reported in the vicinity.

On 20 May 1942, a change in ITA policy enabled the recruitment of hand-picked labourers from the Doom Doom tea estates. Their strength was legendary, and often in June 1942, 4-mile convoys of Doom Doom porters could be seen carrying essential supplies to roadworks on the Simon–Nampong spur road and to the most inaccessible camps between the Pangsau Pass and Shingbwiyang. Porters were also employed to rescue evacuees at night and to carry out emergency repairs on camps. Each group of porters was considered to have a distinctive set of characteristics. Abors were supposed to be loyal and reliable. The tea garden porters would only work for short periods and expected 'special' rates of pay – they also owed allegiance to individual planters and were suspicious of anyone else. The Garos and Khasis were generally considered to be troublemakers, with a tendency to grumble about anything and everything – especially the lack of fish and milk in their diets. The Pnars were often criticized for being dirty and for having low sanitary standards.[56]

Nevertheless, all the porters had to live cheek by jowl with real danger and were frequently *genuinely* sick. They were especially prone to foot sores. By mid-June so many of porters were dying (twenty-three in one week alone, and many more at Shamlung) that on 16 June they were all recalled to Lekhpani. Only a few Garos and 1,300 tea garden labourers were fit enough to work on the road. During the evacuation *at least* fifty-two Pnars, eleven Abors, fifty-nine Khasis, sixty-three Garos and thirteen tea garden porters died in the course of their duties. One Abor porter who had carried two refugees on his back for many miles was awarded the Albert Medal.

Fourth, the ITA Road Commander was responsible for coordinating the RAF airdrops. These were absolutely vital. Poor visibility between 12 and 18 May prevented RAF planes from dropping supplies. Many evacuees went hungry in that time. During the third week of May, the weather improved just long enough to allow the RAF to drop food at Shingbwiyang, Shamlung, Ngalang Ga and Tagup Ga. The main problem was that RAF planes were needed for combat duty, but here they had to be unarmed in order to reduce weight. The pilots were therefore vulnerable to Japanese attack. The planes had to descend and climb steeply because of the deep valleys and high mountains, so it was impossible to drop loads with any degree of accuracy. Packages that went off target by even a few feet might be lost forever in thick jungle. To counter this, pilots began to attach cotton streamers to the packages. However, airdrops remained an inexact science.[57] The main coordination issue was getting porters to the right place to recover airdropped loads. It could take a team of porters a whole day to cover four miles, by which time the packages would probably have been looted.

ITA officials on the ground were unable to communicate with aircraft crews. As a result, inappropriate types of food were often dropped. For example, the evacuees rarely had dry matches with which to light fires and to cook. Not for a long time did RAF crews realize that they should drop food that required no cooking. RAF technicians eventually designed packaging that was less likely to burst on impact. Gradually the percentage of packages hitting the targets improved. By the end of May, most evacuees were receiving plenty of European or Indian food, and hot tea, vegetable stew, meat, biscuit and Bovril and fresh milk for women and children regularly featured on menus in the camps.[58]

Fifth, the new Simon to Nampong 'cut' was a triumph of civil engineering. On 12 May, 900 Abor labourers were recruited in Miao. They were sent to Simon, and it took them just nine days to cut a track through the virgin jungle to Nampong. Teams of labourers worked with elephants and mahouts to construct a very difficult section of the track between Namgoi and Yangman. The route was opened on 21 May and by 25 May, 150 loads per day were being brought through from Simon to Nampong. It was a complex logistical exercise that involved boat transport from Simon to Namgoi Mukh, and on elephants to Yangman. Then porters carried the goods on to Nawngyang. Soon enough food had been stockpiled on the route to feed 9,500 Indians and 500 Europeans, enabling the Simon–Nampong cut to play a vital role in the military retreat.[59]

***

On 26 June, General Wood, General Irwin, Brigadier Whitworth, R. E. McGuire and senior ITA representatives took the decision to close the Hukawng Valley route. It merely confirmed a process that had already begun.[60] McGuire had recently walked over the Pangsau Pass to Lekhpani, and he was strongly in favour of keeping the refugee organization in place until the very last evacuee had arrived in India. ITA officials gave assurances that they would not close the route early.[61] The following factors contributed to the decision. ITA officers were worried about the declining health of many evacuees. The ITA Road Commander feared that ITA staff might be marooned in isolated camps. The Indian Tea Association Projects Sub-Committee wanted to close the Hukawng Valley operation. The Military High Command wanted the ITA to divert resources *from* refugee work *to* construction sites, roads and aerodromes, and finally there were great concerns about the welfare and safety of porters.[62] However, the whole procedure took many weeks to complete.

The closure strategy was very simple – at least in *theory*. First, all the evacuees still in Shingbwiyang (of whom there were many) would be ordered to stay put in the camp, where at least they had shelter and plenty of food. Second, the large numbers of evacuees already walking along the track towards the Pangsau Pass would be ordered to return to Shingbwiyang immediately. Third, ITA field officers agreed to provide assistance to all the evacuees making their way along the Jeep Road towards Lekhpani. And, fourth, there would be ITA and RAF collaboration to ensure that no one was left on the route.[63]

A start had already been made when ITA engineers began work on emergency-withdrawal bridges over the Tagung Hka and Nawngyang Hka and when RAF planes flew over Shingbwiyang dropping leaflets ordering the evacuees *not* to move. Moreover, between 13 and16 June, planes had flown back and forth along the track to Tagap Ga dropping leaflets signed by General Wood. They *ordered* the evacuees to return to Shingbwiyang immediately. On 3 June the ITA Road Commander announced the imminent closure of the Namlip Camp.[64]. It had an effect because the last evacuees arrived on 8 June. Thereafter the Road Commander let it be known that all camps between Shingbwiyang and the Pangsau Pass would close. However, he made it clear that it would happen in an orderly sequence.

The first major snag had already appeared. On 16 June. R. E. McGuire went to the Namyang Hka where 2,500 evacuees were waiting to cross the river. He read out a message from General Wood instructing evacuees to return to Shingbwiyang immediately. None of the evacuees took any notice. They flatly refused to return to Shingbwiyang. In due course, the water level fell and the evacuees began to cross the river. Between 16 and 20 June about 2,000–3,000 evacuees got across.

Meanwhile porters carried food from Shingbwiyang to the camps up to the Pangsau Pass, the RAF dropped enough food on Tagup Ga to feed up to 700 evacuees, and supplies of Indian and European food were stockpiled at Nampong.

However, the situation worsened after 14 June when the Simon–Nampong route was closed. It prevented supplies from reaching several camps on the Jeep Road. A few courageous acts helped to mitigate the situation. For example, on 16 June in appalling weather conditions Captain England took 20 mules from Nampong over the Pangsau Pass. He brought back scores of disabled refugees to Lekhpani, and on 17 June an ITA Liaison Officer and a doctor took two elephants up to Shamlung where seventy exhausted evacuees (including several very sick children) were trapped. They completely cleared the camp by 20 June.

There followed an amazingly thorough mop-up operation. Nothing was left to chance.

First, Captain Keene and 200 Assam Riflemen did a remarkable circuit. Starting from Tipong, they reached the Pangsau Pass on 28 June, Nampong on 2 July, Shamlung on 3 July and Nawngyang Hka on 4 July. They got back to Nampong on 5 July and arrived back in Tipong on 11 July. As they travelled, they picked up many sick and exhausted evacuees, including twelve stretcher cases and thirty walking wounded.

On 27 June Captain England set out once again from Shingbwiyang to Nampong with a string of mules. He left a few mules behind to help those stranded on the Paungsau Pass, and he rescued many evacuees. On the same day, the Chief ITA Liaison Officer and Principal ITA Medical Officer walked from Nampong to Shingbwiyang – then went back and forth several times between 28 June and 10 July, picking up many refugees each time. On 1 July, the ITA Medical Officer launched a census of the evacuees still making their way over the route. He discovered that 2,000–3,000 evacuees were still on the move (see Table 4.1).

By the middle of July 1942, the ITA was more determined than ever than to close its operation on the Hukawng route. It was short of officers, medical staff, porters and labourers and there were few evacuees. For example, on 11 July there were only four evacuees in the Nawngyang Camp and by 12 July the Nampong Camp was empty. The ITA Road Commander announced that all the ITA camps between Shingbwiyang and Lekhapani would close by 31 July. Between 12 and 18 July the camps at Nampong, Namgoi, Namchick, Buffalo, Kumlao and North Tirap closed one by one.

On 18 July sixty-eight stretcher cases were brought from North Tirap to Lekhpani. On 20 July two ITA Liaison Officers and ninety tea garden coolies walked up to Shamlung and found sixty-nine evacuees on the way out and fifty-eight on the way back. On 27 July an ITA Liaison Officer and seventy-five tea garden coolies went out to Shamlung yet again. Between Shamlung and Nampong they picked up twelve stretcher cases and a hundred exhausted evacuees.

Table 4.1 Census of refugee movements Hukawng Valley, 4–8 July 1942

Area of Activity	Activity
Namyang Hka to Tagung Hka	400–800 refugees walking
Tagung Hka (daily arrivals)	60–70
Beyond Tagung Hka	150 refugees walking
Shamlung	100 refugees arriving daily
Nampong to Margherita	500 on move (7 July)
Margherita	1,600 refugees arrived (8 July)

Source: Indian Tea Association Chief Liaison Officer Report, 10 July 1942.

At the end of July 1942, the Chief ITA Liaison Officer flew over the entire length of the route from Lekhpani to Shingbwiyang in an RAF plane. He sighted one European at Shamlung, but otherwise the camps were deserted. The Namyang Hka was in full flood and unfordable. The aircraft circled Shingbwiyang a dozen times and dropped a last load of food and medical supplies. On the return flight, they flew low over Tagap Ga where they saw an SOS message marked out on the ground. There was no evidence of human life, but in case any stragglers arrived the pilot dropped a package of food and a message instructing remaining evacuees to return to Shingbwiyang as quickly as possible. A chowkidar was left in charge of each camp and also a store of food in case any evacuees turned up.

In September 1942, despite all these herculean efforts, a group of evacuees arrived unexpectedly at the Pangsau Pass. Presumably they had 'broken out' of Shingbwiyang. The camp at Shingbwiyang was not finally cleared until November 1942, when it was feared that advancing Japanese forces might be approaching the town. The work of the ITA finally came to an end on 15 August 1942 when it handed over to the Army.

The last evacuees to emerge from the Hukawng Valley were 'verminous and filthy' and they had survived looting, robbery and extortion. One mystery remained unsolved. The murdered bodies of twenty-six 'better-class' women evacuees were discovered at Nampong. They had no jewellery, money or any form of identification.[65]

***

5

The Chaukan Pass Evacuation Route

This is as strange a maze as ever a man trod

Shakespeare: *The Tempest*, Act 5. Scene 1

The civilian evacuees who streamed through the Chindwin and Hukawng valleys between February and May 1942 took part in a *mass* exodus. Many thousands of men, women and children struggled along each of the routes. The evacuation through the Chaukan Pass was a different kettle of fish. It was a small, niche affair in which attention focussed on the fifty or so British and Anglo-Indian civilians involved, although a few hundred Gurkhas and Indian troops struggled alongside the European evacuees. Large numbers of Kachin, Mishmi and Hnung mahouts, guides and porters were inveigled into providing assistance.[1]

A huge amount of public interest in London and Calcutta centred on the fifty or so British colonials involved in the escape. It also sucked in a disproportionate amount of official resources. Many intrepid rescuers were put in harm's way, and there was more than a hint of arrogant irresponsibility about attitudes at the time. The exodus through the Chaukan Pass also exposed a measure of distrust between the parties involved. The rescued and rescuers in Burma in 1942 often misunderstood one another. In this episode, as in several others, the 'rescued' tended to underestimate the enormity of the demands they placed on the 'rescuers'.

The civil and military authorities in India were well aware of the dangers posed by the Chaukan Pass route. They made their position crystal clear at the beginning of May 1942. Brigadier Whitworth, Commander in Chief in Assam, warned the Burma Government not to allow *anybody* to go that way.[2] By that time, the Government of Burma had disappeared without trace and was in no position to prevent *anyone* from doing *anything*. It was left to individual evacuees to decide what they should or should not do. Most did as

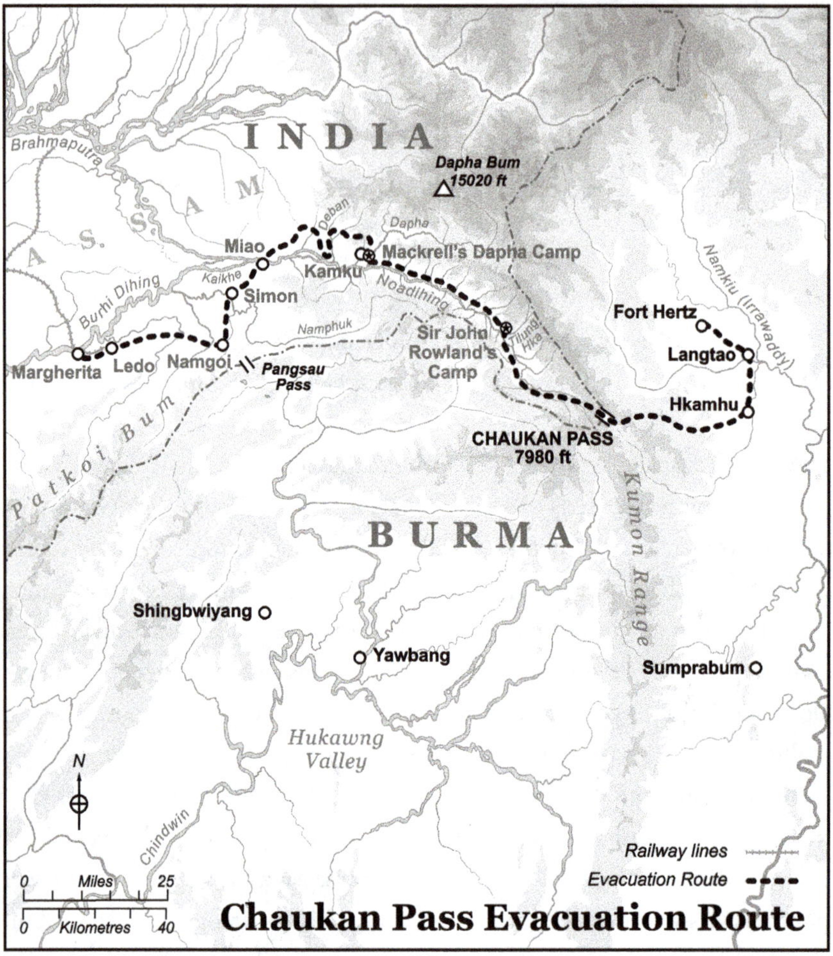

Map 5.1 Chaukan Pass evacuation route

they were told, but a few did not. Predictably, perhaps, a number of prominent colonials considered they knew best and ignored the advice. Sir John Edward Maurice Rowland was one of the most notable.

Notices had been displayed prominently around Myitkyina warning evacuees not to attempt the Chaukan Pass escape route. When the evacuees fled to Sumprabum after 6 May a huge poster repeating the warning was displayed in the town centre. Meanwhile RAF planes dropped leaflets on Fort Hertz ordering people not to move until the cold season.[3] Why people ignored such clear advice is something of a mystery. Some might have thought that the Hukawng Valley was overcrowded. Others seemed to object to diktats delivered by 'pen pushers' in Margherita and Calcutta. Others probably relished the prospect of a glamorous adventure, and some senior evacuees blamed subordinates for unwittingly leading them astray.[4]

Geoffrey Tyson billed the Pangsau Pass as 'grisly trench warfare' and the Chaukan Pass as a 'dashing cavalry charge'.[5] He was right on the first count but wrong on the second. The Chakan Pass route was neither glamorous nor dashing. No European had attempted it since the 1890s – and *no one* had *ever* attempted it during the monsoon season or in a time of war.[6] At the best of times, it lay through a miserable, unhealthy, dangerous, uncharted and unpopulated region.

Against this forbidding backdrop, a surprising event happened. On 2 August 1942 a group of exhausted evacuees – one of them Sir John Rowland – staggered into Margherita. They had had no direct contact with the outside world since starting out from Burma three months previously. The men (some of them rather elderly and very unsteady) had just trekked through some of the most difficult terrain in the world via the Chaukan Pass and the Dapha River. A few of them had died on the way, but most managed to get through. In itself this was a miracle, for they had teetered the whole time on the edge of *complete* disaster.

Unfortunately 2 August was not the end of the story, for the last bedraggled remnants of Rowland's expedition were rescued at great cost. They were carried into Margherita on 6 October 1942, a full six months after they had started out from Burma. They were broken in body and mind. That they survived was due in part to their own steely will, but mainly to the skill, resources and courage of others – including RAF pilots, porters, mahouts, Assam Riflemen and officers of the ITA.

In due course, the escapade acquired the golden glow of a *Boy's Own Paper* adventure yarn. It was presented as the saga of high-ranking colonial officials and faithful native bearers being rescued from the jaws of death by intrepid tea planters and sturdy elephants![7]

It was inevitable that fact was more prosaic than fiction. For, the corporate muscle of the ITA was the key to the rescue mission, and the chef de mission, Gyles Mackrell, was not a swashbuckling privateer. He was the hard-nosed director of a Calcutta Agency House, who had earned his keep as an ITA inspector. He had built up a team of working elephants, was an expert on jungle conditions and knew the frontier region like the back of his hand. In May 1942, Mackrell had volunteered for ITA relief operations in the Hukawng Valley and had become the liaison officer in Ledo before transferring on 17 May to the front-line depot at Simon, where he took charge of 100 working elephants.[8]

***

To begin at the beginning: on 5 May 1942 Sir John Rowland started out from Sumprabum for the Chaukan Pass with a small party of Europeans. He was a colonial grandee, self-confident and with bags of gravitas. He was probably well used to ignoring the warnings of subordinates. He had been a distinguished Chairman of Burma Railways, Chief Railway Commissioner and Managing Director of the Burma-China Construction Company (BCCC).[9] When Rowland was knighted in 1941, it catapulted him into sixteenth position in the colonial pecking order. Furthermore, he became a heroically compassionate icon when he turned down a place on an evacuation flight on the grounds that he 'would lose all self-respect' and 'would never be able to look a woman in the face again'.[10] He let the fact be well known. Unfortunately, when faced with completely new challenges, Sir John was soon out of his depth.

Groups of varying size joined Rowland's party and the collective assemblage became a *coalition* of groups each with its own leader, rather than a *single* party. Twenty Europeans from Fort Hertz had met up with Rowland in the remote village of Hkam Ho on 12 May, and a 'dashed fine crowd' of fifteen commandos led by Major Lindsay and Capt. Cumming joined him sometime later. Another group included Jardine of Lever Bros. and Lecky Thompson and Molloy of the BFF. On 30 May, 104 Punjabi troops turned up, and two days later (1 June) sixty-five Gurkha troops joined the party. On 17 July a very large group of forty Sepoys, and twenty-five Burma Riflemen together with a number of Burma Mines workers descended on Camp 22 by the Dehing River. Rowland's party had already been stuck there for many days.[11] While all this was happening, a number of subgroups broke away from the main party. They went off on their own. Consequently, the numbers increased and diminished day by day. They peaked on 31 May when, for a time, Rowland had to feed no fewer than 250 evacuees and porters. This was a particularly tall order in a region that was completely devoid of food. On many occasions starvation seemed almost inevitable,

Initially at least, most of the evacuees were willing to defer to Rowland's leadership.[12] However, his decision to walk out of Burma by this route in particular placed the British and Indian governments on the horns of a dilemma. Rowland was too important (and too famous) to lose, but he was also too difficult (and too expensive) to save. They also had to take into account the fact that Rowland was sixty years old in 1942. It would have been callous to leave someone so old to die! Meanwhile Rowland's influential friends never missed an opportunity to speak up for him in high places, and the general public regarded him as a sort of latter day General Gordon.

Edward Wrixon Rossiter was leader of the group that had met Rowland at Hkam Ho on 12 May. Rossiter had intended to walk from Fort Hertz to China, but he was persuaded by his friend John Leyden (Extra Deputy Commissioner, Myitkyina) to make his way to Sumprabum, recruit some coolies, gather supplies and take the Chaukan Pass route.

Rossiter was a complex character.[13] An Irish Protestant, he had joined the BFF in 1937 before becoming assistant superintendent at Fort Hertz. He was an authority on Shan politics, and had married Nang Hmat, a Shan Buddhist woman much younger than him. Nang Hmat was already three months pregnant with their *second* child when she started out on the trek. Their first child – six-month-old John Michael Rossiter came with them.[14] It was Rossiter who spread the rumour that the Indian authorities would send a relief party to meet them at the Chaukan Pass. They had made no such undertaking.[15] There were signs that a feud had developed between Rowland and Rossiter. They had toiled cheek by jowl for months on end, yet Rossiter never mentioned Rowland in his letters home and Rowland studiously ignored Rossiter in his diary, and (except in pejorative terms) never mentioned him in letters to his wife.

It is impossible to say at any one time *exactly* how many people there were in Rowland's party. Those that departed in splinter groups offset those who continuously arrived in groups to join. Nevertheless, when he started off from Hkam Ho on 14 May, Rowland's party consisted of about 150 souls. In general, the numbers then tended to vary between about 80 and about 150. By far the largest proportion were Kachin, Garhwali, Hnung and Naga porters and 'menials' together with Punjabi, Sepoy, Burman, Gurkha and Indians soldiers.

Suffice it to say that many of them risked their lives for the greater good, but they were anonymous at the time – and have remained anonymous to this day, receiving little or no recognition for their efforts.

We must remind ourselves that at no time were there more than thirty genuine evacuees in the group – senior British officials, administrators professionals businessmen, managers, army officers and the like. There were also five or six 'executive-class' Anglo-Indians and Indians. Attention in London and Calcutta focused almost exclusively on this small, elite group of around thirty and the local rescue efforts concentrated on bringing them back safely.

Who, then, was in this group of thirty Europeans? In addition to Rowland and Rossiter. The party included: Edward Lovell Manley, Chief Engineer, East Bengal Railway; Yunnan–Burma Railway; Eric Ivan Milne, District Traffic Superintendent, Burma Railways; Dr Burgess-Barnett, medical doctor, curator of reptiles at London Zoo, Superintendent of Rangoon Zoological Gardens and author of *The Treatment of Snake Bites*; C. L. Kendall Surveyor, Burma–China railway project; Captain A. O. Whitehouse, Royal Engineers; Frank Kingdon-Ward, botanist, explorer, writer and secret Military Survey Service operator; Guy Millar, tea planter (Kacharigaon Tea Company) and secret government service officer, and John Lamb Leyden, Additional District Commissioner, Myitkyina, and son of a distinguished poet and physician. The following members of a special operations unit: Ritchie Gardiner (Chief Executive McGregor's), Rangoon City Councillor and 'last ditcher'; Lieutenant Eric McCrindle (Manager, MacGregor's); Captain Noel Ernest Boyt (Steels), forestry expert; Lieutenant William Arthur 'Bill' Howe (Anglo-Burma Rice Company); and Major Lindsay, Captain Cumming (Royal Marines) and Corporal Sawyer (specialist radio unit), R. E. Jardine (Lever Brothers); Captain John Fraser, George Reginald Lecky-Thompson, Patrick Reginald Hembrough Molloy (BFF); and Sergeant Pratt (Seventh Hussars) and N. Moses (railway surveyor) whom Rowland referred to as 'the Dutch Jew.[16] E. Eadon (Health Inspector) was Anglo-Indian and there were three Indian Burma–China Railway Construction Company officials – S. T. Rajan (Divisional Accountant), R.V. Venkataraman (Office Superintendent) and C. V. Venkataraman (Store Clerk). The following 'menials' deserve a special mention: Applaswamy (Manley's faithful butler) and Goal Miri (an elephant tracker).

Here, we must pause to note that at least seven members of the party were in their late fifties – and of course Rowland himself was sixty years of age. This was a punishing ordeal for any gentleman of a certain age. The youngest person in Rowland's party (apart from Rossiter's pregnant young wife and their six-month-old child) was thirty years of age.

Rowland and his colleagues soon got into considerable difficulty. Their maps were hopelessly inaccurate – they showed non-existent villages and omitted major rivers.[17] At the same time, Rowland and his colleagues seemed to overlook the fact that the monsoon was about to break, and that in this part of the world it was always extremely severe. Indeed it was to rain continuously for eighty-six out of the next ninety-eight days. The track was treacherous. They had to trudge through ankle-deep mud for day after day, and naturally became very exhausted. Rowland bemoaned the fact that (whatever their maps indicated) they did not pass a single village between Hkam Ho and Miao – a distance of 232 miles – and that there was no sign of human activity of any sort from 14 May when they crossed the N'pyengaung Hka and 21 June when they reached the Dapha Camp.

The most difficult time was when Rowland's party was forced to spend forty-one days at a camp at the confluence of the Dehing River and the Tilung Hka. They had no porters and very little food – and no contact with the outside world for the whole of that time. Rowland seemed to think that about 300 other evacuees came over the Chaukan Pass and passed by the camp while he was there, and that sixty of them had died on the way.[18] Nothing had prepared him for the sight of 10,000-ft high mountains or the desperate scrambles across sheer rock faces; or the dangerous crossings of twenty-three rivers in full flood or of coming up against the tumultuous obstacles of the Dapha River. Nor was he prepared for the endless trudges through stretches of thick jungle, and for traversing muddy banks strewn with huge boulders. It was an unexpected sort of hell.

***

Rowland kept a detailed diary of the evacuation. He started out from Sumprabum on 5 May with two elephants, ten mules, ten Kachin coolies, two mahouts and several muleteers and he recruited another twenty-three coolies on 11 May. The muleteers, mahouts and thirty-three of the porters ran away on 15 May and the remaining porters threatened to go on strike. Every day the path became more and more treacherous and they spent several days struggling along the Paungma and Yam Yak rivers. Between 22 and 24 May they had to criss-cross from one bank to the other fifty-six times – sometimes wading waist-deep in fast-flowing water, sometimes crawling over low-hanging trees. It was dangerous and energy sapping and several members of the party fell ill. Morale dropped sharply.

On 19 May, Millar and Leyden, two of the fittest and most experienced men in the party announced that they were going ahead, supposedly to spy out the lie of the land and chase up the rescue party. However, Rowland did not hear from them again and he had no idea whether they were dead or alive.

He had no need to worry for Millar and Leyden were well organized. They took with them fourteen Hnung porters, a cook, an elephant tracker and some food and their story ended well. After following the Nam Yak River up to the Chaukan Pass they came up against the Dehing River. It was completely impassable. They attempted to circumvent it by climbing up to 8,000 ft. and hacking through miles of thick bamboo jungle. On 26 May they reached open country teeming with wildlife. It was pouring down with rain and there was no shelter. Their clothing and kit became saturated and they could find no dry firewood. They were plagued by swarms of leeches, blister-flies and sandflies. Their physical condition deteriorated rapidly and to make matters worse their food was running low. They reached the Dapha River on 31 May.

The river was still in full spate and they were unable to cross it. They had run out of food altogether and might well have died had a group of Mishmis not given them three fish. On 3 June they arrived at the small settlement of Bishi, where there was a government rice dump. They reached Simon Camp the following day and were delighted to discover that Gyles Mackrell's base was only five miles away at Namgoi. He had at his disposal eighty-four ITA elephants. Millar and Leyden arrived on Mackrell's doorstep on the evening of 4 June. They were dirty and exhausted and handed him a note from Sir John Rowland explaining his plight. Their mission complete, the two men set out for Margherita on 5 June with a clear conscience.

***

Back at the Tilung Hka, Rowland had no idea that Millar and Leyden had managed to make contact with Mackrell. He had heard nothing from them since they went off on 17 May. After Millar and Leyden had left, Rowland's party made painfully slow progress, covering only eight miles in the next two days. They stopped for four days in order to recover before moving forward again on 22 May. They followed the course of the Hpaungma Hka criss-crossing back and forth over it thirty-seven times. On 25 May, a small party consisting of Capt. Boyt, three other British officers and an NCO caught up with Rowland's party. They all moved off together up the Namyak River and reached the Chaukan Pass on 27 May. At this point all the coolies departed, refusing to go on any further. Rowland and his colleagues had no option but to stay put and built a temporary camp on the pass.

Rowland naively believed that the authorities in India would send a relief party to meet them there, so they lit bonfires to attract attention just in case.[19] In any case, without porters it was impossible to move on so they had to dig in until help came. Some of the fitter and more adventurous members of the party – including Jardine, McGrindle, Howe, Fraser, Pratt, Sawyer, Boyt, Gardiner and Moses – got itchy feet and decided to 'jump ship'. They left the main party and pressed on ahead.

Rowland was not too worried at this stage. He was sure that a relief party would arrive soon and he calculated that they had two-months' supply of food. The situation changed unexpectedly on 1 June. A party of forty-five Gurkhas arrived out of the blue from Fort Hertz.[20] The problem was that they would consume vast quantities of food, but on the other hand, they were willing to carry all Rowland's party's food and kit. Rowland and his colleagues were caught between Scylla and Charybdis. If they decided not to move on, they would run out of food very quickly. On the other hand, the weather had taken a turn for the worse. They knew they would quickly run into difficulties if they decided to move on. It was a difficult choice, but they decided to move.

On 2 June, they all upped sticks and set off in a very violent storm. The rain continued unabated for the next ten days and finally on 11 June the party had to halt at the Tilung Hka. The river was impassable. It was raining heavily; their food stocks were running low and, in any case, they were too exhausted and too weak to go further.

A strange reunion took place in the middle of this cloudburst. Jardine's party (which had parted company with Rowland a few days previously) had also come to a halt at the Tilung Hka. They had been there for several days waiting for the river to subside. Jardine was anxious to get going again and on 12 June the river subsided a little. He decided to risk it. His party attempted to cross the still turbulent river but, in the process, Corporal Sawyer was drowned, Captain Fraser was almost swept away, and all the party's baggage containing food and supplies sank in deep water. Jardine was determined that his party should press on regardless of the losses. Nine days later they reached Mackrell's camp at the confluence of the Dapha and Dehing rivers. They got there in the nick of time for they had 'only four ounces of semi-putrefied rice' to share between them. Indeed they had existed for the past seven days on 'nothing but 2 ounces of rice per day without salt or anything else whatsoever'.[21]

A few weeks previously Major Lindsay, Captain Cummings and group of commandos had joined Rowland's party very briefly. They were one of the first groups to leave the main party. They made good progress and arrived at the Dapha Camp a couple of days before Jardine and his party got there. They were immediately transported to Margherita on elephants, and were able to provide information on Rowland's whereabouts.

Jardine's party took longer to reach Margherita. It took them five days to get from Dapha to Miao. They were held up because one of their elephants was swept away in a swollen river and because Kendall, one of Jardine's closest colleagues, became very ill. Indeed, he died two days after they reached Margherita. Along the way Captain Noel Boyt, joined Jardine who praised him for keeping the party together and displaying all the finest qualities of a leader and a Christian gentleman.

***

Rowland was stuck in Camp 22 at the Tilung Hka for forty-one days, and Rossiter for much longer. They arrived on 11 June. The river was impassable and they had only six days' supply of rice.[22] Manley's servant, Applaswamy, died and two members of the party, Venkataraman and Capt. Fraser, were swept away in the river and nearly drowned in the midst of a huge thunderstorm.

Things went from bad to worse. Violent storms occurred on twenty-six of the next forty-one days and the food situation became ever more critical. Rowland set up a 'food committee' to conserve food. It comprised of Manley, Capt. Whitehouse and Molloy and their first action was to put everyone onto quarter rations – effectively two cups of skilly per day. They became weaker

Figure 5.1 Group of Chaukan Pass Evacuees. Credit: Geoffrey Tyson. A group of evacuees who had been in Sir John Rowland's party in May and June 1942. This party had already trekked through the Chaukan Pass into Assam. They included Jardine, Fraser, Howe, Boyt, Pratt, Ritchie Gardiner, Kendall, McCrindle and three Indian servants.

and more depressed by the day and many of them felt giddy. On 25 June the Dehing River burst its banks, flooded the camp and soaked all their clothing and bedding. Two very long, exhausting days were devoted to moving the camp and all the kit to a higher level.

By 29 June the food had run out *completely* and almost everyone was suffering from an ailment of one sort or another – malaria, septic sores and typhoid were the most common. Rowland feared that they all faced long, lingering deaths. In the nick of time on 30 June the skies cleared just long enough for an RAF plane to fly over the camp. The pilot spotted them and returned the next day and again on 6 and 13 July. Each time he dropped sacks of rice, tinned stores, atta, tea, sugar, salt and essential medical supplies. The airdrops saved the day. One package contained a reassuring note from Rowland's old friend, Wing Commander George Chater.

The Camp Food Committee gradually salted away sufficient food to feed twenty-seven people for two months. However, this was not enough. The problem was that several new groups had descended on them. On 1 June a group of sixty-five Gurkhas and Garhwalis had tagged along. Forty Sepoys turned up on 18 July and on 19 July twenty-five men of the 9th Burma Rifles arrived together with several Burma Corporation employees. The new arrivals shared three things in common. They were all extremely hungry, they had no food, and most of them were sick. It was true that at the same time several smaller groups (like Lindsay, Cummings and the commandos) had gone off on their own, but the numbers of mouths to be fed grew exponentially. It rained on most days so the RAF was unable to drop food, and it was now absolutely clear that the Indian authorities had not dispatched a relief party.

On 22 July Rowland summoned a crisis meeting at which it was agreed to split into two unequal groups. Rowland led the bigger of the two groups consisting of seventy-three *relatively* fit members of the party. They included Milne, Naidu, Venkatachalam, Rajan, Venkataraman, two coolies, forty-nine Sepoys and twelve Burma Corporation men. Their objective was to get to Mackrell's camp on the Dapha River as quickly as possible. Rossiter led the smaller of the two groups. It included twenty-five of the sickest and least mobile of the evacuees – people like Manley, Dr Burgess-Barnett, Captain Whitehouse, Nang Hmat and her baby, six servants and twelve very sick Sepoys.

Rowland party left the Tilung Hka on 23 July. Their journey would prove to be extremely demanding. In the next few days they would have to cross seven swollen rivers and traverse an avalanche of mud and boulders. It rained heavily the whole time, so they were perpetually soaked. They arrived at the confluence of the Dapha and Dehing rivers on 30 July 1942. Captain Street of the 2nd Rajput Rifles was waiting to meet them. He took them to the Dapha Camp where they spent the next two nights recuperating. On 2 August Mr R. B. Black of the ITA accompanied them to Simon with two elephants. At Simon, they transferred to dugout boats and continued their journey via the camps at Miao and Simon and ended up in Margherita on 7 August. Here they were entertained and debriefed by Thomson, Mackrell and Lambert. Rowland, Howe, Milne, Lecky Thomson and Molloy were then taken to tea estate bungalows, while the others stayed in the Margherita Evacuee Camp. Rowland calculated that since leaving Myitkyina they had travelled about 452 miles – most of it on foot. On 11 August, Wing Commander Chater flew Rowland to Calcutta, where he checked into the Grand Hotel.

Three things had become very clear. First, even in such vile conditions it became evident that moderately fit evacuees like Rowland could cover the

Figure 5.2 Gyles Mackrell, DFC, GM, (1888–1959). Credit: Cambridge Centre for South Asian Studies. Mackrell was a tea planter in Assam, an agent for Octavius Steel & Co., and he had his own elephant transport business. He served in the Royal Flying Corps in World War I and in 1942 he rescued about 200 evacuees from Burma for which he was awarded the George Medal in January 1943. This horribly politically incorrect photograph captures the rather swashbuckling life of frontiersmen in the 1940s.

distance between Camp 22 and the Dapha Camp in eight to ten days. It was perfectly doable for able-bodied evacuees, but virtually impossible for the stretcher-bound. There was a huge gulf between Rowland's 'leave party' and Rossiter's 'remain party'. Second, provisions were a constant worry. It was made worse because supplies had had to be split up into smaller and smaller portions and divvied between splinter subgroups. Third, the evacuees' physical condition deteriorated rapidly in a short space of time. The longer things were left, the worse they became.

Twenty-four souls remained hopelessly trapped in the Tilung Hka Camp after Rowland's departure on 23 July. Several of those who remained were disabled and sick and they were all despondent. They had little food and few medicines. Whenever the clouds lifted (which happened infrequently), RAF planes returned to drop supplies, but absolutely no one outside the camp knew what was happening inside it. Only one communication had emerged – an SOS from Manley complaining that many of the RAF food parcels had dropped in the river, and that they were all cold, wet, ill and miserable. They waited anxiously, he said, for a rescue party to arrive.

***

Attention must now shift from rescued to rescuers.[23] When Millar and Leyden arrived on his doorstep after dark on 4 June, Mackrell listened carefully to what they had to say, and read Rowland's message with interest. He was not one to waste time and later that night he assembled a team of porters and twenty elephants.

Mackrell's party set off at dawn the next day (5 June). It was raining heavily. They crossed the swollen Dehing River in the morning and then a Mishmi guide took them by an obscure track through the jungle to the Dapha River. At one point they had to negotiate a very dangerous situation when their own elephants were caught up in a herd of sixty wild elephants on the rampage.

On 9 June they reached the Dapha Camp, which was unoccupied. The river was too full to *risk* a crossing. During the night they heard shouts emanating from a low-lying island in the middle of the Dapha River. On investigation they located sixty-eight Burma Rifles and BFF men. They had been stranded there for several weeks and the island was disintegrating under the constant force of the river. Mackrell worked with the elephants throughout the night,

Figure 5.3 Elephants on Dapha River. Credit: Geoffrey Tyson. A team of Mackrell's mahouts led by the famous elephant, Rungdot, in an operation to rescue a party of men trapped on an island in the Dapha River on 9 June 1942.

and by first light they rescued all sixty-eight men shortly before the island was swept away.[24] All the men were smothered in septic sores and on the verge of starvation. It was a reminder of the perils in this area. Mackrell treated the men's sores, fed them and sent thirty of the sickest of them on elephants to Simon. The Mishmi guide went with them and returned with the elephants, extra stores, and fifteen additional porters the next day.

By 13 June the river had dropped sufficiently to allow Mackrell and his porters to cross the river. He then sent a few of them on, under the trusted Sirdar Iman Singh to look for Rowland's party. Each of the porters carried 20lbs of European food. Mackrell stayed behind at the Dapha Camp to direct operations. On 14th June twenty-seven Sikhs arrived, followed the next day by thirty-eight Gurkha and Sikh soldiers. On 16 June six more Gurkhas, Nepalis and Garhwalis turned up. They all had to be fed and accommodated, and their ailments were treated. Mackrell's stocks of food and medicines were seriously depleted.[25]

On 17 June, Mackrell sent a note to Dudley Hodson, the ITA's Chief Liaison Officer in Simon, explaining his predicament –139 refugees had descended on him. Each of them had required food and medical treatment. One man had died. He had sent ninety-eight of the fitter men on to Miao. The Naga Sirdar and sixteen Mishmi porters had gone forward to try to find Rowland's party. They had taken with them considerable quantities of food and medical supplies. Mackrell explained that he desperately needed medical supplies, rice, sugar, dhal and salt, and that it was vital that the RAF started dropping food supplies as a matter of urgency.[26] A Mishmi 'runner' took the letter to Hodson in Simon, with instructions to return to Dapha immediately with more elephants and supplies of food and medicines.

The runner did not reappear. The reason later became clear. A Captain Wilson had recently been posted to the area. He was inexperienced and unaware of the desperate lack of food at the Dapha Camp. He intercepted the Mishmi runner and Mackrell's elephants and misunderstood Mackrell's instructions. For some reason he assumed that Mackrell wanted building materials. He sent the runner and the elephants on a wild goose chase around local suppliers for tarpaulins and other building materials. Several days later Wilson and his colleague, Dr Bardoloi had stocked up with what they (wrongly) believed Mackrell wanted and with their haul they set out themselves for the Dapha Camp.

Wilson then made a second mistake. He recruited 60 so-called political porters to take with him to Dapha. The Political Porter Corps' (PPC) were notoriously unreliable: Some of them absconded. Others went off sick or took very long rest periods. Progress slowed to a crawl. The porters demanded full rations, and consumed a large proportion of the food that was desperately needed at the Dapha Camp.

Wilson and Dr Bardoloi reached the Dapha Camp on 20 June. They arrived in the midst of a crisis. A large party of Gurkhas had just arrived, and at exactly the same time several members of Rowland's party – among them Ritchie, Gardiner, McCrindle, Howe, Captain Cummings, Lindsay, Kendall, Captain Fraser and Sergeant Pratt – also arrived.[27] They were all in a very bad way and in need of medical attention. Lindsay had a big abscess on his leg and Kendall was desperately ill. The next day Jardine, Boyt and several other members of Rowland's party appeared on the far bank of the river. Mackrell had to devise a Heath Robinson contraption to send food over to them. It was understandable therefore, that he was not best pleased when Wilson and Bardoloi arrived with scores of porters, but *without* food.

To add insult to injury, on 23 June the Dapha River burst its banks and flooded the camp. Mackrell had to spend the next two days moving all the fuel, food, kitchen equipment, beds, tables, chairs and bedding to a drier site. While this was going on, his Mishmi porters got separated and spent several nights sleeping in the open on a nearby hill.

Because of Wilson's and Bardoloi's misjudgement Mackrell's provisions began to run dangerously low. On 30th June some more members of Rowland's party arrived on the other side of the river. Among them were Eadon, Moses, a rifleman and five porters. Mackrell was pleased to see them, but it meant yet more mouths to feed. Fortunately, the RAF dropped food supplies the next day – but there were no medical stores. The logistics were becoming extremely complicated because Mackrell had to send large quantities of food to the growing numbers of evacuees waiting on the other side of the river. On 1 July, Mackrell put Boyt, Moses and their colleagues onto three elephants and sent them to Simon.

The mood lightened on the morning of 5 July. An RAF plane flew over and dropped more stores. Unusually, there was also an important looking bag, which contained a message from the political officer. The note said that Rowland's party had been spotted on 30 June, and that an RAF plane had flown over their camp at the Tilung Hka on 1 July to drop food parcels. The note added that fourteen elephants had been sent to the Dapha Camp. The Political Officer asked Mackrell's opinion on two issues. First, he asked whether Mackrell could send thirty porters to reach the Tilung Hka Camp within the next fifteen days, and second, he asked whether the party could be rescued during the monsoon season. The plane circled overhead as Mackrell laid out his answers on the ground. To the first question he answered '*yes*', and to the second, '*we will try*'. The plane then flew off. It returned later in the afternoon. By prearrangement the pilot fired a green verey light to indicate that he had successfully dropped more food on Rowland's camp.

On 8 July, Sirdar Iman Singh's porters (but without the Sirdar) returned to the camp having failed in their attempt to reach the Tilung Hka Camp. The porters explained that Sirdar Iman Singh and a few porters were continuing the quest to get to the camp. They also explained that one of the Mishmi porters had died on the way, that several others had deserted and that the rest were sick. Indeed, only three or four out of the original sixteen porters were well enough to continue. On 12 July, Sirdar Iman Singh arrived back at the camp. He had reached Sir John Rowland and Rossiter.[28] He brought back with him a letter from Rowland saying that everyone in the camp was extremely ill and debilitated and that sixty or seventy porters would be needed to carry out the sick and disabled. Rowland warned that they were all close to death, and that help was needed *very* urgently.

***

A curious sequence of events had taken place at the Dapha Camp, events which were to alter the dynamics of the rescue operation. First, Mr R. B. Black was brought in to replace Captain Wilson (who was recalled to Simon). On 10 July, Mackrell sent Black to Margherita to make contact with the authorities. In particular, he was instructed to hand Rowland's letter over to Major-General Wood (Administrator-General Eastern Frontier Projects), which Mackrell hoped would galvanize Wood into action.

Second, Mackrell decided to abandon the Dapha Camp. It seemed a very odd decision, but he had two good reasons for doing so. First, the previous day a suspicious plane with strange markings had circled low over the camp before flying off towards the *east*. This was most unusual and Mackrell assumed that it was a Japanese spotter plane. The second reason was that Mackrell had developed a very high fever and felt very ill. On 12 July he spelled out the following message on the ground. 'Am vacating camp and moving west'. At the very same time six elephants arrived from Miao with fresh supplies of food and medicines. Nevertheless, Mackrell had made up his mind and on 17 July he set fire to the camp for security reasons, upped sticks and took all the elephants, porters and mahouts straight back to Miao. A few days later Mackrell travelled on to Margherita.

In the meantime, there was an inexplicable misunderstanding. An RAF pilot flew over Dapha Camp and mistook the Dapha Camp for Rowland's camp at Tilung Hka. The pilot sent a garbled message back to base reporting that the Tilung Hka Camp had been burned to the ground and that Rowland and Rossiter were making their way towards India. In fact, the burning huts in question were at the Dapha Camp, and it was Mackrell, not Rossiter or Rowland who was moving to the west.

Mackrell turned up in Simon on 19 July. He was physically and mentally exhausted having spent the previous six weeks and five days in unremitting toil as he lived on his own at the Dapha Camp. On his way to the Simon Camp, Mackrell met Captain Webster (Political Officer) and Captain Street of the Assam Rifles. They were travelling in the opposite direction towards the Dapha Camp. Street explained that he and Webster had been sent to replace Mackrell at Dapha. The three men had a brief but useful discussion about the situation at Dapha Camp, and then went off in opposite directions.

Twelve days later, on 31 July, Captain Street was sitting in the camp looking across the Dapha River when a remarkable apparition loomed up on the opposite bank. Sir John Rowland suddenly appeared together with some of his colleagues. It was entirely unexpected, and Street was taken aback.

***

Mackrell reached Margherita on 23 July. Immediately afterwards he had a life changing experience. He and Dudley Hodson were taken up in an RAF plane. It was a beautifully clear day. They circled over the whole area, gazing down in awe on places Mackrell had dreamed about constantly in recent weeks. It was as if they were looking down, God-like, at a very familiar map. They flew over Shingbwiyang, the Pangsau Pass, Shamlung, Nampong and down the Hukawng Valley before crossing over the jungle to fly low over the Chaukan Pass. There was no evidence at the Tilung Hka that Sir John Rowland's camp had been burned or had been evacuated (as the RAF pilot had recently reported). Indeed they could make out people walking around and presumed them to be members of Rowland's party. The plane then flew low over the Dapha Camp. Mackrell looked down on Captain Street who was standing on the riverbank where he, Mackrell, had so often stood.[29]

It was a 'Eureka moment'. It confirmed an idea that Mackrell had been mulling over for the past several weeks. The plan crystallized during the course of the flight. He was now utterly convinced that there was *only* one possible way in which to rescue the immobile remnants of Rowland's party from the Tilung Hka Camp. He would evacuate them by boat. He knew that it would create enormous difficulties – not least because the boats would have to be manhandled *up* the rapids – but as the area unfolded below the plane, Mackrell became convinced that his idea would work.

Another thing helped him firm up the idea. Soon after their unexpected arrival at the Dapha Camp on 31 July Sir John Rowland, Lecky Thompson, Molloy and Milne met with Mackrell in Margherita. They gave Mackrell a better idea of the dire situation in which Manley and others found themselves in the Tilung Hka Camp. So it was that a completely new rescue strategy evolved.

On 6 August, Mackrell met with senior ITA and Indian Government officials in Margherita. He explained his ambitious idea, and the officials agreed that he should go ahead with the plan. A flurry of urgent activity followed. Three boats were purchased in Bardapur and nine expert boatmen were engaged to take them to Margherita, where they were loaded with food, clothing and medicines. The boatmen then took the boats on to the Dapha Camp, which would be the base for the final push to the Tilung Hka Camp.

Mackrell returned to the Dapha Camp on 22 August.[30] Morale in the camp was very low. R. B. Black was in charge because Captain Street had died. Black had a complement of twenty-five men of the 2nd Assam Rifles and several PPC porters. However, many of the men were sick and they were desperate to get back to Miao.

For his part, Mackrell felt re-energized and he was raring to start on the final push towards the Tilung Hka Camp. He decided to move the entire camp up to a 150ft-high plateau on the opposite bank of the Dapha River. Everything had to be ferried across the river and then winched up to the new camp. Then he set about improving the track from the river to the new camp, so that elephants could climb more easily up and down the bank.

Mackrell outlined his plan to his trustworthy lieutenant, Havildar Dharramsing. He explained that the main objective was to rescue a few members of Rowland's party who were still trapped in the Tilung Hka Camp. They were starving and some of them were extremely ill. The RAF had been unable to drop food to them because of the bad weather and therefore speed was of the essence. Mackrell explained that he was going to leave R. B. Black in charge at the Dapha Camp while he (Mackrell) and Havildar Dharramsing made their way towards the Tilung Hka Camp. They would take a number of porters and several elephants with them. At regular intervals, along the way they would set up and provision a series of temporary camps, which would then be used on the return journey. The idea was that they (i.e. Mackrell, Havildar Dharramsing and the rest of the party) would continue until it was impossible for the elephants to go any further. At that point they would find a suitable site by the side of the river and set up a forward base camp. A small 'strike force' of the fittest porters would be selected to continue on foot towards the Tilung Hka Camp. Then came the coup de grâce. Mackrell explained that he and the remainder of the party would wait at the forward base camp for the arrival of three boats and nine boatmen from Bardapur.

Mackrell did not attempt to conceal or minimize the difficulties. He emphasized that many things could go wrong and that it was a very dangerous mission. He asked Havildar Dharramsing to explain the plan to the porters, and to find out if they were willing to proceed with the mission. The next day Havildar Dharramsing reported that all the men wanted to go along with Mackrell's plan.

***

On 1 September 1942, Mackrell, Havildar Dharramsing, a few dozen porters and eight elephants, set out along the Dehing River on the final phase of the rescue mission.

Three days later, on 4 September, Mackrell was stunned to see Rossiter, Nang Hmat, the six-month-old baby and thirteen other individuals emerge through the undergrowth. They were all on their last legs and in a bad way.[31] One of the Gurkhas had been stung and blinded by a swarm of wasps and was in a very serious condition. Rossiter explained that he had left E. L. Manley behind with the rest of the party, and he clutched in his hand a letter addressed to Pearce. It was from Manley who was writing from the Tilung Hka Camp on 28 August. Manley explained that he, Burgess-Barnett and four servants were too weak and ill to move and that Whitehouse was in a critical state because of peripheral neuritis. They had barely enough food to last the next eight days. Manley concluded with the plaintive words, 'do please do your utmost to deliver us from a situation which is becoming desperate'.

As luck would have it, later that same day a runner brought Mackrell a letter from Eric Lambert, the Political Officer in Margherita. Lambert ordered Mackrell to abandon the rescue mission (which he said was altogether too risky) and to return immediately to Miao.[32] Mackrell was on the horns of a dilemma. Within a few minutes of each other he had received one letter imploring him to proceed with all haste to rescue Manley and others, and another letter ordering him to abandon the mission and return to base forthwith.

After some thought Mackrell decided to ignore the Political Officer's instruction and to respond instead to Manley's plea. He loaded Rossiter's party onto six of his elephants and sent them on to the Dapha Camp with some porters. Then he, Havildar Dharramsing and the rest of the porters continued on their trek towards the Tilung Hka. They reached the Tilung River (but not the camp) on 6 September. Heavy rain meant that the river was rising at the rate of six feet per hour. After a superhuman effort they managed to get all their gear across the river, and it was here that they set up their forward base camp.

The next day Mackrell selected the 'strike force', which (as planned) consisted of nine of the fittest men.[33] Their packs were loaded with fresh onions, cigarettes, potatoes, sugar, butter, apple rings, milk, bully beef, soap, Lysol, ointment and gentian violet, together with a blow-up airbed for Whitehouse. The 'strike force' then went off as quickly as possible, while Mackrell and the rest of the party stayed behind with the elephants at the forward base camp. Later that day an RAF plane flew low over Mackrell's camp.[34]

Thursday 10 September was a red-letter day. The three boats and nine boatmen arrived right on cue. Mackrell had been anxiously waiting for them. They were the final element of a complex project. The boats were reloaded with enough rations to last two weeks and Mackrell, Havildar Dharramsing, some porters and the nine boatmen paddled up the river towards the Tilung Hka Camp. It was an extremely difficult journey. On no fewer than seven occasions they had to drag the boats over rocks. Each time they had to unload the rations and kit and then reload them again when they reached water. After twelve hours of this excruciatingly hard work they set up camp at a place called Tulwar. They were unable to go further because of a huge whirlpool, so they unloaded the boats for the last time and Dharramsing and six porters went on to stock up camps 5 and 6 with provisions. They were loaded with enough food to feed themselves and nineteen other men for a week.

Mackrell stayed behind and waited anxiously for news. On 18 September Havildar Dharramsing and his party returned to report that they had successfully provisioned Camps 5 and 6. However they had been unable to contact either Manley or the 'strike force' (which had now been away for twelve days).

The 20 September was another red-letter day. At 5.00 pm in the evening the 'strike force' suddenly turned up, carrying Manley and all his colleagues. The evacuees were 'emaciated, weak and worn'. Whitehouse, who was paralysed below the waist, had been slung across his shoulders of Tami, one of the porters, who then carried him for the next forty miles. Dr Burgess-Barnett and Whitehouse both had high fevers.

By this time Havildar Dharramsing and some of his men were also feeling unwell so the journey back proved to be more difficult than ever. The river had risen rapidly and rations had to be reduced for Mackrell was feeding a total of sixty-three people – twenty-six mahouts, four Europeans, twelve Assam Rifles and porters, four Indians, five servants, two Burma Rifles and ten boatmen. Against all the odds, they all reached Dapha safely on 29 September, and their ordeal ended on 6 October 1942, when they finally arrived in Margherita.[35]

***

So ended an extraordinary story. Celebrations at the ITA headquarters were muted. By mid-September 1942 the directors in Calcutta took the view that they could carry on no further. The Association's commercial and altruistic imperatives were in conflict and war-weariness had set in.

The tipping point came at a Liaison Committee meeting on 23 September 1942. Major General C. M. P. Durnford, the Army's Deputy Quartermaster

General, asked the ITA to provide the Army with an additional 71,000 labourers. There had been a string of such requests. On this occasion the Army needed the labourers for vital defence installations in Chittagong, and for work on aerodromes and military roads. Durnford disclosed that he was under pressure from London, Washington and Chunking to complete a motor road from Ledo to China via the Patkoi mountain range, and for this he would need an additional 4,000 coolies immediately. He urged the ITA to provide at least half that number.

In the past, the ITA had always responded to such requests. On this occasion, however, Mr J. Jones, the most senior ITA official present (who also happened to be Chairman of the Liaison Committee) refused to help. He explained that the ITA could no longer afford to haemorrhage managers and labourers, that tea production had taken a nosedive and that the association could no longer recruit enough volunteers.[36] Jones suggested that if the Government was prepared to pay the full cost of the labourer, the tea estates might be willing to provide the number required – but that unless and until this happened, the ITA intended to withdraw its labourers and supervisors from all existing military projects.

A lively debate followed in which Jones unexpectedly found that he had allies. R. H. Hutchings (Secretary to the War Department) agreed with Mr Justice Braund that in future the Army should take responsibility for *all* civilian evacuees. Indeed Hutchings expressed misgivings about the deployment of *any* civilians in conflict zones. Mr E. T. Coates ICS (Financial Adviser to the Military High Command) agreed. He also had reservations about employing ITA labour for military purposes. Durnford became more isolated and exasperated, until he reminded the meeting that the survival of India was at risk. Jones stuck to his guns and the golden goose was slain.[37]

***

On one level, the Chaukan Pass evacuation can be read as an enthralling adventure yarn. At another level, it was a very sobering episode that had serious implications.

Four points must be made in conclusion. First, it revealed how poor judgement and human frailty in the upper echelons of colonial society had created great risk. Second, it was the last straw that broke the back of the ITA.

Third, it confirmed the impotence of the Government of Burma and suggested that there was absolutely no way back for it. Fourth, an enormously complex and dangerous operation had been required to rescue a handful of British civilians, some of whom were very sick indeed.

Finally, one is left with the impression that within the context of the civilian evacuation as a whole, a completely disproportionate amount of effort had been required to rescue a very small, elite, group.

6

The Indian Tea Association

A victory is twice itself when the achiever brings home full numbers

Shakespeare: *Much Ado About Nothing*, Act 1. Scene 1

The ITA played a pivotal role in the civilian evacuation from Burma. It is abundantly clear from the preceding chapters that the Association was the common thread running through every aspect of the civilian evacuation between March and September 1942. Indeed, had it not been for the ITA, hundreds of evacuees perished on the routes through Chindwin Valley, the Hukawng Valley and the Chaukan Pass.

The ITA filled the vacuum left by the collapse of the Government of Burma in April 1942. It was a state within a state, providing resources on a grand scale, managing a huge labour force, constructing and supervising facilities, providing professional services, supporting sick refugees, and mounting daring rescue operations. Put quite simply, but for the ITA the civilian evacuation from Burma would have ground to a halt in May 1942.

The fortunes of the ITA and the province of Assam followed similar trajectories. Tea was the largest industry in Assam, and Assam was the leading tea producing area in India. British planters carved their tea garden estates from virgin jungle during the nineteenth and early twentieth centuries and their successors maintained these estates impeccably.[1] They kept 600 square miles under tea cultivation in Assam. The average size of an ITA estate was 4,000 acres and they produced 280 million lbs. of tea annually. This represented 60 per cent of India's total output.[2] The ITA garden estates also sustained over a million workers and their dependents.

Before partition in 1947 Assam was a vast, sprawling province, which was hard enough to administer in peacetime, let alone in times of war. The military authorities made constant demands on the Government of Assam. Matters came

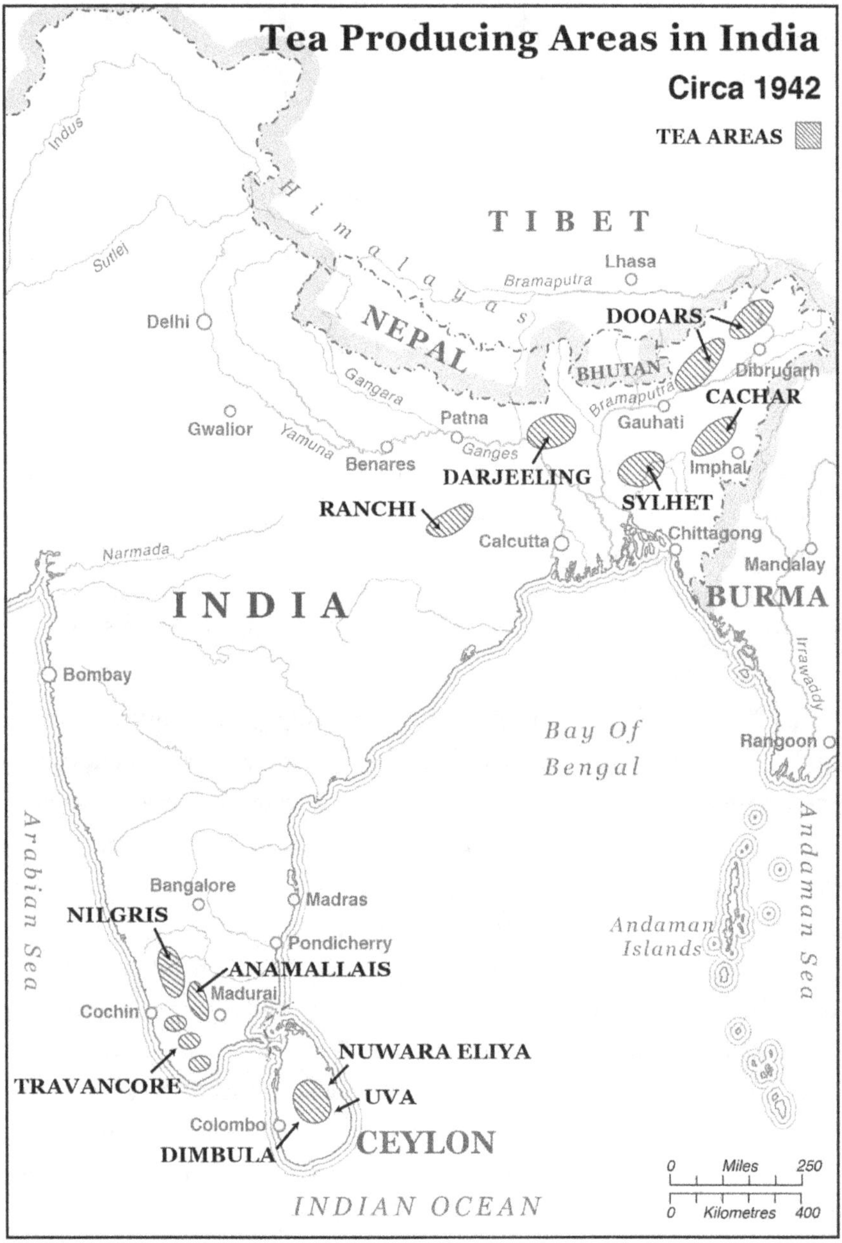

Map 6.1 Tea-producing areas of India, circa 1942

to a head in February 1942 when the political agent of Manipur was asked to recruit thousands of manual labourers for military road-building work and to supervise the large numbers of civilian refugees who were now passing through his 'patch'. At the same time, he was expected to feed columns of retreating troops.[3]

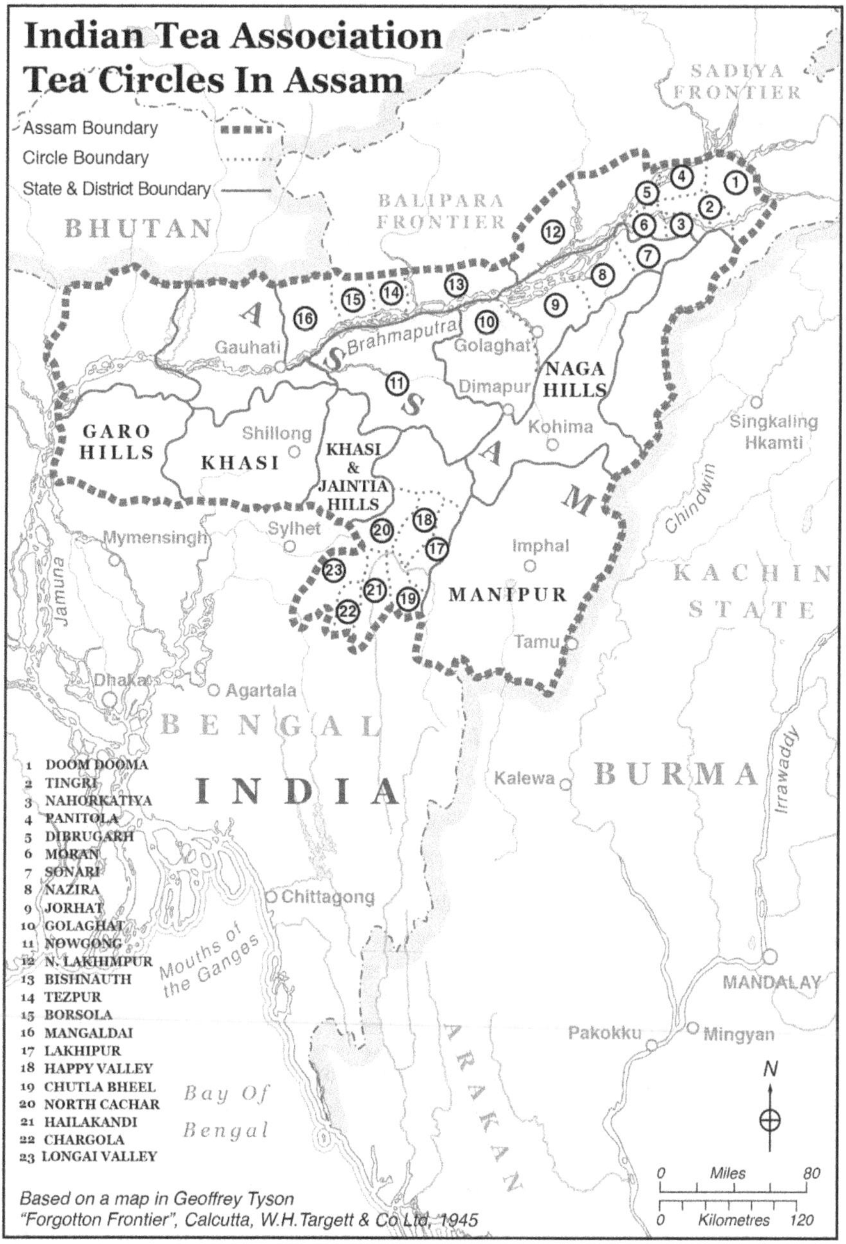

Map 6.2 Indian Tea Association tea circles in Assam

Manipur was the largest state in Assam and it lay next to Burma. The refugee route passed right through it. The Political Agent had limited resources at his disposal so was unable to meet these heavy demands. He sought help from the Government of India, which in turn called on the ITA.

The ITA was one of the largest, if not *the* largest commercial enterprise in pre-war India. It was certainly the most serendipitous. It was well managed, capital-rich and a huge employer of labour. The ITA's board of directors set the tone for the whole organization. The directors were unstuffy men capable of making big decisions in double quick time. They had vast resources at their disposal, and employed a huge and multiskilled workforce. Moreover, members of the board were personally committed to defeating the Japanese, and were willing to make commercial sacrifices to achieve that goal. Unusually, while many other Indian companies buckled under the strain in 1942, the ITA enjoyed its best year ever, producing and selling more tea than ever before.[4]

At the grassroots level, hundreds of British tea planters and managers made up the core membership of the association. They were its real backbone. The planters were no-nonsense businessmen and determinedly practical. They were balancers of books, tillers of soil, innovative producers, employers of labour, elephant-wallahs and vehicle mechanics rolled into one. They looked after their workers in a paternalistic sort of way, and often the spirit of loyalty and mutuality between planter and workforce spanned several generations. In their spare time, planters were inveterate big game hunters. They were familiar with the frontier region and unfazed by jungle conditions. They had well-honed skills as trackers, orienteers, elephant men and marksmen – almost genetically programmed for the task ahead. The tea planters' adventurous and slightly quirky lifestyle attracted maverick nonconformists like Gyles Mackrell, Eric Lambert and Alexander Beattie – charismatic personas, whose swashbuckling public faces belied their inner steel. Most of planters were well organized, hardworking characters with an eye for detail.

In 1942, most of the tea estates in India were still British owned and almost all of them belonged to an ITA 'circle'. These were branch organizations that proliferated in all the tea growing areas. In Assam alone, there were twenty-three circles and a total of 496 ITA tea estates.[5] (See Table 6.1).

At first sight, it may have seemed odd that individualistic and independently minded tea planters were enthusiastic members of ITA circles. However, this was because the circles provided commercial protection, economies of scale, cooperative marketing structures and purchasing clout. They also insured individuals against hard times and offered convivial fellowship throughout the year. Each circle elected a committee, and sent representatives to one or

Table 6.1 Tea Garden Circles in Assam

Circle	Number of ITA gardens	Registered Acreage	Yield per acre (lbs)
Doom Dooma	54	40,609	1,037
Tingri	26	11,331	1,115
Nahorkatiya	24	10,653	1,120
Panitola	20	13,224	1,301
Dibrugarh	39	21,000	1,190
Moran	20	14,410	1,207
Sonari	17	9,982	956
Nazira	17	14,711	808
Jorhat	37	30,882	905
Golaghat	42	28,855	769
Nowgong	14	11,059	675
N. Lakhimpur	10	7,154	873
Bisnauth	24	19,082	984
Tezpur	20	17.155	955
Borsola	22	11,864	962
Mangaldai	19	12,833	998
Lakhipur	9	9,919	647
Happy Valley	13	8,208	870
Chutla Bhfel	16	11,012	502
North Cachar	17	11,041	592
Hailakandi	16	11,848	545
Chargola	6	6,899	430
Longai Valley	14	11,553	730
Total 23	**496**		

Source: Indian Tea Association: General Committee Report, Calcutta, 1943.

other of nine ITA districts. Assam was the largest of the districts. The others included Travancore, Anaimalai, Nilgiris, Ranchi, Dooars, Darjeeling, Sylhet and Cachar. The district committees offered the circles advice about markets, labour relations, materials and husbandry and supported the circles and growers in time of need. The district committees were required to submit quarterly reports to the Indian Tea Association Executive Committee in Calcutta. This body represented all the main agency houses in Assam and Bengal. The Calcutta Executive Committee was also closely linked with the London Tea Association Committee, to which all the world's largest sterling tea companies belonged. Thus the ITA, and in particular its Assam district, was at the heart of a global organization.

At the beginning of 1942, it was clear that even in India trouble lay just ahead. The ITA took the precaution of setting up a small projects sub-committee. This was a light-touch body that had the authority and cash to make quick decisions and to respond to exceptional demands. It was not long before the projects sub-committee was called into action.

The ITA's wartime story really began in February 1942, when representatives of the Indian Government and the Military High Command met for the first time with officials of the ITA in Calcutta. They discussed the growing international crisis. Burma had imploded, China was isolated and there was even danger that Japan would invade India. The Indian Army was under pressure to embark on a series of ambitious military road projects.

The Manipur Road was just one of these projects, and the ITA was pressed into service right from the beginning. The Manipur Road was the northernmost extension of the Chindwin Valley evacuation route. It demanded immediate attention because thousands of civilian evacuees were already walking along the route in February 1942 and retreating troops and tons of military hardware were expected to arrive at any time. The Military High Command envisaged that once it was built, the Manipur Road would become part of a more permanent defence system. In the long run too, it would be essential if *offensive* action were to be launched against the Japanese. For the moment, however, only the short term mattered. The immediate priority was to bring the Burma Army back to India intact, and the secondary aim was to rescue as many civilian evacuees as possible.

There were other projects in the pipeline as well. The forced closure of the Burma Road to Kunming in March 1942 meant that an alternative link to China was urgently required. It spawned a vast and sprawling long-term road-building programme intended to link India, Burma and China. It was code-named the 'two frontier road project'.[6] This was needed to bring Chinese troops south to fight the Japanese, and to take essential supplies north to keep Chiang Kai-shek's Government in the war.

The Army desperately needed European engineers, supervisors and managers and Indian labourers to get the project underway and, as always, it turned to the ITA to provide the workforce. Indeed, no other organization in India was capable of providing either the number of personnel required or the variety of skills required. The Army's 1942 'personnel shopping list' is shown in Table 6.2.

The fact that the ITA responded positively to these demands was due, in part, to its patriotism and, in part, to self-preservation. The planters

Table 6.2 Eastern Frontier Projects: Statement showing ITA labour required for each project

ITA Districts	**Projects**	**Labourers**
Lakhimpur, Sibsagar, Nowgong	Dinjan Airstrip	300
	Chabua, Nagaghoolie, Mokal Bari, Sookerating and Jorhat Airstrips	5,600
	Various quarries	3,000
	Imphal Road	3,000
Darrang	Missamari Airstrip	3,000
Cachar and Sylhet	Khumbigram Airstrip	6,000
	Hailakundi Airstrip	0
	Aijal Road	10,000
Dooars	Hasimara Airstrip	6,000
	Rupsi Airstrip	1,000
ITA Labourers required		52,000
TDLA Labourers required		9,000
Sylheti Labourers required		4,000
Total Labourers required		**65,000**

Source: Indian Army, Eastern Frontier Projects Report, 1942.

knew that if India fell, they would fall with it. Therefore, they were willing to abjure commercial considerations in deference to the higher goal. To get the ball rolling, the ITA appointed four of its highest ranking officials to direct operations. Lieutenant Colonel A. H. Pilcher and Mr R. L. McLennan (chairman of the ITA's Assam Branch) became the association's chief labour liaison officers and Mr R. MacDonald and Mr N. Dawson its senior project managers.[7] For its part the Government of India promised to remunerate the ITA for any services it provided.

Over the course of the next seven months, government, military and ITA representatives met regularly. At each meeting the Army demanded more labourers and more resources. The ITA responded to each request in full.[8] The cumulative scale of its contributions was astonishing. In a matter of weeks, 609 of the ITA's 1,655 European managers had volunteered to serve in the armed services and 240 of them had been seconded to 'special projects' in northeast Burma. Moreover Table 6.2 indicates that 65,000 tea garden labourers were employed on defence and construction projects in northern Burma and Assam.[9]

In effect, the association had voluntarily sacrificed its commercial viability and by September 1942, the ITA's overall workforce (including managers and supervisors) was reduced by 50 per cent. Clearly no commercial organization could sustain such a regime for long.

As the war continued trading conditions deteriorated in India. Commodities and transport were in short supply. There were too few railway carriages, too few steamer-flats and too few motor lorries. The ITA was often unable to move its products and it had too little coal or oil to power its machines. Moreover, because (for security reasons) commercial shipping was often excluded from the Chittagong and Calcutta harbours, it was necessary to take tea for export all the way across India to Karachi and Bombay on the west coast.

Essential imports suffered too. Plywood from Scandinavia and lead and paper from Burma were in short supply. This affected the manufacture of tea chests and thereby affected the ITA's ability to handle the tea produced. Tea garden labourers went hungry because rice imports from Burma had dried up completely, and austerity measures threatened social unrest. Although no major industrial strikes happened in 1942, the tea garden labourers began to flex their muscles and to demand higher wages.

The increased likelihood of social and political unrest prompted the Government of India to expedite several emergency measures intended to appease the labour force. Trade unions were recognized for the first time, the Trade Disputes Act (1929), Workmen's Compensation Act (1923) and the Factories Act (1934) were amended, and a War Injuries Ordinance (1942) was enacted. Compulsory insurance schemes and provident funds were set up to support industrial workers and politicians stepped back from the introduction of national service.[10]

The ITA projects sub-committee had to deal with a deluge of complaints from the Assam tea planters who were concerned about the military's never-ending demands for ITA help. The projects sub-committee promised to relieve the pressure on the tea garden estates by recruiting ITA labourers from other parts of India. However, these efforts were rarely successful.

One of the ITA's requirements was that gangs of labourers working on military projects had to be supervised by British estate managers and planters (see Table 6.4). It placed heavy demands on senior managers. The stakes were high. The labourers had to be fully equipped with tools, clothing and stores, and they had to be transported to and from distant work sites. Each gang had to be self-contained with medical staff, camp-builders, pay-clerks and so on. Moreover, the ITA stipulated that only *volunteers* could work on these projects – so no conscripted labourers were allowed. At the same time the

Table 6.3 ITA labour deployed on Eastern Projects September–November 1942[a]

Activity	Projected Figures[b]			Actual Figures[c]		
	Tea Garden Labourers	Tea Garden Labourers	Tea Garden Labourers	Tea Garden Labourers	Tea Garden Labourers	European Supervisors
Roads	September	October	November	**September**	**October**	**October**
Manipur	12,000	17,000	22,000	**14,5584**	**19,5004**	**73**
Aijal	10,000	10,000	8,00	**12,614**	**11,9025**	**20**
Golaghat	1,000	1,500	1,500	**1,000**	**1,5366**	**7**
Sub-Total	23,000	28,500	31,500	**28,174**	**32,938**	**100**
Aerodromes						
Dinjan	300	300	300	**36**	**208**	**3**
Chabua	3,000	2,500	2,500	**2,804**	**2,694**	**12**
Mohanbari	2,000	1,200	1,200	**894**	**1,197**	**6**
Sookerating	2,000	3,000	3,000	**2,763**	**2,206**	**7**
Nagaghoolie	1,000	500	500	**708**	**697**	**3**
Jorhat	2,800	3,500	3,500	**2,500**	**3,700**	**8**
Lillibari	300	300	300	**416**	**5496**	**2**
Missimari	0	1,500	2,500	**0**	**1,369**	**7**
Sorbhog	0	1,500	5,000	**201**	**1,081**	**8**
Kumbhirgram	4,000	6,000	6,000	**4,249**	**8,9675**	**8**
Hailakandi	2,000	2,000	2,000	**1,250**	**1,297**	**9**
Hasimara	0	2,000	4,000	**0**	**1,5007**	**3**
Sub-Total	17,400	24,300	30,000	**15,871**	**25,465**	**76**
Other Projects						
Dibrugarh Ghat				**627**	**420**	**2**
Nahorkata Stone				**1,011**	**1,217**	**3**
Nazira Stone					**328**	**1**
Hazelbank Sand				**179**	**179**	**1**
Digboi Oilwells				**570**	**592**	**1**
Miscellaneous				**810**	**488**	**1**
Sub-Total				**3,197**	**3,224**	**9**
Summary						
Roads	23,000	28,500	31,500	**28,174**	**32,938**	**100**
Aerodromes	17,400	24,300	30,800	**15,871**	**25,465**	**76**
Other Projects	0	0	0	**3,197**	**3,224**	**9**
Total	40,400	52,800	62,300	**47,242**	**61,627**	**185**

Source: Ernest J. Nicholls: Report to the ITA European Personnel and Tea Garden Labour Committee, November 1942.

Notes

a The figures were prepared by Ernest J. Nicholls, Member of ITA Committee with responsibility for European Personnel and Tea Garden Labour

b The target figures were revised as military/PWD requirements changed

c A handwritten note dated 5 November 1942 from the Chief of the General Staff was appended: It read 'The security of this information must be carefully guarded.'

Table 6.4 Total number of ITA labourers promised on projects

	Acres	Total Acres	Number of Labourers[a]
Lakhimpur	101,088		
Sibsager	94,076		
Nowgong	11,045	206,209	20,000
Darrang		54,763	5,000
Kamrup		1,536	150
Cachar	49,886		
Sylhet	75,286	125,172	12,000
Dooars		117,529	11,000
Sub-Total		**505,209**	**48,150**
TDLA			9,000
Sylhetties			4,000
Total			**61,000**

Source: ITA General Committee Report, Calcutta 1943.

Note

a The number of labourers to be contributed was calculated on a ratio of 1 labourer per 10 acres of cultivable land

Army insisted that all operations must be conducted in the strictest secrecy. Consequently, tens of thousands of labourers had to be moved around the country without the enemy knowing. Tea estate managers did a good job in persuading their coolies that this work was for a greater 'good', and that in volunteering they were helping to keep India safe. The ITA's public relations techniques were sophisticated and effective.

For the first time, politicians in London became fully aware of the quality of the ITA's work. One of the association's advocates in Westminster was the right-wing Conservative politician, Sir John Wardlaw-Milne, MP. He was a champion of private enterprise and voluntarism. On 13 October 1943, Wardlaw-Milne tabled a question for the Secretary of State for India, Lord Munster. He asked whether the Secretary of State was aware 'that local planters had voluntarily supplied food and assistance to evacuees who came through the trackless country between Burma and Assam. [And] that several planters had risked their lives [by succouring] the evacuees [while] several others met their death as a result of their labourers'? (See note 11.) Wardlaw Milne went on to enquire 'what recognition, or Government appreciation has been given to those who gave their services in this way'?

Before answering the question, Lord Munster thought for a moment then jotted down the following ideas on the back of a parliamentary notice form. 'I did not know' he said, 'that some of the planters actually met their death as a result of this relief work' – although he agreed that it was common knowledge 'that the companion of Mr Gyles Mackrell, 'who was decorated for his [bravery] up on the Chaukan Pass Route, died on the outward journey'. Munster was at pains to point out 'that in several cases these conspicuous services have been recognised by the conferment of an honour by His Majesty'.[11]

In fact, Munster's response did scant justice to the ITA's efforts. It was true that nine ITA staff and associates were honoured, but Munster never fully recognized that more than 600 planters and managers and 62,000 labourers had been involved in operations relating to the evacuation and military retreat. Three years later, Geoffrey Tyson attempted to set the record straight. He drew up a comprehensive list of the 238 Europeans involved in the evacuation scheme – included among them were many planters and sixty-four women. Tyson calculated that 130 ITA managers had been engaged on the Ledo Road project and fifty-eight on the Chindwin Valley–Manipur Road project. He singled out for special mention the thirteen ITA doctors and nurses who had provided such spectacular medical support, and named the nine ITA personnel who were subsequently honoured for their work on the evacuation routes.[12] (See Table 6.5).

These men and women earned their spurs between February and September 1942 in three theatres of the civilian evacuation: the Chindwin Valley and Manipur Road; the Hukawng Valley and Pangsau Pass; and the Chaukan Pass.

By August 1942, the ITA was extremely worried about its burgeoning operational costs. Commercial operations and humanitarian motives were clearly bad bedfellows. The Calcutta directors of the ITA carefully scrutinized the company's accounts. They were especially concerned about the cost to the ITA of the evacuation operation. In mid-September 1942 it was decided in principle that the evacuation work must end.

The tipping point came on 23 September 1942. At a meeting of the Liaison Committee, Major General C. M. P. Durnford, the Army's Deputy Quartermaster General, asked the ITA to provide the Army with an additional 71,000 labourers. There was nothing unusual about such a request, except that it was very large. Durnford explain that the Army needed the labourer for vital defence installations in Chittagong, and also for work on various aerodromes and military roads.

In the past, the ITA had always responded positively to such requests. On this occasion, however, Mr J. Jones, the most senior ITA official present

Table 6.5 Roll of honour: ITA personnel involved in Burma evacuation

The names of ITA personnel working on the Ledo Road Project
Messrs Alexander, J.H., Alexander, J.C., Aitken, G., Archibald, A.N., Dr Anderson, J.R., Major Brennand, C.H., Messrs Black, R.B., Burgh, J.H. (A.R.&T. Co.), Bruce, J.D., Bennett, N., Bishop H.C., Blair, A., Barron, J.C., Berry, A.G., Brodie, A.T., Birnie, C.D., Blacklaws, T.A., Burnside, P., Dr Bertram, D.M., Mr Bryant, E.W., Dr Baruah, P.N., Messrs Collins, J.C., Creech, C.L., Crombie, E.L., Cruden, T., Connell, W.A., Cooksey, W., Duchart, D.R., Dempster, H.F., Duckworth, L.S., Everett, H.L.F., Evans, F., Lieutenant Esslemont, N.M., Messrs Fitt, H., Flux, C.J., Farquarson, R.F., Fairhurst, G., Fairfield, T.A., Major Gilroy, A.W., Messrs Gordon, Gellatley, J.W., Greig, J., Gleed, F.G., Griffiths, G.S., Grant, G.H., Major Henniker Heaton, C. Lieutenant-Colonel Hodsn, D.C., Messrs Haslewood, W.B., Hill, J.C., Harris, H., Hayne I.C.G., Hunter, S., Heaney, H., Hughes, H., Hardwick H.J., Harrison, C.J., Hutchins P.P.P., Hunter, J., Heefke, G., O'C., Captain Haywood, H.D., Messrs Irwin C.T., Ingram, G.E., Johnston, I., Johnston, F.A., King, W.T.H., Kervood, D., Kay, M.W., Kenny, E.W., Lovie, J.M., Low, A.J.D., Lessels, H.C., Lindsay, D.D., Levick, N., Lury, H. Dev., Captain Lancaster, D.W., Messrs McDonald, W.M., Murray, H.S., Mackrell, G., Masson, J.A., McGown, R.G., Marshall, J.F., Mackie, W.F., Macaulay, M., Moor, F.A.W., Marshall, R., Macara, N., McIntyre, C.D., Millett, H., McIntosh, J.L., Owen, H.G., Olding, W.G., Pooley, K., Rowden, W.A., Reid, W.A., Dr Rose, T.H., Dr Robertson, J.R., Mr Ross, J.C., Lieutenant Smith, J.T., Messrs Stuart, I.G., Spurr, G.E., Scott-Fowler, R., Stoneman, J.O., Scott, W.J., Spurling, A.P., Smith, J.A., Stewart, W., Smyth, C.G., Swannell, H.O., Captain Street, H.T., Lieutenant Simpson, G.A., Messrs Thomson, R.M., Taylor, W.A., Thom, R.P., Tate, L.J., Tapner C., Tew, C.W., Taylor, K.A.S.R., Vipan, R.H, Wooley-Smith, F., Warren, A., Wilson, J.R., Watson, A.C., Williamson W., Warner, M.C., White, H.A., Wilkie, C., Warner, N.A.B., Young S.G., West, L.R.,

The names of ITA Personnel, wives and relations working at the Dibrugarh Reception Camp

Messrs Aiton, J., Lawrie, A., Palmer, R.A., Thomson H.C., Stevenson, R.C., Mrs R.A. Palmer, Mrs J. Aiton, Mrs B.H. Routledge, Mrs W. Gow, Mrs F.W. Hockenhull, Mrs R.C. Stevenson, Mrs J.A.D. Main, Mrs A Lawrie, Mrs A. Bell, Mrs L.R. Harvey, Mrs P. Gothorp, Mrs L.F. Paget, Mrs H.C. Thomson, Mrs J.G. Mitchell, Sister E.M.Oliver, the Misses M.V. Salberg, Stevenson, Montague and Franklin.

The names of ITA Medical Staff at Panitola Hospital

Dr D.J.Lapping, Miss E.M. Davies, Mrs E.D. Hooper

The names of ITA Personnel working on the Bishenpur-Silchar Refugee Route

Messrs Clark, H.F., Dutt, S, Ferrier G.A., Joss, J, Patterson, W.A., Mountain, C.W., Robertson, J., Sibbald, E.R., Sinclair, J., Smith, A.M., Mundy, N.S., Taylor, J.

The names of the wives and relations of ITA personnel who worked at the Silchar Dispersal camps

Mesdames E. T. Taylor, H.P. Taylor, W.E. Leggee, I.D. Stephens, J.H. Heaney, K.O. Smith, T.A. Thomas, T.A. Edward, Misses E.M. Lloyd, O.Rees

The names of ITA Personnel engaged on the Manipur Road Evacuation Route

Messrs Beattie, A., Blennerhassett, F.W., Coutts, A., Davies, C.A.P., Crearar, A.N., Dumma, W.S., Gardner, O.*, Hay, D., Hearn, F.T.H., Hamilton, A.C.*, Meaton, D.*, McNeill, H., Middleton, C., Morris, D.R., Palmer, S.G.H. (also worked on the Bishenpur-Silchar route, Pizey, R.M.*, Petch, G.F., Reed, H.R., Rogers, T.R.*, Robertson, G., Spaull, C.M., Thomas, F.V., Tullie, J., Whittaker, A., Whyte, V.C., Wilson, D., and Mesdames F.W. Blennerhassett, R.B. Boswell, T.R. Clark, A.Anderson, C.G. Humphery, H.A. Lakin, A.H.Pilcher, K.L. Phillips, F.V. Thomas, A.C. Tunstall

(* The ITA switched these men to roadwork soon after their arrival. This was because of the shortage of experienced planters available for the construction of the Palel-Tamu Road to enable the Burma Army to withdraw,)

The names of the wives and relations of ITA personnel who worked at Chapermukh, Pandu, etc

Mesdames T.R. Clark, G.K. Farquharson, F. Jamieson, E.G. Taylor, S. Reid, G.S. Ross, W. Henry, F.M. Carmichael, M.V. Palmer, R.S. Wood, Booth, A.E. Ross, G.B. Alexander, W. Milburne, R.B. Scott, H. Sheldrake, K. Danter, E. Showers, R.F. Stephen, Thomas, Anderson, Miss Mary Simmonds

Names of ITA personnel honoured because of their work during the evacuation

H.F. Clark, C.I.E., Secretary of the Surma Valley Branch – Silchar; C.J. Harrison, O.B.E. Director, Tocklai Experimental Station, Assam; F. Woolley-Smith, O.B.E., Tingri Tea Estate, Assam; Mrs A.C. Tunstall, M.B.E., Tocklai Experimental Station; Dr D.J. Lapping, M.B.E., Jokai Tea Company, Panitola, Assam; Gyles Mackrell, D.F.C., G.M., Messrs Octavius Steel & Co. Ltd.; Mrs T.R. Clarke, K-i-H, Salonah Tea Estate, Assam; Mrs G.S. Ross, K-i-H, Bhooteachang Tea Estate, Panerihat, Assam; Dr D.M. Bertram, M.B.E., ITA Base Hospital, Ledo, Assam.

Source: Tyson, Forgotten Frontier, pp. 145–146.

(who also happened to be chairman of the Liaison Committee) refused to help. He explained that the ITA could no longer afford to haemorrhage managers and labourers, that tea production had taken a nosedive and that the Association could no longer recruit enough volunteers.[13] Jones suggested that if the Government was prepared to pay the *full* cost of the labourer, the tea estates might be willing to provide the number required – but that until this happened, the ITA intended to withdraw its labourers and supervisors from existing military projects.

A lively debate ensued in which Jones found support from unexpected allies. R. H. Hutchings (Secretary to the War Department) agreed with Mr Justice Braund's view that in future the Army should take responsibility for *all* civilian evacuees. Indeed, Hutchings expressed profound misgivings about the deployment of civilians in conflict zones. Mr E. T. Coates ICS (Financial Adviser to the Military High Command) also sided with Jones, saying that he had reservations about employing ITA labour for military purposes. Durnford became more and more isolated and exasperated, until unable to contain himself any longer, he reminded the meeting that the security of India was at risk and that the Army needed help. Notwithstanding this appeal, Jones continued to stick to his guns.[14] It was the swan song of the ITA's involvement in high politics and military affairs.

Although the high-level issues were important, in the final analysis the ITA stood or fell by the everyday endeavours of its men and women on the ground. Trivial though it might have seemed, it was important that evacuees were moved to tears when ITA men greeted them at camps with cups of sugary tea, or when ITA porters turned out on dark, wet nights to help limping evacuees along muddy tracks. Some of the most unforgettable characters were also some of the most ordinary. The ITA was proud of its ordinary decent men who tended to blisters or mended leaks in roofs. In the end the association's reputation was based on meticulous organisation, attention to detail, knowledge of local conditions and innovative ideas.[15]

7

Returnees and Émigrés: India 1942–1945

Now my co-mates and brothers in exile, Hath not old custom made this life more sweet?

Shakespeare: *As You Like It*, Act 2. Scene 1

Every day, during May, June and July1942, refugee trains bound for Calcutta steamed from the railheads at Dimapur, South Tirap and Margherita. Every train was crammed to the roof with emaciated men women and children. They had escaped from the Japanese, trudged for miles out of Burma and were physically and mentally drained. Most of the passengers were Indians, but scattered among them were groups of British and Anglo-Burmese evacuees. Each of them clutched a pathetic little bundle containing all his or her worldly belongings. At Sealdah Station in Calcutta, they spilled out onto the platform to a cacophony of noise – clanking machinery, hissing steam, bells and myriad voices advertising wares and yelling instructions. Lofty British administrators shuffled into Boubazar Street alongside poor Indian labourers. This brief communion of suffering was fleetingly shared before the Europeans went one way and the Indians another. They would never meet again.[1]

They dispersed to the four corners of India, each one struggling to come to terms with nightmarish experiences. They had all had close encounters with death and now mourned lost friends. Each experience was unique, but there were common strands. This chapter offers a few grainy snapshots of lives spent in an exile from which the fallout was catastrophic. The period of exile in India seemed almost anticlimactic, but it cast a long shadow over post-war Burma.

The Government of India was used to receiving refugees. The U K Government had sent boatloads of civilian personnel from Poland, Ukraine, the Baltic States, Greece and Malta. Camps had been built, and wardens had been recruited to deal with thousands of evacuees from all over the world.

From 1942 onwards refugees from Burma, Malaya, Hong Kong, Singapore, the Dutch East Indies, China, Korea and the Philippines began to arrive. Some of the camps were occupied for many years, while civilian internees waited to return home. The process of winding up was slow, and the last camp was not closed until 1950.

***

Relatively few European evacuees had arrived in India before 1942. They came in their tens and hundreds rather than thousands. The National Services and Aliens Act required all European immigrants to register so the Government knew who they were and where they lived. In addition, most of them kept diaries, wrote letters and spoke to journalists, so a great deal is known about them. By contrast, almost nothing is known about the returning Indians. To find out more about them, the Government of India required all evacuees arriving after 8 December 1941 to register their details on a census. No fewer than 393,735 names were listed.

Many more evacuees left Burma than seemed to have arrived in India There are several reasons for this. Those arriving before 8 December 1941 – mainly Indian nationals – were not included in the census, and about 10,000 evacuees were thought to have died before they reached India. Many Indian evacuees refused to register – menials, porters, coolies, chaprasis, chowkidars, sweepers, peons, paniwallahs, khalasis, cultivators and the like. They had propped up the colonial regime in Burma and had no wish to prop up the imperial regime in India as well.[2] Anonymity seemed to be the best defence against exploitation. Moreover, many of the menials were illiterate, so they left no records or diaries and wrote no letters. Very little is known about them or their experiences on returning to India.

Two interesting subsidiary facts *did* emerge from the census. Most of the evacuees or their parents had originally come from Madras (153,440), Bengal (121,609) or the United Provinces (41,428) and, 34,799 of those who had been born in Burma or were domiciled there were complete strangers to India; they had never visited it before.[3] (See Table 7.1.)

It did not really matter whether 393,000, 400,000 or 500,000 evacuees arrived in India at this time. Whatever the number, it was a very large number of extra mouths to feed and a lot of people to absorb, even in a country the size of India.

Table 7.1 Census of evacuees: November–December 1943

	Total	Male	Female
Total number of Evacuees Registered	393,735	300,285	93,440
Indians	352,235	280,176	72,059
Anglo-Indians	4,214	1,944	2,270
Anglo-Burmans	4,775	2,165	2,610
Burmans	9,368	4,524	4,844
Indo-Burmans	3,543	1,807	1,736
Zerabadis	17,113	8,516	8,597
Others	2,477	1,153	1,324

Source: Government of India, Register of Evacuees, December 1943.

More information about the Indian returnees began to emerge after 2011, when Amitav Ghosh started to gather their accounts. One account sticks in the mind.[4] Dr Krishnan Gurumurthy was an evacuee, a boy of nine at the time. He vividly remembered his family's feeling of relief when they finally arrived home.[5] The 'air of sympathy and fellow feeling' was palpable as 'our Indian people regardless of caste, community or language welcomed us with open arms'. It took ten days to travel from Calcutta to Madras by train, and the evacuees were packed in like sardines. But the most memorable thing about the journey was the warmth of the reception the evacuees received along the way.

> At every major station, people from the villages flocked to the train and showered us with delicacies, fruits and beverages. The affection shown to us by Bengalese, Oriyas, and Andhras en-route was touching. At that time … the fervour of patriotism and freedom from British rule was such, [that] everyone was vying with each other to do their bit for their fellowmen. Slowly, the evacuees were trying to recover from the trauma of fear and anxiety. Sometime during the first week of April 1942 we reached Madras Central Station. A big feast was arranged by the local philanthropic organisations on the platform of the Station itself for about 2,000 people. All the evacuees thanked the Almighty for getting us [home] safely against all the odds. (Amitav Ghosh 1941)

After such heady outpourings of public joy, one can only guess how thousands of Indian evacuees faced the frostier reception that lay ahead. By some proleptic irony, impoverished families began to discover that their husbands, sons and fathers had arrived home empty-handed. These were men who had worked so hard, endured celibacy, lived in squalid hovels and withstood hostility and disdain for so little reward. They had then had to endure the indignities of the trek out of Burma.[6]

'Menials' were not the only people to suffer such indignities. Street traders, small-time moneylenders, durwans, contractors and semi-skilled industrial workers shared in their misery. They had underestimated the speed of the Japanese advance and fled from Burma in a very great hurry. Most of them left fixed assets behind – agricultural land, uncollected rents, un-harvested crops, unsold merchandise, unpaid debts and wages still owed to them. Indeed, they were scarcely better off than the menials below them.

At the other end of the scale, the wealthiest Indians were extremely rich. For example, the Sinha family owned the largest sugar factory in Burma, the Jewanlal family, the largest aluminium factory, Adamji Haji Dawowodd, the largest match factory, and the Birla family, the only starch factory in Burma. Nath Singh's Oil Installations and Neogy's flourmills were among the largest employers in Burma. R. K. Pal, the Malakars and the Chowdhuris operated substantial networks of inland waterways transport services. Many of the major property developers, entrepreneurs, merchants and financiers were Indians, and Abdul Bari Chowdhury was perhaps the wealthiest Indian businessman of all. His Bengal Burma Steam Navigation Co. had merged with the Scindia Steam Navigation Co. to form a vast conglomerate.[7] All these men had been squirrelling their wealth away into safe havens for many years. Such families could buy their way out of Burma, and they paid huge sums to secure berths on boats or seats on planes. Some of them chartered whole planes in which they transported their extended families back to India. Once there, they continued to live in luxury. Of course, it was not all plain sailing. A number of Indian businessmen suffered huge losses. S. N. Haji and R. G. Ayengar estimate that Indian landowners forfeited holdings totalling Rs.5000m and J. Russell Andrus suggests that the Chettyars lost in the region of £56m (Rs 74.5m).[8] (See Table 7.2).

***

'Money' might have played *the* most important part in protecting the wealthiest Indian families during their exit from Burma, but 'memory' deterred most of them from returning. Communal troubles were etched in Indian memories. Ethnic tension had never been far from the surface and the tensions often

Table 7.2 Indian investments in Burma on the eve of the Japanese invasion of 1941

Type of investor	Rs. (millions)
Chettyars	750
Debt owed to Government of India	486.9
Export and import trade	120
Local Indian traders and shopkeepers	160
Industrial establishments	150
Rangoon real estate	160
Investments in foreign corporations	63
Approximate total value	**Rs.1, 889.9 (£142m)**

Source: Chakravarti, Table 7.6, p. 93.

Note: Indian investments in shipping; inland waterways; road transport; insurance corporations; banking corporations; money-lenders (other than Chettiars); real estate in other towns and cities; plantations and mines cannot be estimated.

flared into violence. The most recent episode was in 1938–1939. These atrocities were fresh in Indian minds.[9] The sudden collapse of British rule left the Indians even more exposed than before. They were fearful of Burmans and realized that they could expect no mercy from the Japanese. Indians of all classes and castes were extremely nervous as they trekked out of the country. They suspected that dacoits lurked around every corner. There were certainly cases of harassment – some of them serious – but there were relatively few verifiable incidents, and most Burmese communities showed remarkable restraint. Nevertheless, the myth of Burmese treachery persisted in the Indian psyche, and by the time they crossed the border into India very few Indians – even the most open-minded – considered returning to Burma.

B. R. Pearn hit the nail on the head when he described Indian émigrés in 1942 as 'unwanted in Burma and equally unwanted in India'.[10] Before the war, they had returned to India with money in their pockets and were welcomed with open arms. The situation was very different in 1942. The labourers' families scolded their impecunious menfolk, who resented the British for letting them down and detested the Burmans for stabbing them in the back. These resentments stood in the way of an equitable post-war settlement.

A vigorous debate got underway in India. In 1943, Mr Vellayan Chettyars claimed that Indian labourers and financiers had been responsible for cultivating 20 million acres of land in Burma, and therefore had a right to be consulted before any plans for the reconstruction of Burma were implemented. Indeed, he contended, Indian claims 'to rights and privileges in that land' were far greater than British claims. Sir Annamalai Chettiar supported this argument and added that because Indian troops had played an important role in Burma's development, they should also be permitted to retain their property rights in Burma, and should be allowed to return to Burma as soon as possible. Dr N. B. Khare (member of the Governor General's Council for Commonwealth Relations) was unconvinced. Mindful of Burma's recent history, he called for cast-iron guarantees of protection for any Indian citizen who returned to Burma. The guarantees were not forthcoming.

***

The sudden influx of evacuees caused major social problems in India. Most ordinary Indian evacuees slipped back into their home communities and the wealthiest European evacuees stayed in the most expensive hotels, but between the two extremes were thousands of others. There was insufficient 'affordable' accommodation to go around.[11] Middle-class European and Anglo-Burmese refugees who were unable to afford hotel prices rented rooms in Roman Catholic convents and charitable institutions. But even this was expensive.[12] Many of the poorer evacuees became homeless. At the beginning of 1942 Reuters had reported that the Government of India was employing thousands of coolies to build thirty enormous refugee camps for Burma refugees.[13] It was a very enlightened approach, and as the camps came on stream they housed thousands of evacuees. They were then given temporary benefits to tide them over, until they found paid work in private companies or on government-funded projects.[14]

Ian D'Mello spent the war years in an evacuation camp. Born in Rangoon in 1933, he was the eldest son of a Eurasian family and was eight years old when the bombing of Rangoon began.[15] Ian's father was in the Army, but he and his mother and younger brother were evacuated by boat to Calcutta. Initially they were passed from one refugee camp to another – first to Ranchi, then Jhansi and finally to Chunar Camp on the River Ganges, midway between Benares and Allahabad, where they stayed until the end of the war.

The camp at Chunar accommodated about forty evacuee families from Burma. Each family was housed in a modest brick-built bungalow in the old military cantonment. There was no electricity and tongas, or horse-drawn rickshaws, made a deafening noise as they trundled back and forth along the stone-flagged lane outside the houses. The Camp Commandant, W. A. Gibson, was such a distant figure that Ian D'Mello never once clapped eyes on him. A Royal Army Ordnance Company R.A.O.C. unit was also garrisoned in the camp together with several former military and Indian Civil Service (ICS) families. Each day the evacuee children had to attend the camp school for a couple of hours. The school was housed in a large four-storeyed brick building that towered incongruously above the surrounding bungalows. Life in the camp was fairly relaxed – indeed it was almost idyllic. Ian and his brother spent a lot of time playing around tombstones in an old military cemetery and swimming in the nearby River Ganges. Mrs D'Mello could come and go as she pleased, and would occasionally go on shopping trips to Allahabad. On these occasions the boys visited their old Uncle Horace.[16] Behind the scenes, camp-life was probably rather more onerous than Mrs D'Mello would admit. She had very little money to spend and no doubt had to scrimp and save. Even the most independent of evacuees probably became institutionalized. Some camps were worse than others, accommodating the evacuees in very basic, regimented huts, and treating them almost like prisoners. However, life in Chunar was perfectly bearable, if a little tedious.

***

There was no such thing as a 'standard' British evacuee. Indians and Europeans were carefully segregated and attitudes towards Anglo-Indians were perennially ambiguous. Within the British community it mattered who you were, where you were educated, how well you were connected, what work you did before the war, and how much money you had. There was a world of social difference between white oil rig operators and white High Court judges. Much depended on how well a person was treated by his company or organization. In 1942, every European organization grappled with the same thing – shifting foundations, collapsing structures and stretched resources. Whereas most organizations tried to maintain their employees' morale and to keep them together, everything felt temporary and nothing seemed safe.

Curiously, this 'corporate challenge' was well illustrated by a group of about thirty Methodist missionaries who escaped to India from Upper Burma in 1942. They occupied a sort of sociological no man's land. They were classless, outsiders, nonconformist, straight-laced and teetotal. Unusually for colonial Burma, they were motivated by service not money. They eschewed the normal colonial pursuits and rarely, if ever, frequented European clubs and restaurants. They were sometimes critical of the antics of their more flamboyant compatriots and had little in common with public-school educated administrators or smart Rangoon-based lawyers. Yet they were English through and through and deeply patriotic. In India they had to go through exactly the same hoops as, say, Steels managers, Burma Oil Corporation (BOC) drillers or IFC captains – they clung together and tried to recreate familiar routines and structures.

The Methodist missionaries had one particular virtue. They were compulsive record-keepers and letter writers, and the vast Methodist Missionary Society Archive casts light on the issues facing many of the exiled organizations in Burma and India.[17] The missionaries had begun to arrive in Calcutta from mid-February onwards. Most of the women and children had flown from Shwebo to Chittagong and most of the men had trekked through the Chindwin Valley to Dimapur.[18] They were homeless, jobless, penniless, demoralized, exhausted and emotionally drained.[19] They were sent to live and work with fellow Methodist missionaries in India, so were scattered to the four corners of the subcontinent. In Burma, they had been part of a close-knit fellowship – a team – that had common goals. They missed this very much. Rev. Clement Chapman, chairman of the Burma Methodist District, was an exile himself. He understood how his colleagues felt, so he summoned them all to a District Synod. In fact, he organized two synods during the period of exile. It gave them all a chance to meet, to share gossip, and to feel wanted.

The first synod was held in Benares in July 1942. No real business was done but information on the whereabouts of absentee colleagues was pooled.[20] The missionaries had had *no* news from their congregations in Burma.[21] They shared their experiences during the evacuation, they grieved over things they had lost, and compared notes about life in India.[22] It was a cathartic experience and a number of organizations adapted the idea of the Methodist synod to their own needs.

The second synod was held in January 1943 in Bangalore.[23] Here the missionaries were able to get their teeth into a 'live' moral dilemma. The Army had asked Rev. Acheson, one of the missionaries, to join the Military Intelligence Department. Acheson was a fluent Burmese speaker (as were all his colleagues). He was keen to join the Army but Chapman was adamant that he should not. The Missionary Committee in London was dismayed by Chapman's refusal. After all the military had already enlisted at least three Burma missionaries.[24] Nevertheless, the pros and cons of military service were discussed at great length. In the end, it was felt to be 'unwise and most prejudicial to our standing as missionaries to undertake work for the intelligence service', which might affect 'the treatment of all missionaries who fell into Japanese hands'.[25]

Another tricky issue lurked just below the surface at this synod. The evacuation had provided the missionaries with an extraordinarily vivid experience. Those who arrived in India considered themselves to be part of special fellowship – a sort of exclusive club.[26] It divided the missionaries of the Burma Methodist District into two factions – those who had evacuated to India versus those who had not. In a way, the two factions were never properly reconciled. The Methodist experience was not unique. The same dichotomy occurred in several other Burma organizations as well.[27]

***

Calcutta was awash with impecunious displaced 'middle-class' British exiles. There were lawyers, administrators, engineers, ships' captains, teachers, doctors, businessmen and the like. All had lost their livelihoods and sources of income, and although most of them had plenty of money in the bank at home, they could not get their hands on it. The banks were in the same pickle as everyone else. They too had evacuated chaotically. When they arrived in India, the exchange bankers feared that the rapid Japanese advance through Burma might engulf India too.[28]

On 5 March 1942, senior bank officials met in Calcutta to discuss whether they should move to safer locations in India. The meeting was inconclusive. However, the war situation had improved sufficiently by mid-1943 for the Burma Banks' Reconstruction Committee (BBRC) to open its office in Calcutta. The other managers remained jittery. Senior bankers like Sir Arthur Morse, chairman of HSBC, argued that the exchange banks should stay together in Calcutta.[29] Others favoured moving well away from the frontier. Several bankers decided to take immediate action. One bank leased a strongroom in Lucknow, and three other banks relocated to Lahore. Sir Robert Bruce, general manager of HSBC in Rangoon toyed with the idea of moving his branch to

Simla so that he could be near the Burma Government and the Rangoon Corporation. Bruce calculated that it would put HSBC in a privileged position in the event of a return to Burma. Simla also happened to be much safer and cooler than Calcutta.[30] Accordingly in May 1942, the HSBC staff, records and securities were moved lock, stock, and barrel to Simla.

In Simla HSBC officials compiled the so-called *Books of Agency*, which described how they intended to transfer accounts from Burma to India (a legal minefield), and how they intended to distinguish between 'non-enemy' and 'enemy' depositors.[31] HSBC also campaigned for parity to be established between the Burma rupee and the Indian rupee and urged the Government of Burma to establish a limited moratorium for debt repayments. It entered into discussions with Chinese officials about the establishment of an agency in Chungking, although it was fully committed to move back to Burma.[32] While these ambiguous, cloak-and-dagger negotiations were underway the bank kept its ordinary customers waiting a very long time for their cash. This was a matter of deep frustration for many cash-strapped evacuees, whose effectiveness was compromised and whose style was cramped.

***

Reginald Clark was a good example of those cash-strapped middle-class colonials. He was a city lawyer, who had lived in the fashionable Rangoon suburb of Windermere Park. He was smart and ambitious but had not quite made it to the top. He had gone to Burma for the adventure, to make money and to provide his young family with a better quality of life. The Japanese invasion was a nuisance, but Clark decided to stick it out for as long as possible. When the bombing in Rangoon became unbearable he travelled up to northern Burma with some friends and they walked to India, arriving only with 'the clothes they stood in'. He lost two stones in weight and looked like a skeleton when he arrived in Calcutta. Like many other young men at the time he would say very little about his ordeal, but suffice it to say, in July 1942 he was admitted to the Rainsay Hospital with tertian malaria.[33]

Two themes stand out from the rest in the newsy weekly letters Clark wrote to his wife in England. The first was that he had an astonishing number of acquaintances in India – most of them dated back to his Burma days. They included former neighbours, work colleagues and business contacts. Clark had only vaguely known some of them in Burma, but they soon became bosom companions in India.[34]

Few of Clark's new acquaintances were to be found in the Dorman-Smiths' address book. This spoke volumes about the strict social stratification that had operated in colonial Burma, and which continued among ex-Burma Europeans in exile. When he first arrived in India, Clark had stayed in clubs and budget hotels. He often felt quite lonely, but soon got into the swing of things and began meeting people in exotic places like the Lockwood Hotel in the Northern Frontier District, Faletti's hotel in Lahore, the Cecil hotel in Simla and in yacht clubs, gym-dance clubs and even in the cinema in Karachi. He was eminently clubbable, enjoyed the high life and dined frequently with friends in colonial watering holes like the Sind Club in Karachi, the Punjab Club in Lahore and the very smart club in Ootacamund. More domestically, old Burma friends often invited him to Sunday lunches in their mansions in Karachi or their bungalows in fashionable Nilgiris.

The second issue that leaps out from Clark's letters was his desperate search for gainful employment. He had not been paid since he had left Burma and was becoming hard up. He sounded out a number of law firms, tried to find a way into the judiciary, assiduously courted legal contacts from Burma, and kept a very careful watch on the New Year's Honours list. In January 1943 he noted, with more than a hint of envy, that Lord Justice Dunkley and Sir Robert Bruce had both been honoured and that John Wise and John Francis Sheehy were off to Buckingham Palace to receive their knighthoods. He noted too that Harold Roper and June Hobson had received CBEs in the Supplementary Burma Honours List. He needed to keep an eye on acquaintances whose stock was rising.

Clark's persistence eventually paid off. In April 1943 he was commissioned into the Army. He owed this piece of good fortune to the good offices of 'Shorty' Marsh and Major General Freddie Pearce – both of whom were 'Burma men', although neither had known Clark in Rangoon. He found himself in the thick of things in Delhi, for he was given a desk in Army General Headquarters. He also received several congratulatory telegrams, including one that he relished particularly, from Sir Reginald Dorman-Smith.

One thing led to another, and on 5 September 1943 Clark was invited to serve on a military commission that had been set up to investigate corrupt

Army contracts.[35] It meant that he was 'gazetted' – his name appeared in print on 26 September 1943 – Lt Col. R. Clark, Bar-at-Law. Sir John Wise was the senior member of the Army Contracts Panel. He was a man worth cultivating. It obviously paid off, for within a month, Clark had been headhunted by the civil judiciary and was appointed to be one of the three members of the Lahore Tribunal. His new calling card now read, '*Lieutenant-Colonel Reginald Clark, Punjab Club, Lahore*'.[36]

Promotion gave Clark an appetite for more. His old friend, Cyril Paget, (senior partner in a large Rangoon law firm) came up with some helpful suggestions, but in July 1943 the Government of India announced its intention to absorb Burma judges into Indian High Courts. Several Burma judges were already in place. Mr Justice Blagdon was in the Calcutta High Court, Mr Justice Sharpe was in Lahore and Clark's old bosses in Rangoon, Sir Goodman Roberts and Sir Lionel Leach quickly followed suit. Indeed when Clark met Sir Lionel at a function in Karachi he tipped him the wink that a judge in the Madras High Court was ill and was about to resign.[37] To his bad luck, the sick Judge recovered and no more was heard on the subject. However, on 29 March 1944 the *Southport Guardian and Southwest Lancashire Chronicle* announced that Reginald Clark had been appointed as a judge in the Indian High Court.[38] He had finally made it, and was subsequently able to retire to a beautiful house in the English Lake District, where an imposing photograph on the wall shows Mr Justice Reginald Clark beaming down, clad in the robes of a judge of the Madras High Court.[39]

Many of Reginald Clark's friends found it more difficult than he did to climb the greasy pole, and many of them were less well equipped to seize opportunities. They found exile in India hard to bear. Their careers had to be put on hold and many of them disliked the necessity of having to grovel to strangers. They felt it was an exercise in humiliation. Few of them returned to Burma after the war. Indeed there was very little appetite among the expatriate British community to return to Burma in order to help build the future.

***

The British evacuees at the top of the social pyramid had the most to lose and furthest to fall. They had lost their status, self-respect, beautiful homes, exquisite possessions, businesses and industries, and in many people's eyes they were responsible for losing a Crown colony. At the same time, they suffered the same personal grief and anxiety that afflicted everyone at the time. Lady Dorman-Smith's diary bears witness to this. She belonged to the privileged colonial upper class, but also had peculiar burdens to carry.

Lady Dorman-Smith had no affection for Government House in Rangoon and was much more upset about the loss of her personal things.[40] When she and the Governor had arrived in Rangoon on 1 May 1941, a string of coolies had carried forty-five large boxes full of their possessions into Government House. Exactly one year later when they left Government House, each of them carried one small bag. They had had to leave everything else behind – Lady Dorman-Smith's 'dressing case … photographs, books, and cigarette boxes' and Sir Reginald's valuable silver salver that had been presented to him by the National Farmers Union (NFU). Miss Gibbs (their beloved pet monkey) and their dogs, upon which they doted, had to be put down. As she left Rangoon Lady Dorman-Smith had sighed, 'so that is the end of all our possessions'.[41]

On Saturday 2 May Lady Dorman-Smith flew from Myitkyina to Calcutta.[42] Her husband followed two days later, just thirty-six hours before the Japanese marched into the town.[43] They stayed for a while in Government House, Calcutta – such opulence! In 1942, Myitkyina and Calcutta belonged to different planets.

'Ordinary' evacuees would have given their eyeteeth for that quick flight and the few nights of luxury spent in Government House. Instead, they endured weeks of mud, exhaustion, squalor and danger on the way out of Burma. But 'privilege' came at the price of responsibility, in Dorman-Smith's case, he was made to feel responsible for the collapse of Burma. Even his superiors in London were unimpressed by his performance. In *All Our Tomorrows* Douglas Reed nicknamed him 'Dormant-Myth', and O'Dowd Gallagher accused Dorman-Smith of being too ashamed to show his face in public and of surrounding himself by a phalanx of '*burra-sahibs*'.[44]

In December 1942 an American journalist called Alfred Wagg turned up unannounced on the Dorman-Smiths's doorstep. He was the author of a yellow-press bestseller, *A Million Died* in which he had attacked the colonial establishment including Dorman-Smith.[45] The Governor was away from home when Wagg called, but Lady Dorman-Smith invited him into the house. It was a mistake. He launched into a tirade of abuse against her husband, whom

Figure 7.1 Lady Dorman-Smith (1896–1988). Credit: National Portrait Gallery. Lady Doreen Agnes Edith (née Watson) Dorman-Smith recorded in her diary the daily events of her husband's career in Burma from Wednesday 12 February 1941 when they were bidden to lunch at Buckingham Palace to Monday 5 August when her husband's resignation was announced.

he accused of botching the Battle of Kawkereik, driving the banks out of Burma, causing depositors to lose their money, and messing up the Air Raid Precaution system in Rangoon. According to Wagg, the Governor was hated by the military, and a laughing stock in India, London and America. He sneered at Richard de Graff Hunter, Dorman-Smith's protégé and dubbed the two of them 'the chorus-boy and the playboy.'[46] Lady Dorman-Smith was shaken to the core and her diary crackled with resentment.

Maybe it was because she was so fraught that caused Lady Dorman-Smith to live life at a frenetic pace. On her very first full day in Calcutta – Sunday 3 May – Reggie Ledger, Mr Jordan of *The Times* and the Allens from Chunking came to tea and General Irwin came to dinner in the evening. Sir Reginald arrived the next day looking gaunt and ill after flying from Myitkyina.[47] On 5

May, Dorman-Smith flew straight to Simla. Lady Dorman-Smith followed by train, and she immediately picked up where she had left off in Calcutta. She provided tea and sympathy for endless streams of guests – many of whom had trekked out of Burma. In public she was the life and soul of the party, but in private she suffered from bouts of depression. On 11 June she wrote in her diary, 'the outlook fills [me] with deepest gloom … I only hope I can find something to do to fill in the time. Everything at the moment is horrible. I just feel awful'. She was not alone in this, for most exiles in India in 1942 experienced moments of uncertainty and oscillated between despair and irrational hope.

Dorman-Smith was often away on government business and he was recalled to London at the end of June 1942. He did not return to India until the end of August. While he was away Lady Dorman-Smith continued to entertain without a break. She listened to countless accounts of evacuation adventures. Each person's anguish added to her own. Eric Battersby arrived on 19 June after walking 250 miles from Myitkyina to Margherita in thirty days. He had malaria and looked 'a ghost of his former self'. McGuire dropped in for a drink on 4 August after a harrowing trek from Shingbiyang during which he had had to pick his way through unburied corpses. He claimed to have brought with him 2,500 Indians, although many had died on the way. Sir John Rowland was another visitor. He had taken his party along the Chaukan Pass route from Fort Hertz. They were stuck for many weeks at the top of a. 9000ft pass – it wasn't his fault of course, but despite his unblemished reputation, Rowland was criticized for following this route against all advice and for showing bad judgement. He was still nursing psychological scars when he arrived for lunch at the Dorman-Smiths on 3 September.

Every visitor to Simla brought fresh news of tragedies they had endured on the way out of Burma, and at dinner parties each slight exaggeration notched up the 'evacuation-inflation' level just a little. Distances walked, numbers of corpses, depths of mud and widths of rivers seemed to expand with each retelling of a story. The constant drip, drip of the woes of evacuation took its toll, and seemed to enhance the gloom, corrode confidence, magnify self-doubt and undermine collective determination. One day a journalist named Mr Lees turn up to interview Lady Dorman-Smith about 'evacuees and their problems'. It was particularly harrowing for her, because at that time she was grappling with personal grief of her own. However, she was the Governor's wife and had to carry on.[48]

Even the most senior of Dorman-Smith's colleagues felt disgruntled for another reason. Many of those who gathered at his house in Simla had been told that they were on twelve months 'gardening leave'. They would receive full pay for four months and half pay for eight months. It was hard to make ends meet – or at least to live in the manner to which they had become accustomed. India was a very expensive place and suitable employment was hard to find. Many of the senior people were technically unemployed and felt rather ashamed to be so.[49] On New Year's Eve 1942 Pat Dorman-Smith danced the night away at a ball with Richard de Graaf Hunter and the Dunkleys. Lady Dorman-Smith sat at home alone. She reflected on the events of the past twelve months and wrote in her diary, 'What a Year! Very little to recommend it!'

Of course, not everything had been bad. Lady Dorman-Smith loved shopping and when things got her down she could always hop on a train for some 'retail therapy' in Calcutta or Delhi. Moreover, Simla was awash with interesting people. Sir John Wise and Ian Wallace often popped in for lunch, and she frequently met up with her old chums Mrs Webster, Mrs Roper, Mrs Blagden, Mrs Brewitt and Lady Paw Tun for a good old gossip.[50] She also enjoyed being pampered by Edna and Phyllis, her old hairdressers from Rangoon, who had set up a salon in Calcutta. And now a stream of exotic *new* acquaintances beat a path to her door – people like Freya Stark, Sir Maharaj Singh, Sir Edward Benthall, Sir Clarence and Lady Bird, Raja Charandjit Singh and Lady Hope. On one occasion, Sir Reginald even brought Gandhi home for a meal.

***

On the other hand, Sir Reginald Dorman-Smith found little to smile about. He was beset by problems. There was infighting in Simla; Churchill did not seem to think highly of him; and he felt responsible for the terrible destruction inflicted on Burma. In February 1944, he invited the exiled Anglo-Burmese community to attend a conference in Simla.[51] He gave it the title 'Towards a Greater Burma'. Rarely could a title have been more wildly optimistic. If the intention was to inspire and motivate, it failed miserably.

Dorman-Smith and the Bishop of Rangoon were the keynote speakers. The Bishop opened proceedings. He complimented the Anglo-Burmans on their upright families, high moral standards and dynamic faith.[52] They had, he averred, demanded nothing and given everything. Indeed, they had been 'magnificent to the last man [and] the last typist'.[53] On the other hand, Burma was teetering on 'the front-line of history'. It faced a stark choice. It was about to become either a backwater or a beacon. It was up to the people to decide. He was sure it was to be the Anglo-Burmans' 'hour of destiny'. They must lead the way. Their patriotism could transform Burma into a 'living unity'. The audience was mystified. Their blank expressions seemed to say that this was great rhetoric, but what on earth did it mean?

The next speaker, U Tin Tut, was Adviser to the Reconstruction Department. He was less supercharged and more down to earth. He spoke about the animosity that had prevailed between Burmans and Anglo-Burmans and urged his audience to rise above such petty squabbles. They should accept that the Burmans really respected them and should avoid demanding special privileges. Nor should they 'stand aloof from the great tasks' that lay ahead. Instead they should put their trust in the Burmese people with whom they shared 'ties of blood and common interest'. Another delegate, Mr H. C. Campagnac, agreed wholeheartedly. He for one was proud to have Burmese blood flowing through his veins and declared himself to be determined to play a full part in the new Burma. Another delegate, Mr H. Mc. G. Elliot, urged the audience to do everything they could to help the reconstruction of Burma. He reminded them that Anglo-Burmans had always been willing to fight for good causes.[54]

Sir Reginald Dorman-Smith was the principal after-dinner speaker at the conference. Everyone looked forward to hear him. They expected to be given specific details about what needed to be done and to be lifted by an inspiring speech from the Governor. It was not to be. Sir Reginald seemed very downbeat. He referred to the Bishop as, 'a Bishop without a diocese', to his colleagues as 'Commissioners with no districts' and to himself as 'a Governor with no country to govern'. He confessed that he found such occasions unbearably sad. Ghosts hovered over every table – ghosts of the fallen in battle and ghosts of the hundreds of evacuees who had died in the Hukawng Valley. His heart bled for the Anglo-Burman community because it had suffered 'grievous trials and tribulations'. He reminded his audience (as if they needed reminding) that when the war ended, their troubles would not be over and that the future would still look rather bleak.

It was unfortunate, he said, that the evacuees in India were so scattered. For they needed to buoy each other up. Unfortunately, only one exile could understand how another exile felt. Then he spoke very personally. He had been badly hurt by the jibes and sneers of detractors, who said that he was living off the fat of the land in Simla while ordinary people in Burma suffered. It was untrue. He and his colleagues had been working day and night. He invited his audience to look at people like his colleagues Arnold and McGuire who 'used to be light-hearted young men, full of the joy and gaiety of life ... but', he said, 'look at them now'![55]

Dorman-Smith was aware that pessimists had predicted that the British would never return to Burma – and he agreed that there were no quick fixes. Many years of hard work lay ahead before any of them could contemplate returning to Burma, and even then, there was no guarantee of success. Some of his listeners may have felt that this was one of the most pessimistic of pessimistic speeches they had heard.

Finally Dorman-Smith turned to the thorny question of communal relations. The trouble was that Burmans had no respect for religions, cultures and languages other than their own, and that minority groups showed little loyalty to the country that nurtured them. He offered no solutions but urged everyone to pull up their socks, and the Anglo-Burmese community in particular to bring the two sides together.

On this note the conference closed. The delegates had felt physically and emotionally drained when they arrived at the conference and most of them felt no better when they left. They had wanted to be informed and inspired, but the stench of defeat and failure hung over the proceedings. The Governor had lost his swagger, his sense of humour and his belief in the future of Burma. The period of exile was beginning to leave its mark on everyone, great and small.

Dorman-Smith could be forgiven for having lost his sparkle, for he had been subjected to a great deal of criticism. He was accused of deserting a sinking ship, of cowardice, and worse.[56] Journalists lampooned him, his own officials criticized him and senior civil servants in London viewed him with suspicion. Even Churchill damned him with faint praise. Indeed, Dorman-Smith appeared to be thoroughly deflated.[57] In February 1944, the war in Southeast Asia rested on a knife-edge. The decisive battles of Kohima and Imphal were still to be won. India was under threat from within and the reconquest of Burma was a distant pipe dream. There was little positive to say, and maybe empty rhetoric and morbid introspection were the only things that the Bishop and the Governor could offer their audiences.

***

Three years of exile in India had sucked the life out of the colonial project in Burma. Evacuees from the poorest Indian to most powerful British official were pausing to take stock and to assess their futures. Indians of all castes distrusted the British and Burmans in equal measure. Few would return to Burma, but most demanded compensation for their losses. Without Indian labour and Indian finance colonial rule in Burma wouldn't work. Several European groups had once vowed to return to Burma for humanitarian reasons – people like the Methodist missionaries, for instance. But even they had become lukewarm after three years in exile and few of them went back. Everyone was five years older, less robust, less confident, less enthusiastic and more tired than before. A minority did eventually return to Burma, but they found that local 'subalterns' resented them and they were not always made welcome. Commercial companies, businesses and many middle-class professionals simply could not afford to return. The future for them was too uncertain.

The Governor and his senior officials had a *duty* to pick up the reins once again – it was a case of noblesse oblige. Some of the officials mourned their loss of status, and not many had used the period of exile to good effect. They had ignored the need for radical change, and pretended that things would be the same as before. They were surprised to discover that everything had changed. It escaped their attention that Burmese political leaders had tasted power and they would not be satisfied with marginal concessions.

Ordinary Burmese people certainly did not feature in the celebrations to mark the Dorman-Smiths' return to Rangoon. Most were emotionally and physically exhausted and felt little enthusiasm for another change of regime. Few, if any of the new group of Burmese politicians featured in the official events and there was no mention of Aung San or of independence. The 14th Army had won the war, but there was little sign that the colonial regime had won the peace. Humility and cultural sensitivity were still in short supply. Colonial rule had returned, but with less of its swagger and with few new understandings.

8

The Post-War Mess

We go to gain a little patch of ground that hath in it no profit but the name
Shakespeare, *Hamlet*, Act 4. Scene 4

In the early hours of 16 October 1945 HMS *Cleopatra* sailed up the Rangoon River.[1] Sir Reginald and Lady Dorman-Smith were passengers on board the vessel and they had come to regain their little patch. They had spent the past forty-one months in Simla, as exiles in a gilded cage. They were about to set foot on Burmese soil for the first time since May 1942. The *Cleopatra* berthed at the Sule Pagoda wharf in Rangoon and Sir Reginald and Lady Dorman-Smith appeared on the gangway at precisely 9.30 am. There was a gun salute, a squadron of RAF planes with dipped wings flew past, and a guard of honour met them on the quay. Then they were whisked along Sule Pagoda Road and on to the cathedral.

There were no cheering crowds. Armed British troops lined both sides of the route and beyond them the Dorman-Smiths caught glimpses of gutted buildings. After a short service in the cathedral, the Dorman-Smiths continued to Government House.[2] Rangoon had changed out of all recognition in the three and a half years they had been away.

By the end of October very few European evacuees had been allowed back into Burma, and many of them had a nagging suspicion that the Governor had jumped ship in May1942 and had left them in the lurch. Their opinions had not mellowed during the years in exile. Rangoon was still under martial law and a depressed and edgy mood hung over the place.

The Dorman-Smiths paced themselves carefully. They attended a few carefully choreographed events during the first week or so. The most important of these events was the official Japanese Surrender Ceremony, which was held on 24 October. That evening the Governor and his wife attended a victory dinner hosted by Brigadier Thomas in the British Army Officers Club.[3]

A flurry of engagements followed in November and December 1945. Whereas Sir Reginald was fully occupied with affairs of state and with tours to far-flung parts of the colony such as Toungoo and Mandalay, Lady Dorman-Smith had more than thirty official engagements to attend. She visited leper colonies, old people's homes, orphanages, convents, dispensaries, schools, Salvation Army hostels, hospitals and canteens and attended services in the cathedral. The Governor and his wife hosted receptions, dinner parties (one was for twenty-three guests), tea parties, lunch parties and cocktail parties in Government House. Air chief marshals, brigadiers, aristocrats, diplomats, trade commissioners, senior British civil servants, foreign diplomats, loyal Burmese politicians and US congressmen were among the guests.[4] Five hundred needy children attended a huge party on Christmas Eve. During this whole time, they were free of guests on only two days. Despite this, Lady Dorman-Smith managed to fit in several race meetings to which she was escorted by an array of dashing military officers, including General Thomas, Captain Robertshaw RN (Commander of HMS *Cleopatra*), Captain Hughes-Hallett (Captain of HMS *Jamaica*) Brigadier Wright and General Stopford.

The Governor and his wife endured some awkward moments. For example, the American journalist Alfred Wagg (whom they distrusted) turned up unannounced on 22 October, and the swearing in of the new Executive Council on 3 November proved to be another very tricky occasion. General Aung San cast a long shadow over their lives. Lady Dorman-Smith recorded in her diary that Aung San had been especially non-cooperative on 30 October (we don't know why), and that on 18 November there had been great excitement when he addressed a huge crowd of 30,000 at the Shwedagon Pagoda. Lady Dorman-Smith was painfully aware that her husband's lack of charisma was in inverse proportion to General Aung San's massive popular appeal. Her misery was completed when on 28 December she discovered a cache of letters full of bitter complaints about Dorman-Smith sent by colleagues, Burmans, Indians, Europeans, and even British soldiers. The year seemed to end as miserably as it had begun. To compound it all, on 30 December, Dorman-Smith had a difficult meeting with 'trade union people'. On 31 December 1945, Lady Dorman-Smith wrote forlornly that it was the end of 'another queer year'.

It is not absolutely clear why the Dorman-Smiths insisted on punishing themselves by engaging in frenetic action, but perhaps it was an attempt to recreate life as it had been before 1942. However, the world had changed. The Dorman-Smith's spent a great deal of time with passing 'celebrities' and very little with ordinary 'subjects'. Indeed, the familiar faces from the European, Indians and Anglo-Burmese communities of pre-war Rangoon were singularly absent from the new world. Clearly many twists and turns were to come but, on 16 October, few could have predicted that in less than 1,000 days Burma would have become a fully independent self-governing state.

Dorman-Smith was soon under a great deal of pressure. He was not in the best of health and seemed to have few friends. Churchill and the British political elite regarded him as a liability, General Aung San and Burmese nationalists regarded him as the enemy, hostile journalists, senior army officers briefed against him, and British and Indian evacuees did not trust him. In June 1946, Dorman-Smith returned to England for medical treatment, and he and his wife returned to their house in the village of Stodham in Hampshire for the first time in over five years. Stodham was a place of pure relaxation and reflection, but Burma was never far from their thoughts. Dorman-Smith knew he was out of favour with the powers that be, and suspected that he would be dismissed if he did not to resign.

While at Stodham, the Dorman-Smith's learned that Sir Hubert Rance was to replace him as Governor of Burma on 31 August 1946.[5] It was a blow to Sir Reginald's self-esteem and Lady Dorman-Smith was angry and frustrated on his behalf. They decided to invite Sir Hubert and Lady Rance to lunch in Stodham on Sunday 4 August. The mood did not lighten when Rance revealed that over a period of several weeks he had discussed the issue of the governorship in succession with Attlee, Mountbatten and Lord Pethick-Lawrence (Secretary of State for India). Lady Dorman-Smith was disgusted to discover that so much had been happening behind her husband's back and without his knowledge. It was, she said, 'a mean way of treating Reg'. The very next day (5 August 1946) Sir Reginald Dorman-Smith's resignation was announced in the press, and after that there were no more entries in Lady Dorman-Smith's diary.

Sir Reginald Dorman-Smith felt that he was under attack from all quarters. Churchill had criticized his leadership during the civilian evacuation, and there is evidence that senior military officers plotted against him. Brigadier Jehu (the Army Senior Public Relations Officer) claimed that senior army officers had instructed him to 'use Dorman-Smith as a scapegoat … for the collapse of Burma in 1942 … so as to divert attention from the Army's failures'.[6] Dorman-Smith had an unfortunate tendency to make unguarded comments. In October 1943, for example, he had ruffled feathers in the Burma Office. During an address to the East Indian Association he had criticized Britain for frequently promising self-government but never delivering it, so that 'neither our word nor our intentions are trusted … we have fed such countries as Burma on political formulae until they are sick at the very sight and sound of formulae' [it is merely, he suggested,] 'a very British means of avoiding a definite course of action'. Nor was Dorman-Smith always as sure-footed politically as he might have been. For example, he was determined to arrest Aung San for a murder he had allegedly committed in the course of the war in 1942.[7] His colleagues warned him that it would lead to civil unrest, and even Rance advocated a more conciliatory approach on the grounds that a policy of closer cooperation with Aung San and the Anti-Fascist People's Freedom League (AFPFL) would pay dividends. Dorman-Smith complained that Rance's intervention was designed to undermine his authority.

***

The continued resurgence of Burmese nationalism seriously undermined colonial rule in Burma. It will be recalled that, after a great deal of activity in the 1930s, nationalist protests fell strangely silent in 1940. The colonial authorities were distracted by world events, and were unaware of the major developments taking place behind the scenes.

Even before the war, Thakin Aung San had been the leading figure in nationalist politics and was well known to the colonial police. In 1939, he had been arrested and released without charge. He suspected that it was just a matter of time before he was arrested again. From beginning to end Aung San uncompromisingly advocated full independence, and he planned to take the nationalist movement in a completely new direction. In his view, the invasion represented a new opportunity and the Japanese had emerged as a potential ally.[8]

To further his plans and in order to pre-empt the inevitability of arrest, Aung San and one of his colleague, Thakin Hla Myaing, sailed secretly to Amoy. Their immediate objective was to link up with Chinese communists, but Japanese agents intercepted them and took them to mainland Japan. Here

Aung San was introduced to Colonel Suzuki and the two men joined Suzuki's secret organization. It was preparing to undermine British Rule in Burma.

They were then shipped back to Burma with instructions to recruit young Burmese nationalists willing to undertake training under Japanese military instructors.[9] The recruits were subsequently nicknamed the 'Thirty Comrades' and eventually they formed the core of the Burma Independence Army (BIA), which was inaugurated in Bangkok on 26 December 1941.[10] BIA units had fought alongside Japanese troops in the invasion of Burma in January 1942. Therefore they were able to claim that they had been involved in the military campaign that drove the British Army out of Burma in May 1942.

Aung San lived by his wits. He unashamedly *used* the Japanese military in order to serve his long-term objective of Burmese independence. He readily accepted the promotion to the rank of major general in August 1943. He was then drafted into Dr Ba Maw's quasi-independence government as Minister of Defence.[11] However, by this time he was disenchanted with the Japanese New Order and openly criticized Japanese practices. Behind the scenes, he assembled an anti-Japanese nationalist coalition, which was known as the Anti-Fascist Organisation (AFO).[12] On 27 March 1945 – just a few weeks before Japanese forces in Burma finally surrendered – General Aung San switched his support from the Japanese to the British Army. The BIA fought with the British Army *against* the Japanese in the final battles of the war. Critics were appalled at these double-dealings, but it was evidence of his mastery of opportunism.

General Aung San's meteoric rise continued after the war, when he used democratic processes, rather than military means to seek power. In 1946, he was elected President of the AFPFL and he worked night and day to hold it together. When a bitter dispute in the Communist Party threatened to blow the coalition apart General Aung San took the momentous decision to expel the Communist Party from AFPFL.[13] In September 1946, Aung San and the AFPFL controversially decided to take part in the general strike.

Many British officials heartily distrusted Aung San. They were highly critical of what they considered to be his double-dealings at the end of the war, and were disgusted that AFPFL chose to support the general strike in 1946. In return Aung San accused British officials of attempting to undermine his authority. In the midst of these claims and counterclaims a particularly frosty relationship developed between Aung San and Sir Reginald Dorman-Smith.

Dorman-Smith's problem was that by 946 Aung San was in an unassailable position. He enjoyed popular adulation in Burma, and was supported by two of the most influential luminaries of the day. General William Slim praised Aung San and his supporters for their 'patriotic resistance' (Tinker 1984: 250). Lord Mountbatten complimented Aung San on his decision to be 'a Churchill rather than a Wellington,' thereby enabling him to speak on behalf of all Burmese peoples (Bayly and Harper 2004: 64). It was no coincidence that one of Sir Hubert Rance's first acts when he succeeded Sir Reginald Dorman-Smith as Governor in August 1946 was to persuade Aung San to become Deputy Leader of the Governor's Executive Council. At the same time, Aung San also headed up two of the most important departments of government – Defence and External Affairs.

Meanwhile, under Aung San's tutelage, the AFPFL broke new ground in November 1946 when it issued an ultimatum *publicly* demanding *full* independence from Britain (outside the British Commonwealth), insisting that the transfer of power should take place within one year. It set the stage for a head to head clash between Burmese nationalist leaders and the British Government.

***

To understand what happened next it is necessary to focus on developments in London, thousands of miles away from Rangoon.[14] Britain's domestic difficulties at the end of the war were directly (although not solely) responsible for Burma's rapid progress towards independence. It must be remembered that successive British governments before 1945 had resisted all demands for Burmese independence. In January 1946 the British Government suddenly made it clear that it was willing to grant independence to Burma – and indeed, that it intended to grant it as quickly as possible.

There were four main reasons for this unexpected volte-face.. First the British economy was in crisis. Second, the United States now exercised a strong influence on British colonial foreign policy. Third, the Labour Party had won a landslide majority of 146 seats in the British General Election of 26 July 1945, and finally, post-war British governments became entangled in a series of damaging semi-clandestine military engagements in Southeast Asia.[15] At precisely the same time, between 1945 and 1947, Britain faced simultaneous demands for independence from India, Burma and Ceylon. The weight of these factors hung over the heads of British negotiators at the Burmese independence talks held in London in January 1947.

***

The first of these reasons was Britain's parlous financial situation. In fact Britain's economic woes predated the war. They stemmed in part from the financial crash of 1929, in part from the devaluation of the pound in 1931, in part from complications in the sterling area, and in part from the convertibility of the pound. Britain emerged from World War II in more debt than any of its allies. The Treasury had borrowed £18 billion – or seven times its gold and dollar reserves and the equivalent of 10 per cent of its GDP (about £50.5 billion in today's values).[16]

The United States remained neutral until December 1941 because it was unwilling to offer financial assistance to combatant nations. Therefore the British Government had to pay cash for any purchases of food and military supplies. Under the terms of the 1939 Cash-and-Carry arrangements the United States made a concession to its principal ally, Britain. It agreed to commute some payments into services-in-kind (such as access to Britain's overseas bases), nevertheless it still left Britain stranded. Fortunately, the terms of the 1941 Lend-Lease scheme were less stringent. Under it the United States was willing to *donate* equipment to Britain.[17]

It was a curious fact that Britain incurred less debt *during* the war (when America did not insist on repayments) than it did *after* the war when America continued to provide huge loans to see Britain through the post-war period. In December 1945 the United States made available $586 million of credit and a loan of $3.75 billion at 2 per cent interest. This had to be repaid in fifty annual repayments starting from 1950. Nevertheless, Britain defaulted on six occasions – and indeed the final instalment of $ 83 million (£45.5 million) was not repaid until 31 December 2006.

Britain was further hampered by the fact that its expected export boom failed to materialize after the war and because essential post-war reconstruction work proved to be costlier than had been anticipated.[18] At the same time the new Labour Government was committed to a very expensive programme of welfare and health reforms at home. Furthermore, because of the new cold war

Britain had to spend much more on defence after the war than it had expected to spend.

US business leaders used Britain's dependency on American aid to challenge the terms of the Ottawa Agreement of 1932 on the grounds that commonwealth preferences discriminated against non-sterling-area manufacturers and producers.[19] In order to head off US objections, Churchill secretly agreed to abandon commonwealth preferences and to return sterling to full convertibility by August 1947.[20] The effect of this was catastrophic, as countries holding sterling reserves rushed to convert them into US dollars. Convertibility was abandoned in September 1947 when the British Treasury was reduced to its last $850m. Sterling was in danger of total collapse.[21] J. M. Keynes advocated a massive extension of credit facilities and the creation of an artificial currency (the *bancor*) to replace gold. American financiers rejected the Keynesian proposals, adopting instead a modified gold standard and more modest credit facilities. It will not go unnoticed that this desperate situation was unfolding just at the time when the Burmese independence negotiations had got underway.[22]

***

The second reason was that Britain's increasing dependence on the United States had many far-reaching political consequences. On 5 December 1962 the US Secretary of State 1949–1953) made the speech at West Point in which he declared that Britain had lost an empire but had not yet found a role. It was true that by this time Britain's so-called First Empire had all but disappeared.[23] On 9 and 10 August 1941 Churchill and Roosevelt had met aboard the U.S.S. *Augusta* to agree on their joint war aims. They issued a joint communiqué known as the Atlantic Charter, which included assurances that they would not seek territorial expansion and identified several shared aims. The most important clauses recognized the right of all people to 'choose the form of government under which they will live' and promised to restore 'sovereign rights and self-government' 'to those who have been forcibly deprived of them'.[24] This clause was open to different interpretations. Roosevelt insisted that it meant exactly what it said – that is, that all peoples *including* colonial subjects would be guaranteed self-determination.[25]

Churchill insisted that the clause applied *only* to peoples recently subjugated by the Axis Powers.[26] He assured listeners at the annual Mansion House Dinner in London that he had 'not become the King's First Minister in order to preside over the liquidation of the British Empire'.[27] He continued to reject nationalist demands for independence up to the very last moment although privately he acknowledged that the British Empire could not survive without American support. It is the reason why Ronald Robinson considered 1945 to be the node point in imperial history – it was the moment when Britain was forced to dismantle its Empire.[28]

***

The third reason was the Labour Party's landslide electoral victory in 1945. Colonial independence was not an issue in the 1945 General Election. It was an issue voters rarely raised on the doorstep. They were too war-weary, too tired of austerity and too interested in jobs, housing, schools, hospitals, welfare, food, clothing and the availability of fuel. They had little appetite for involvement in yet more overseas conflicts. Indeed the 1945 Party Manifesto, *Let Us Face the Future*, made no mention of the Empire, and British people eagerly awaited the creation of a new, peaceful and socially secure society at home. In any case the parlous state of public finances meant that there was no money to squander on colonial skirmishes. Every aircraft, jeep, machine gun, policeman, administrator and soldier had a price tag.

Nevertheless there were those in the Labour Government who were keen not to relinquish Britain's great power status or to abandon its global role.[29] The party was divided on the issue.[30] 'Little Englanders' considered the colonies to be morally reprehensible, while Fabians were ambivalent.[31] Fabians like R. H. Tawney, G. D. H. Cole, Harold Laski and Annie Besant supported colonial independence movements and colonial leaders like Jawaharlal Nehru, Muhammad Ali Jinnah, Obafemi Awolowa and a host of Ba'athist leaders joined the Fabian movement.[32]

In 1945, most Fabians wanted to abandon the colonies and bring the troops back home, and almost all of them demanded a timetable for decolonization. Left-wing journalists like Woodrow Wyatt and Tom Driberg forthrightly supported colonial independence.[33] Driberg interviewed General Aung San in 1945 and described him as 'honest and incorruptible'. His columns in *Reynolds News* were read by thousands of Labour leaning 'demobbed' servicemen.[34]

Attlee's cabinet was also divided on the question of the Empire. In public Attlee advocated colonial independence, but privately he believed that only India was ready for independence. Even Herbert Morrison (a champion of colonial independence) was loyal to the 'jolly old empire' and Arthur Creech Jones, the Colonial Secretary, refused to grant more freedom to the colonies than was absolutely necessary.[35] Ernest Bevin, the Foreign Secretary was an unapologetic imperialist. He fought to keep a substantial British military presence 'east of Suez' because British workers depended on imperial trade.[36] Moderate trade unionists looked both ways. They campaigned against the brutal treatment of colonial workers, while resisting competition from cheap colonial labour.[37] In the end, Bevin was forced to choose between providing resources for overseas garrisons and paying for health and education at home. He plumped for the latter conceding that domestic spending had to be funded by increased productivity and export earnings.

Most Labour MPs were enthusiastic Keynesians. They were determined to implement the 1942 Beveridge Report.[38] Indeed between 1945 and 1948 the Labour Government enacted at least nine important pieces of welfare legislation and at the same time the railway system, road haulage industry and, coal, and steel industries were nationalized.[39] The proceeds of Marshall Aid were needed to stimulate industry and provide full employment.

This focus on domestic reforms consumed all the Government's meagre resources, and it explains why the British Government was determined to settle the Burma independence issue without delay. It had no will to resist and no wish to prolong deliberations.

***

The fourth reason was rather curious. Few civilians in Britain realized what was happening. Yet it contributed profoundly to the collapse of colonial rule in Burma. After the end of the war, Britain became entangled in a series of military operations in Southeast Asia, despite the fact that British and Indian troops were exhausted and their morale was low. This was particularly true of Indian servicemen who had already made enormous sacrifices. Two and a half million of them had served on the British side between 1939 and 1945 and over 87,000 Indian troops had been killed or wounded in action. In addition, 79,489 Indian troops had been taken prisoner, and at least 11,000 had died in

Japanese camps. British and Indian troops had quite reasonably assumed that they would be demobilized immediately after Japanese forces surrendered on 14 August 1945, but in many cases the process dragged on for months.

In October 1945, sailors serving aboard HMS *Northway* in Singapore harbour demonstrated against poor living conditions. Many British and Indian soldiers attended communist rallies in Malaya, while others enrolled in the Indian Communist Party. In January 1946, airmen at RAF bases in Malaya downed tools and 4,000 men went on strike at the main RAF base in Singapore. The ringleaders were charged with mutiny.[40] In February 1946 a serious disturbance broke out at the Royal Indian Navy base in Bombay. Sailors paraded around the nearby streets carrying Congress Party banners. The demonstration spilled out into the city centre and sparked riots. Unrest spread across India like wildfire. At Kluang airfield in Malaya 243 airmen were found guilty of mutiny and were sentenced to long terms of imprisonment. In May 1946, men of the Parachute Regiment based at the Muar camp in Malaya went on strike.[41] It was the first time ever that front-line combat troops had been involved in demonstrations.

The root of the problem was that after the end of the war and beyond public scrutiny, the British Government had pitchforked its troops into some extraordinary military entanglements. Attlee had inherited from Churchill a two-pronged strategy in Southeast Asia. The first of the prongs focussed on the Malayan peninsula. Churchill was right in predicting that Singapore and Malaya would one day become the 'dollar arsenal' of the sterling area. He believed that whatever happened, and at whatever cost, Singapore and Malaya should be persuaded to stay in the British Empire. Accordingly, colonial office officials were instructed to win over the hearts and minds of the non-Malay Chinese population, and at the same time Britain invested in an ambitious (and expensive) social engineering project.[42] The fact that Malaya and Singapore had been beckoned to the front of the investment queue meant that India, Burma and Ceylon were pushed to the back. Without 'sweeteners' British officials in those territories were unable to counter independence movements. The simple fact was that Britain could not fund several expensive projects in Malaya, Singapore, India, Burma and Ceylon all at the same time.[43]

The second prong to Churchill's strategy almost beggared belief. He was convinced that in order to bring Burma back under British control it would first be necessary to create a ring of Western-influenced territories around the colony.[44] The policy began inauspiciously before the 1945 British General Election – war was still raging and there was turmoil in India and Burma.[45] In the event, the strategy succeeded in doing three things. It alienated the states that Churchill had intended to befriend, it emptied the national coffers and it drove a wedge between Britain and America.

Siam (renamed Thailand on 20 July 1948) was first on Churchill's list. Siam had been one of Britain's 'protégés' before the war. Britain had guaranteed its independence in return for trading concessions. The situation changed abruptly on 8 December 1941, when Japanese troops invaded Thailand. A few days later Thailand declared war on Britain and the United States. Indeed, the Thai troops accompanied Japanese forces into Burma in January 1942. Churchill never forgave them for this. He threatened to wreak revenge by annexing the Kra Peninsula, seizing one and a half million tons of 'surplus' Thai rice, and extracting reparations. Thailand pleaded poverty and claimed (not unreasonably) that it had been forced to declare war.

Roosevelt condemned Churchill's demands and American newspapers accused Britain of colonial expansionism, while US Congressmen threatened to withhold Britain's loans. Attlee had to build bridges. On 1 January 1946, he withdrew Britain's demands and signed an agreement with Thailand.

Indochina was more problematic.[46] In1940 the Vichy Government had become responsible for the 100,000 French residents in Indochina. Most of the residents were Vichy adherents although some were Free French supporters. They had readily collaborated with Japanese forces against Vietnamese nationalists.[47] Chaos ensued on 13 August 1945 when local Japanese forces surrendered. French settlers and Japanese units fought around Saigon, and in Hanoi the Japanese administration established a quasi-independent government under Ho Chi Minh.[48]

Earlier, Churchill had agreed to send British troops to assist the French. General Gracey and an Indian Division arrived on 13 September 1945. Martial law was declared. By this time Viet Minh groups controlled most of Saigon. They killed large numbers of French citizens and torched the central market area. Gracey enlisted the support of fully armed Japanese troops, thousands of whom had remained in Vietnam. For several months they fought alongside British and French forces against the Viet Minh.

A further complication arose on 5 October when General Philippe Leclerc arrived in Saigon. He demanded that he take charge. However Gracey would not give way. The more immediate problem was how to dislodge the Viet Minh. They remained dug-in until hundreds more battle-hardened British troops from Burma arrived in Vietnam.[49]

Roosevelt was appalled by the developments, which he felt smacked of Anglo-French imperialism. But his successor, Harry S. Truman, was willing to tolerate Anglo-French influence in the southern Vietnam, on condition that Chiang Kai Shek (with US support) had a free hand in the north. The arrangement guaranteed continued chaos in Vietnam. The Viet Minh set up roadblocks, attacked airfields, radio stations, power stations, docks and waterworks ensuring regular blackouts and sporadic bursts of small arms fire. British, Indian, French and Japanese troops were stretched to the limit.

By the end of December 1945, the situation had improved sufficiently to enable Gracey to hand over control in Saigon to General Valluy and the French 9th Colonial Infantry Division. Elsewhere intense fighting continued – especially in the highland districts. Even more British reinforcements had to be brought in from Burma together with an RAF squadron. They fought the last major pitched battle at Bien Hoa on 3 January 1946.[50] The Viet Minh continued to carry out ambushes and hit-and-run raids, but Gracey handed his command over to General Leclerc on 28 January 1946 and he left Vietnam. The last Indian troops – a company of the 2/8 Punjab Regiment – left on 15 May 1946, after which the remaining Japanese troops were repatriated

In the seven-month entanglement in Vietnam forty British and Indian troops were reported killed, although the actual number may have been ten times that number. Of even greater importance was the fact that thousands of war-weary British and Indian troops had been dragged into the conflict, and that scarce resources had been diverted away from India and Burma. French and Japanese forces suffered very heavy casualties and it was estimated that 2,700 Viet Minh were killed in the same period. The war in Vietnam continued to rage for many years to come, and it is unclear whether the British forces had mitigated or exacerbated the troubles

The British military intervention in the Dutch East Indies was even more incomprehensible. Once again British forces acted as 'proxy' for a defeated European power. The reconquest of Indonesia seemed to have little to do with

Britain's strategic interests.[51] Supporters claimed that British forces were sent to protect British commercial interests – estimated to be £100m (including a 40 per cent stake in Royal Dutch Shell) – critics denounced it as pure folly and the United States suspected that it was another example of colonial expansionism.

On 15 August 1945 South East Asia Command (SEAC) became responsible for 500,000 square miles of Indonesian territory, a population of 80 million and 250,000 armed Japanese soldiers still at large in the archipelago. Lieutenant General Sir Philip Christison was dispatched to establish law and order.[52] Britain took over the administration of Java and Sumatra, while Australia administered the outer islands. It was a mission from hell.

British troops were parachuted into Java and Sumatra on 8 September 1945 and a week later, thousands more landed in Java aboard HMS *Cumberland*.[53] Their first task was to locate and release in an orderly way the 100,000 men, women, and children incarcerated in prisoner-of-war and civilian internment camps throughout the islands. The Dutch internees were not interested in waiting for an orderly release. They wanted to return to their homes as quickly as possible, and in some cases to reassert their authority over local communities. However, the world had changed fundamentally in the previous three years.

Indonesia was politically complex. The Dutch had never *directly* controlled large swathes of the archipelago before the war. They had ruled Sumatra (which had become a hotbed of Moslem intellectualism) indirectly through Islamic sultanates. Dutch settlers in Java had ruled with rods of iron, and had cohabited openly with 'temporary wives'. There was therefore a large and politically ambiguous Eurasian community.

Nationalist leaders were quick to act. Dr Sukarno and Mohammad Hatta declared the country a republic and there were calls for jihad. Former Dutch internees were attacked when they attempted to regain their old homes and businesses. Tensions rose further when unpopular Dutch officials like Dr Hubertus van Mook (the Lieutenant Governor) and Charles van der Plas (the Governor of East Java) returned from exile.[54] Neither nationalists nor the Dutch community were willing to put their faith in Christison and the British troops.

At the end of October 1945, very serious clashes erupted when the 49th Infantry Brigade of the 23rd Indian Division disembarked in Surabaya.[55] An estimated 120,000 civilians, 24,000 British and Indian troops and tanks and aircraft were drawn into battles that raged for several weeks. During that time all sides suffered heavy casualties.[56]

It was the signal for civil disturbance to flare up in towns and villages across an archipelago. Local youths, Dutch vigilantes, British military units, Japanese stragglers and nationalist groups piled into the conflict.[57] Problems were exacerbated because the whole place was awash with discarded Japanese weaponry. Estimates of civilian deaths varied from 10,000 to 15,000. Rarely a day went by without reports of British and Indian deaths. Christison became deeply despondent. He withdrew all British and Indian troops into Jakarta, which he attempted to transform into a fortress.

The political situation was equally fraught. In November 1945 Sutan Sjahrir became Prime Minister and Sukarno, the President. On 1 January 1946, a People's Congress was held at Purwokerto. The radical Tan Malak dominated proceedings. He was imprisoned in March 1946 after calling his supporters to arms.

The British position in Indonesia was now untenable. In February 1946, a senior British diplomat, Sir Archibald Clark Kerr, arrived in Jakarta to negotiate a way out. He announced a withdrawal of all British and Indian forces troops by the end of November 1946. Just before this deadline (on 15 November 1946) Dutch and Indonesian leaders met at Linggajati They agreed terms for a ceasefire to start in March 1947. It did not last long. British forces withdrew as planned at the end of the month. In July 1947, fighting resumed between Dutch and Indonesian forces.

These extraordinary post-war adventures were veiled in secrecy. The population in Britain was kept in ignorance, but as casualties rose the facts could not be concealed. It added more pain as British and Indian families racked up the costs, at a time when Britain was almost bankrupt.

Churchill had pitchforked British troops into needless battles in Vietnam and Indonesia, but Attlee was also complicit in the sense that his Government was slow to stop the process. After enduring three and a half years non-stop fighting in the toughest combat zones of the world, exhausted British and Indian troops arrived in Saigon and Surabaya to fight other people's battles in some of the most remote, humid and unglamorous corners of Southeast Asia.[58]

These actions reached their nadir during 1946 when Burma was in crisis. It was no wonder that, a few months later, Aung San discovered that the British Government was desperately anxious to 'offload' Burma.

The British Government was bankrupt and had to dance to America's tune, and it was determined to introduce social reform at home. At the same time, Malaya and Singapore had been pushed to the top of its priority list. It had been hopelessly entangled in foreign entanglements, could no longer rely on Indian soldiers to suppress if and when it was to occur in the colonies unrest and British troops were exhausted. It was not surprising that the colonial office believed that the Empire (in its current form) was beyond redemption.

It was inevitable that Britain would have to hand over control to nationalists in the colonies. It just happened that Burma was one of the first in the firing line.

9

Anglo-Burmese Relations 1942–1947

This world is like a lasting storm whirring me from my friends
Shakespeare: *Cymbeline*, Act 4. Scene 2

Long before military hostilities had ended between the Allied and Japanese forces on the battlefields of Burma, fierce arguments began to erupt behind the scenes. The arguments flared up intermittently between 1942 and 1945 and continued long after the war had finished. Government ministers, nationalist leaders, businessmen and aggrieved individuals quarrelled about the spoils of war, the displacement of civilians, and compensation for damaged property. These remained measures of discontent long after the troops had laid down their arms.

By 1945, the opposing armies had inflicted a colossal amount of damage on the land as they surged and retreated across Burma. They left behind a toxic legacy that choked civilians, politicians, shareholders, managers and the exhausted evacuees alike. Arguments reverberated down the corridors of power of Rangoon and Westminster, in smoky Burmese tea shops, panelled boardrooms and at dinner parties in the English shires. Burma had been scarred beyond recognition and faceless people had lost fortunes. Ordinary men and women grieved over destroyed homes and their looted possessions. Everyone longed for redress.

By the end of 1942, the colonial project in Burma had disintegrated, and one disaster followed another. By 1945 Rangoon, Mandalay and every other major town had been bombed – often twice over – and roads, railways, factories, refineries, bridges, air strips, ports, houses and agricultural land had been ruined. The year 1942 was the nadir. The Governor and his ministers had fled to India, the apparatus of the colonial government collapsed, the British Army retreated and Indian, British and Anglo-Burmese civilians streamed out of the country. Ordinary Burmese people were left on their own to face the Japanese *Kempetai*. Each new disaster left behind it a trail of death, suffering and material damage. It was a time of great uncertainty. Behind it all loomed an unanswerable question. Would the colonial rulers *ever* return to Burma?

Sir Reginald Dorman-Smith and his senior advisers spent the next three years from 1942 to 1945 exiled in Simla. They were in a gilded cage – pampered, but frustrated and powerless. They did not know what was happening in Burma and could not plan for the future. They did not know that charismatic young Burmese nationalist leaders had occupied the ground they had vacated. The world was shrouded in mistrust, economic gloom and constitutional uncertainty.

The first *serious* discussion about the future of Burma took place in the British War Cabinet on 14 April 1943.[1] Sir Reginald Dorman-Smith had asked L. S Amery (Secretary of State for India) to slip it into the agenda.[2] Many cabinet ministers were annoyed to see it there. There were far more pressing concerns, and Churchill was in an impossible mood because of his 'instinctive hatred for self-government in any shape or form and his dislike for any country or people who want such a thing'.[3] The desire to sort out a future independent Burma was not on Churchill's list of priorities.

Nevertheless the cabinet *did* discuss the item – and at considerable length. It acknowledged five principles. First, that one day Burma would probably gain autonomy. Second, that Britain was likely to impose direct rule on Burma, at least for a period of seven years. Third, that demands for independence would be inadmissible within those seven years. Fourth, the lure of dominion status might have to be dangled in front Burmese leaders. Fifth, Burma would be bankrupt, and might need a loan or a grant to repair the war damage.

Churchill was silent. It was a sign that he did not intend to implement any of the principles. Although fine words butter no parsnips, Amery wrote reassuringly to Dorman-Smith promising that the British Government would *not* 'leave a ravished and impoverished Burma to sink or swim on its own'.[4] Dorman-Smith was not reassured.

Late in April 1943, a flurry of letters began to pass between Sir Reginald Dorman-Smith in Simla and L. S. Amery and Sir John Walton in London. Generally the letters were depressingly bereft of hard facts, new ideas or any real conviction. Dorman-Smith (aware of the feelings of people in Burma) was anxious to persuade his colleagues that Britain had a moral duty to repair Burma's infrastructure that had been smashed in the course of Britain's war.

The British Treasury was unconvinced. In 1944, a Conservative Party committee produced a report that put the brakes on proceedings. It claimed that since 1942, 'Burma, had drunk the heady wine of nominal independence ... and had become imbued with the spirit of nationalism'. It warned that after the war the British Government would have to impose on Burma 'a Governor who would be responsible to the Imperial Parliament' in London. The committee realised that this would provoke 'nationalist impatience', but it was a necessary evil, and as an emollient gesture it proposed (not for the first time) that the British Government should offer dominion status to Burma in order to assuage nationalist antagonism.[5] It was breathtakingly arrogant – the assumption that colonial subjects would be unable to resist the honour of dominion status. Indeed, the dominion status controversy would run for years to come.

As the war drew to an end a group of hard-bitten British businessmen challenged what they called, Sir Reginald Dorman-Smith's 'fanciful ideas'. Sir Arthur Bruce was a leading sceptic. He accused the Governor of going soft, of 'smarting under defeat', of feeling 'deeply humiliated by the way in which the civil authorities had been unceremoniously bundled out of Burma', and of being 'imbued with a self-exculpatory feeling of having let down the Burmese people'.[6] He accused Dorman-Smith of assuaging his conscience by overcompensating for his own past failings. The Governor, he said, was bent on designing an *ideal* but impracticable world that would have to be financed *entirely* by the British Government.

Bruce set out alternative proposals based, he claimed, on the kind of carefully budgeted plans beloved of hard-nosed Treasury officials in times of austerity. His aim was to reduce the proposed expenditure to a minimum and to fund *only* productive projects such as ports, roads and railways, agriculture, electric supply systems, oil, mining, timber and rubber industries. Bruce also believed that Burma should be expected to repay in full any loans it received and within rigid time frames.[7] He advocated a network of project boards to administer finance, kick-start essential industries, and be accountable for expenditure.[8] Each project board would be carefully regulated and financed by interest-bearing loans.[9] The idea influenced a nascent Treasury, and a new orthodoxy began to emerge – one that insisted Burma could and should foot the bill for war damage inflicted on their country, while the British Treasury could and should offer support only in extremis.

Before May 1945, British colonial administrators could only *imagine* what had happened to Burma during the war. The actual situation was much worse than anything that the returning evacuees had imagined and they were shocked by the plight of every Burmese town and village. The Burmese people were lacklustre and did not seem at all pleased to see the returning British evacuees. From this point onwards, discussions about war damage, loans and grants became increasingly fraught and battle-lines were drawn.

Thomas Lewis Hughes had been the Governor's Private Secretary before the war. He was one of the first exiles to return to Rangoon.[10] He described what he saw. There was

> a distressing lack of every form of activity necessary to maintain human life ... not a train, tram, bus or conveyance ... save on the outskirts of the city. A few dilapidated pony carts, pulled by mangy scarecrows of ponies were plying for hire at exorbitant rates. The streets were feet deep in filth and the open drains had long since ceased to be other than a depository for excreta and garbage. Both the water and sewage systems were out of action. At night there was a complete blackout and whole blocks of the city had been laid waste by Allied bombing. The once trim well-laid-out residential areas were overgrown with rank jungle and were dirty beyond description. (see note 11)

Hughes reported that the population in Rangoon was less than half its pre-war number, and 'the survivors were ill clad, unkempt and dirty. Of soap there was none and many suffered from skin diseases. The economic devastation was paralysing'. Railways, power plants, oil refineries and port facilities had been demolished in the denial operations of 1942. Wave after wave of Japanese and Allied bombers and the attention of heavy artillery had finished the job. Hughes wrote that hardly a major bridge had survived. Factories and houses had been looted and the 'economic life of the city was at a standstill'. He had discovered that conditions were even worse elsewhere in the country – 'the up-country towns of Mandalay, Meiktila, Myingyan, Myitkyina, Bhamo, Prome, Toungoo and Pegu were flat and lifeless. Burma lay sorely stricken from the battles that had surged over and receded from her shores'.[11]

Sir John Wise returned to Burma at about the same time.[12] Like Hughes he was overwhelmed by 'the enormity of the task of reconstruction'. As he travelled around the country he noted that 'hardly a town had escaped almost total annihilation' and that agriculture was in a precarious state. In this land of plenty, local food had run out in some areas of the country and Burma had no rice to export. It was too late in 1945 to begin planting for the following year's crop. Even to the casual observer it was clear there was an existential crisis in Burma.[13]

Sir Raibeart MacDougall was a very senior civil servant in the Burma Office. He had been despatched to Burma on a fact-finding mission and returned to London in November 1946. He presented an extremely gloomy report to the Cabinet.[14] The Burmese economy was indeed in a dire state. The Port of Rangoon was in shambles. Ships had to unload their cargoes manually because quayside cranes were still not available. Consignments of consumer and other goods had piled up on land adjacent to the port because there was no transport to take it onwards. There were no storage facilities, pilfering was rife and wrecked vessels obstructed the Rangoon River, creating all manner of serious navigational hazards. There was an acute shortage of housing in the city and the Rangoon Corporation was powerless to act. It needed huge sums of money to replace the bombed tenement blocks.

Sir Raibeart was shocked to see profiteering and 'spiv-very'. He noted that a small number of Burmans had made vast sums of money during the Japanese occupation, and that a few blue-collar workers had benefited from wage inflation. How different things were for the population as a whole. While a tiny minority became affluent, tens of thousands of unemployed, semi-unemployed daily labourers and poorly paid government servants suffered terrible hardships. Consumer prices rocketed and there was rampant inflation. The vast majority of the population had been ground down by the very high cost of living. It was true that some products – for example, cooking oil and fish – were available in city bazaars, but the collapse in agricultural production and the severe disruption to road and rail transport meant that most stallholders had very few products to sell.

The disappearance of Chettiars from rural Burma had caused capital to dry up almost completely. There was no money to finance the rice crop and cultivators were entirely dependent on meagre government loans. Over a third of the paddy fields had gone out of cultivation, and it seemed that they were likely to fall out of use permanently. Moreover, because of widespread lawlessness in rural areas, villagers were afraid to cultivate paddy fields distant from their villages. The transportation of rice had become almost impossible because of the prevalence of highway robbery.[15]

***

The new Labour Government in Britain took Sir Raibeart MacDougall's report very seriously. However, Britain was also in a very bad way. British cities had suffered terrible bomb damage, there was an acute housing shortage, British schools, hospitals, ports, railways and roads, were all in urgent need of investment and repair. The black market also flourished in British towns. There was rationing and an acute shortage of food. The British Government was also bankrupt, and the British merchant fleet had been decimated. It was not surprising therefore that ordinary British voters had little interest in Burma's problems.

The British Government refused to write blank cheques. It was in no position to lend or give away large sums of money. The Chancellor of the Exchequer made it clear that Britain would only contribute to Burma's reconstruction costs in the last resort, and that grants or loans would only be given to 'prime the pump for the future development of British trade with Burma'. The Cabinet insisted that it must be allowed to supervise the whole process of spending grants or loans from beginning to end.

***

Burmese nationalist leaders presented a different side of the story. General Aung San was the most vocal of the nationalists. He broadcast to the nation at the end of December 1946 in terms that perfectly captured the mood of the Burmese people. He said:

> We have not forgotten how directly and grievously we have been affected by events in Southeast Asia in the course of the last World war. Burma became a battlefield for nearly four years through no fault of her own and for no cause in which our people were interested. Today the ravages of that unwanted war are still with us to a very great extent.[16]

Aung San maintained that the fundamental difference between war-torn Britain and war-torn Burma was that the British people were fighting their own war, for their own national survival, and of their own volition. They were willing to suffer because it was in their interest to do so. On the other hand, Burma had become a battlefield in the British Empire's war. Japanese, British and American forces had fought across their land and laid it to waste. It was not Burma's war, and nor was it a war in which the people of Burma had the slightest interest.

The arguments between the UK and Burma continued for many months, and in September 1947 Thakin U Nu reminded Sir Stafford Cripps (if he needed reminding), that between 1942 and 1945 Burma had been completely devastated by two military campaigns. There was just enough food to feed the populations of the larger towns, but rural Burma (which amounted to 95 per cent of the country) had descended into abject poverty. U Nu described the tragedy in which most Burmese people were destitute in a country rich in natural resources. Before the war, the lion's share of the country's wealth had been stolen by foreigners and, even now in post-war Burma, the country's natural wealth was being diverted away from the Burmese people. U Nu warned that there was a great deal of suspicion and mistrust of non-Burmese capital interests. We have a duty, he said, to foster the growth of Burmese industrial undertakings and industries, even if this should mean a substantial restriction of the present spheres of operation of non-Burmese capital.[17]

There was increased interest in a number of financial issues in the two years leading up to January 1947 – the date of the Burma Constitutional Conference in London. Principal among the issues were the 'divorce settlement' prior to independence and compensation for the damage inflicted on Burma's infrastructure.

Lord Pethick-Lawrence, the new Secretary of State for Burma, divided the financial demands relating to war damage into three categories.[18] The first was compensation for loss of *public* property, second was compensation for loss of private property *deliberately* destroyed at the request of the British Government, and third, compensation for private property destroyed or damaged as a result of *enemy action*.

The first category (i.e. public property) was by far the biggest and most complex of the issues, and it also required the most urgent action. This category included repairs to damaged infrastructure, such as roads, railways, airstrips, ports, telegraph installations, hospitals, schools, public buildings and agricultural land. It also included intangible losses, for example, loss of revenue, interruptions to trade and disruption to public institutions. These were deeply political issues, and because the costs ran into many millions of pounds, compensation claims could only be settled on a government-to-government basis by means of grants, loans and trade deals.

The last two categories included compensation for self-inflicted damage to private property as demanded by the Government as part of its 'denial programme'. It also included damage inflicted by enemy action. There were very big variations in the amounts of compensation at stake. At one end of the scale were huge claims submitted by the biggest companies. At the other end of the scale were hundreds of small amounts claimed by private individuals.[19] In general, the British Government did not respond to these claims until the 1950s, and the implications of this will be examined in Chapter 10. This chapter will concentrate exclusively on the first category – the arguments over public finances that raged between British ministers and Burmese nationalist leaders.

There were early indications of confusion. Lord Pethick-Lawrence was trying to find his way. He set out what he believed to be the issues in telegram no. 4590, which arrived with the Burmese Executive Council on 14 December 1946.[20] The fingerprints of Sir Stafford Cripps, the British Chancellor of the Exchequer, were all over the telegram. It contained a bewildering plethora of facts, revised figures (some of them contradictory) and a number of new stipulations. There were references to net loans of £8.5m that had supposedly been given to Burma in 1945–1946, and to another loan (not a gift) of £22m that had to be repaid within one year. Pethick-Lawrence was accused of demanding its immediate repayment, but he vehemently denied this. Members of the Burmese Executive Council were angry. They hotly disputed several of Lord Pethick-Lawrence's figures and began to press for a completely fresh financial settlement, which would *include* a generous rehabilitation grant.[21]

As Lord Pethick-Lawrence was relatively new in his post, he bravely (but rashly) spoke of the *actual* sums of money he thought would be necessary to complete essential post-war reconstruction work in Burma. On 18 December 1945 he mentioned the figure of £87m (equivalent to approximately £35.5 *billion* in today's money).[22] The sum included the money required for key industries £24m; for public utilities £10m; for civil supplies £25m; for government services £11m; and for an estimated revenue deficit over two years £15M.

Pethick-Lawrence became a hostage to fortune. The figure of £87m was no more than a finger-in-the-air guess, but Burmese politicians got very excited about it. They believed that the sum had been carefully calculated, that it represented Burma's *actual* losses, and that therefore the British Government felt obliged to provide Burma with an interest free grant of £87 million to cover the losses. None of these assumptions were correct, but they gave rise to a series of questions, assertions, claims, and counter claims all of which focused on this sum of £87m. It became a source of profound disagreement between the British and Burmese governments and caused confusion and misunderstandings for several months.[23]

By 8 January 1947, Sir Stafford Cripps had become so concerned about the rumours and misinformation flying around that he urged Lord Pethick-Lawrence to deny that he had ever promised a grant or loan of £87m.[24] For some reason Cripps blamed the misunderstanding on Sir Reginald Dorman-Smith for producing 'a fantastical plan in Simla'. However, the plot thickened when Burmese nationalist leaders insisted that the *loan* of £87m should be commuted into a free *grant* of £87m. At the same time, they also demanded that the UK Government should cover the cost of maintaining the BDA. Sir Stafford Cripps was dismayed. He dismissed the demand to pay for Burma's defence forces, suggesting that it made no more sense than asking Britain to fund Burma's education system. He insisted that a grant or a loan of £87m had never been offered. As a sop, he said that he was willing to offer a loan of £35m, but that it would be charged at the standard rate of interest and would have to be repaid within seven years.

Sir Stafford Cripps was utterly convinced that Burma's *primary* aim in the forthcoming Constitutional Conference was to achieve political independence. He tried to persuade Pethick-Lawrence that the Burmese delegation would not be interested in financial concessions, and advised the Secretary of State to resist all Burmese demands for money. Instead, Cripps said, Pethick-Lawrence should 'give the Burmese what they wanted on the political front at the outset', and save 'good British money from being lavished unnecessarily'. In public, Cripps expressed surprise that 'a proud and independent country like Burma' was willing to demean itself by demanding largesse from a foreign state.

Cripps also urged extreme caution on the question of war damage compensation. He feared that these demands could easily become a bottomless pit. He reminded Pethick-Lawrence that Britain was not obliged to pay 'a single penny' for war damages, at least until the bill was finally revealed in its totality.[25]

On 9 January 1947, Clement Attlee chaired a meeting of the India-and-Burma Sub-Committee, in which Burma's 'divorce bill' was discussed. Attlee and most committee members took a much softer line than the one Sir Stafford Cripps had adopted. They agreed that 'Burma had suffered great destruction during the war and that much of this was as a result of the scorched earth policy that had been carried out at Britain's instigation'. They accepted that Burma had a strong moral case, and that it was proper that 'they should call on the British Government for assistance'.

A few British Cabinet members – cheered on, no doubt, by the Chancellor of the Exchequer – still argued that because Burma had once been a wealthy country and was likely to become wealthy again – it should pay its own way. However, the Cabinet acknowledged that its first priority was to protect British commercial interests in Burma, and to safeguard the UK's balance of payments. It agreed with Sir Stafford Cripps that the Government was 'in no position to be unduly generous', but it was equally keen to prevent narrow British interests from 'obstructing the natural political development' of Burma.

At this point, two very significant *new* principles began to emerge. The first was that any financial help Britain provided to Burma would depend on whether or not Burma decided to stay in the Commonwealth. The second was that if the Burmese Executive Council nationalized British companies operating in Burma, (which it threatened to do) the British Government would demand full compensation from Burma.[26]

Even at this late stage in proceedings the Burmese Executive Council made it clear that it was still expecting to receive a grant of £87m from Britain. Sir Stafford Cripps was shocked that the issue had rumbled on, and he was painfully aware that the demand for £87m was widely supported by the Burmese population as a whole. Once again he insisted that a *grant* of this order had never been discussed and nor had a l*oan*. He stuck (albeit reluctantly) to his earlier offer to make available an interest-free loan of £35m for the purposes of post-war rehabilitation, but he added darkly that 'we cannot afford improvident good nature'.[27] As has been said, the uncomfortable truth was that Britain, like Burma was almost bankrupt.

Pethick-Lawrence took a softer line. He desperately wanted to help Burma. He recognized that its infrastructure had been destroyed and that rehabilitation work had not yet started. He also knew that Burma had no money and was in no position to make annual loan payments of even £5m. At the same time Pethick-Lawrence was aware that India had started to demand that Burma resume payments for the debts it had incurred under the terms of the Separation Agreement in 1937.[28]

In November 1946, the AFPFL issued an ultimatum demanding full independence for Burma, *outside* the Commonwealth. This implied that Burma did not wish to accept dominion status. The AFPFL also injected a note of urgency. It insisted that independence should be granted within one year.

***

It was against the background of these factors that in December 1946 Clement Attlee invited a Burmese delegation to London to discuss Burma's constitutional

Figure 9.1 Burma Talks, 23 January 1947. Credit: Fox Photos/Stringer. Delegates at the Burma Constitutional Conference outside 10 Downing Street in January 1947. Front Row: U Ba Pe, Thakin Mya, Sir Stafford Cripps (partly hidden), Clement Attlee, U Aung San, U Tin Tut, Lord Pethick-Lawrence. Behind including U Saw, Arthur Bottomley, and Ernest Bevin.

future.[29] At face value, it was a very bold move considering Britain's profound economic and political problems. The Burma delegation duly assembled in London at the beginning of the freezing January of 1947. General Aung San was the glamour boy of the event. He was frequently photographed and remained the main focus of interest throughout the talks.[30]

Even before the talks officially began, financial issues came to the fore. U Tin Tut was the economic spokesman for the Burmese delegation. He issued a positional statement that set the cat among the pigeons. His case was as follows: Burma had demonstrated financial competence and prudence before the war. It had built up healthy reserves and at the same time had managed to keep up its annual payments to India for the Separation Debt. However, the war had changed all this. The Japanese invasion and the consequent devastation 'had come upon Burma because she was part of the British Empire'. Burma appreciated the UK's financial difficulties but Burma also faced ruin because of the war. U Tin Tut reminded the British Government of its undertaking to meet the deficit in Burma's budget by providing an interest free loan up to £87.5m. Sir Stafford Cripps' blood pressure rose. However U Tin Tut went further. He insisted that the Burma Government should have 'complete freedom in the administration of this budget' and 'should be free to deal with her own finances'. He made this point because there was a suspicion in Burma that the British Government's main interest was to re-establish British commercial firms with funds that really should have been made available to the Burmese tax payer.[31]

U Tin Tut's preemptive strike put Sir Stafford Cripps on the back foot. He responded by pointing out that the UK was in serious financial difficulty too, and that it 'had a limited capacity to make grants or even loans'. Britain's huge deficit had also been caused by the war and its trade gap was widening all the time. Privately he advised Hugh Dalton to 'handle him (i.e. Tin Tut) with care, realizing that he has great knowledge of these matters, but not of international finance'. He urged Dalton to

> try and give them something definite and immediate to show their followers when they get back … which will not be unduly expensive to us while holding off the larger claims upon the basis that we cannot settle them till we know more of the future circumstances. On this basis you would no doubt be able to "give way" somewhat on the £x million or £5M and give them a sense of having accomplished something.[32]

Given these exchanges it was little wonder that both the British and the Burmese delegations approached the talks with trepidation. There was a great deal to lose on both sides.

It was a small miracle that eleven senior members of the Burmese Executive Council had been persuaded to come to London at the beginning of January 1947 in the lowest winter temperatures recorded for more than a century. Indeed the talks opened promptly on 13 January. General Aung San was the key personality. He dominated the Burmese delegation, which consisted of Thakin Mya, U Tin Tut, U Ba Pe, Thakin Ba Sein, U Saw, U Kyaw Nyein, U Aung Than, Thakin Chit, U Ba Yin and U Shwe Baw, ICS. Clement Attlee led the United Kingdom delegation, which consisted of Sir Stafford Cripps, A. V. Alexander, Lord Pethick-Lawrence, the Earl of Listowell, Christopher Mayhew and Arthur Bottomley. Sir David Monteith, Sir Gilbert Laithwaite, Sir Raibeart MacDougall and F.W.H Smith were also in attendance.

To everyone's surprise the talks were conducted throughout in a spirit of civility and mutual respect. The Burmese delegates had fully expected that they would have to fight tooth and nail for independence. However, very quickly they discovered that they were pushing at an open door. Of course Burma was desperate to achieve its independence, but the astonishing thing was that Britain appeared to be even more desperate to grant it.

Two weeks of intensive negotiations followed and the Aung San-Attlee Agreement was signed on 27 January 1947. The members of both delegations duly appended their signatures. There were two notable exceptions. Two members of the Burmese delegation – Thakin Ba Sein and U Saw – refused to sign the final communique, claiming that the concessions made by the British Government 'fell far short' of the demands made by the Burma delegation. Ba Sein, in particular, remained vehemently truculent to the end. The British negotiators were shocked to encounter this unexpected dissent in the Burmese ranks so late in proceedings. Aung San and most of the Burmese delegates were irritated, but sanguine. They took their colleagues' behaviour in their stride, regarding it as par for the course for the two men concerned.

The Aung San–Attlee Agreement bound both sides to Burmese independence. The two trickiest issues were left open – that is, it was not decided whether or not Burma would choose to remain in the British Commonwealth, and no deadline was given for independence although it was agreed that it should happen 'as soon as possible'.

The steps whereby independence was to be achieved were spelled out in detail. A general election for a Constituent Assembly was to be held as soon as possible 'under the 1935 electoral machinery'. A period of transition would follow during which the Constituent Assembly would draw up a new constitution. The Governor's Executive Council would act as the interim government. The Governor would appoint a councillor to be responsible in the short term for Defence, and another to be responsible for External Affairs. However, the Governor's Executive Council would have no more (and no less) power than the interim government of India. This was a sensitive issue, for Burmese politicians were anxious not to be seen as the poor relations of India, and Indian politicians did not wish to see Burma stealing a march on them. It was agreed that Burma should have financial autonomy. The most crucial constitutional question was that of Burma's territorial integrity – particularly in respect of the frontier areas and ethnic minority groups. No final decision was reached at the London conference. However representatives of all the minority groups had already agreed to attend a conference scheduled to meet in February 1947 in Panglong. It was agreed that, at the Panglong conference, General Aung San and the delegates would draw up policy proposals and hammer out the details relating to the minority groups and the frontier areas.

Annex B to the Agreement was read with great interest. It concerned the financial settlement. Most people anticipated that this would be a major stumbling block. In the event financial matters were ushered through with little trouble. Attlee was astonished that U Tin Tut and Sir Stafford Cripps had managed to achieve this miracle. It was confirmed that Burma would have financial autonomy, and that Burma would receive an interest-free loan of £8m for the current financial year. A further loan of £7.5m would be made available in September 1947. Beyond that, a joint commission would be appointed to examine the financial situation in Burma and make proposals for future funding provisions.

Thus it was that the three most contentious issues in 1947 – dominion status, the timing of independence, and the financial settlement had remained unresolved. However their non-resolution did not create friction, it merely underlined the fact that the main prize was the principle of independence. Both sides believed that appropriate solutions would be found and both sides respected one another. The final remarks of the conference summed it up:

> The Prime Minister said that it had been a great pleasure to meet the Delegation and to take part in the talks and that he had every hope that co-operation would continue and that the two countries would go forward as good friends. U Aung San reciprocated these sentiments. He felt sure that the two countries would remain firm friends and allies.[33]

Aung San made a triumphant return to Burma from the London conference and AFPFL won an overwhelming majority in the General Election, which was held on 9 April 1947.[34] The Constituent Assembly opened on 16 June 1947. There followed an extraordinary period of eight months, during which there were terrible tragedies but also remarkable triumphs. The greatest of the achievements was the granting of full independence on 4 January 1948.

***

All was not well. In the months that followed, the Aung San–Attlee Agreement a wave of strikes spread across Burma and there was a loss of 20,000 tons in rice production between February and April 1947. Reconstruction slowed down because of shortages of construction materials the world over.[35]

Provisional agreement on financial issues was not finally reached until after Aung San's death. On 11 October 1947, Hugh Dalton confirmed that the British Government would not require the Government of Burma to repay the cost of the Civil Affairs Administration, and that it had agreed to cancel £15M of the £52M it had advanced towards budget deficits. Burma would repay the balance (at no interest) in twenty annual payments beginning in 1952. The British Government agreed to reimburse the Government of Burma for supplies and services rendered to the Burma Army in 1942, and to release benefits payable to Burma Army personnel for war service. It would also postpone any payments of War Damage Compensation claims in Burma until all claims in the Far East were known. Dalton retained £15m from Burma's indebtedness, in case some contribution had to be made towards the War Damage claims of British interests in Burma.[36]

***

The financial settlement had been inextricably bound up with the question of dominion status and commonwealth membership. British politicians were keen for Burma to stay within the commonwealth. It would have added credibility to the liberal reincarnation of the Empire – the British Commonwealth. However the Earl of Listowell misread the popular sentiment in Burma.[37] He believed that Burma had more to gain from remaining in the commonwealth than Britain had for keeping her there. Therefore he insisted that if Burma was to join 'it must be on Commonwealth terms'. He singled out in particular the requirement that would be placed on Burma to accept 'the position of HM the King'. Listowell promised that Britain would remain Burma's friend even if she remained outside the Commonwealth. On the other hand, he warned that if she remained outside the Commonwealth she would forfeit the possibility of financial assistance, support for UN membership, beneficial bilateral agreements, military protection, and economic cooperation (which would affect Burma's exports to India). Furthermore, he insisted that only 'continued membership of the Commonwealth would persuade the Karens and other minority groups to remain within the Union'.

Listowell assured the Burmese delegates that, if they did decide to remain in the Commonwealth, Burma would be free to leave at any time and that as long as she remained a member she would find herself 'in a strong united group' and would 'have moral support against external aggression'. She would also have access to 'specialist support and equipment'.[38]

A new orthodoxy began to emerge in British Government circles. It was that commonwealth membership was the prerequisite for financial assistance. Ministers frequently reiterated the dire consequences of non-membership. For example, the British Cabinet India–Burma Committee resolved to 'use the prospect of financial assistance to persuade Burma to remain within the Commonwealth'.[39] On another occasion during a discussion on the possibility of financial assistance the committee agreed that 'much might depend on whether Burma decides to become a member of the Commonwealth'. On yet another occasion the British Government indicated that it felt unable 'to make any proposals until it is known whether or not Burma decides to remain in the Commonwealth'. Indeed Burma was constantly being asked to choose between leaving the Commonwealth and receiving financial benefits.

Listowell underestimated the force of Burmese *emotional* resistance to a continued relationship with Britain. Some Burmese nationalist leaders were reasonably well disposed to Britain. For example, U Tin Tut had benefited directly from the British connection. The historian Thant Myint-U once described him as 'the brightest Burmese official of his generation,' and in April 1943 Sir Reginald Dorman-Smith had asked him to explain what Burmese people understood by the word 'freedom'.[40] U Tin Tut got straight to the point. Most Burmese people, he said, simply wanted to gain freedom from Britain. The problem was that many of them misguidedly assumed that everything would be fine once independence had been gained. Few Burmese nationalists, he said, had bothered to consider the implications of freedom. Consequently they were in for a nasty shock. U Tin Tut suggested that Burmans were poor negotiators and had habitually come off worst in business dealings with Indians. They would almost certainly come off worst in their negotiations with the British Government. For example, they were likely to be stampeded into accepting dominion status on the understanding that it was the immutable price of freedom. In doing so, they would miss the point. For commonwealth membership would bring positive benefits that would only become clear in years to come.

U Tin Tut envisaged that the time would come when an independent Burma would find itself squeezed between two predatory powers – independent China on one side and free India on the other – each of which already had teeming populations and would probably soon have huge standing armies. When that moment arrived, he said, Burma would need all the powerful friends it could get in order to survive. U Tin Tut suggested that England was Burma's best friend. Britain's spirit of 'generosity and disinterestedness' had been demonstrated over the years so membership of the British Commonwealth of Nations would be a priceless asset.[41] Of course most leading nationalists at the time would have furiously disagreed with U Tin Tut's assessment, but his response lifted Sir Reginald Dorman-Smith's spirits.

Senior nationalist figures in Burma had been arguing long and hard about the advantages and disadvantages of commonwealth membership and a consensus had emerged by 1947. People like U Tin Tut who saw some benefits in dominion status were in a tiny minority. The long history of disputes between colonial rulers and their subjects had left a legacy of irreparably damaged relationships. It is possible that colonial rule was more deeply resented in Burma than it was in any other British colony.

***

When Sir Hubert Rance replaced Sir Reginald Dorman-Smith as Governor on 31 August 1946 expectations were very high that relations would improve. Rance was relatively new to the game, but he suspected that the Rubicon was about to be crossed at the Constituent Assembly to be held on 11 June 1947. He believed Aung San would use the occasion to declare Burma a sovereign independent republic because he feared that 'India was about to steal a march on Burma'. There were, Rance said, 'psychological factors' at play included the overwhelming 'self-confidence of the Burmese' that underlined their determination 'to attain complete independence'. However, they also wanted to have their cake and to eat it – for 'they also wanted a treaty with the British Government'.[42] Rance believed that emotions in Burma would calm down if and when India decided to stay in the Empire. He wrote to Listowell requesting an update on the current situation vis-à-vis Indian independence. It was a highly sensitive issue, and Listowell's reply to Rance was marked 'For your most secret and personal information, and in no circumstances is it to be divulged'. Listowell was hopeful that 'certain Congress leaders could be persuaded to accept Dominion status' and that this would open up

> new possibility of the whole of India remaining in the Commonwealth when their new constitution comes into operation. He explained that in July legislation was to be introduced in Parliament, which would mean that British India would become two (eventually three) independent States within the Commonwealth. The title 'Emperor of India' would be dropped to enable the Congress Leaders to accept the Crown. Listowell was aware that 'this announcement will have an important bearing on Burma.[43]

On 13 July 1947, just six days before General Aung San was assassinated, the Bogyoke addressed a huge audience in Rangoon Town Hall. His followers listened spellbound to a long, passionate speech that left no one in doubt that Burma had no intention of accepting dominion status and that it would *not* join the Commonwealth. Aung San claimed that India was disunited, and was therefore incapable of severing its links with Britain. It would – he predicted – remain a *semi*-sovereign state and as a Dominion in the British Commonwealth it would be bound by rules, regulations, values and expectations against which it had struggled for so long. Aung San explained that he found Eire's situation confusing. Although Eire *claimed* that it was about to cut free from Britain to become an independent sovereign state, but it was by no means clear whether or not Eire would remain in the Commonwealth and whether or not it would be prepared to accept the King as its figurehead. At the same time, because white men formed the majority in Canada, New Zealand and Australia they did not count in the equation.

Aung San claimed that Burma was unique in the British Empire, for it was at liberty to stay or to leave. He assured his listeners that Burma's constitutional status would remain unambiguous. It would govern itself under a constitution of its own making. He asked the audience to cast their minds back to January 1946 when the AFPFL Supreme Council had voted to seize *complete* independence and *not* to accept dominion status. On 23 May 1947, the AFPFL Convention had confirmed this resolution, and had demanded that Burma should become an independent sovereign republic within the next year. General Aung San concluded his speech with the promise that he would achieve independence by peaceful means if at all possible. But he pointed out that victory had not yet been won, so the clear implication was that force might be necessary.[44]

***

10

Compensation Wars: British Government versus British Interests in Burma

For I can raise no money by vile means, by heaven, I had rather coin my heart, and drop my blood for drachmas.

Shakespeare, *Julius Caesar*, Act 4. Scene 3

Burma was unique in the British Empire. Between 1942 and 1945 it was twice fought over. Everyone – from the poorest cultivator to the wealthiest landowner – suffered in some way or another. The indigenous people were the biggest losers. They had most to lose, and were often left destitute after foreign armies and planes wrecked their houses, possessions and paddy fields. This chapter is about loss, destruction and restitution. It describes bitter arguments that raged between governments, proprietors and individuals long after the war was over.

In the final analysis, no firm or individual profited from the war in Burma; everyone was a loser and no one was adequately compensated. The Burmese Government had neither the resources nor the moral imperative to compensate Burmese citizens, and the British Government refused to compensate non-British citizens.

Whitehall divided British citizens who had sustained losses into three categories. The first category consisted of British companies, whose property was destroyed or damaged as a direct result of the British Government's scorched earth policy. The second category consisted of British companies, whose property was destroyed or damaged as a direct result of enemy action. The third category consisted of individual British citizens whose belongings were damaged or destroyed as a result of enemy action. Many of them sustained their losses during the course of the evacuation of 1942. No other losses or claims for compensation were considered.

The most important unanswered question had deep political implications. What would be done about the terrible wartime destruction inflicted on Burma's infrastructure? Would it be repaired – and if so, who would pay? On 18 February 1943, the British Government *seemed* to make a 'whispered' promise. It would repair any property and replace any goods that had been destroyed anywhere in the British Empire during the war. To implement this undertaking, a War Damage Commission would be established – not immediately, but perhaps one day in the future.

The truth was that in 1943 any talk of war compensation was without substance. The British Government had absolutely no idea what the final bill would be, or who would pay it. For example, the British Government guessed that the final bill for war damages in Malaya might be in the region of about £160m.[1] It suggested that the cost might be borne in part by the British Government and in part by taxpayers in Malaya. It wasn't to be. Nor was it a viable model for any other colony, including Burma.

War damage compensation hung over the British Cabinet like a sword of Damocles. In 1942–1943 the Government chose to procrastinate. It insisted that *no* payments against war damage claims would be made until a War Damage Commission had been set up and had reported, and, of course, that event was a long way off. Yet, there was an underlying assumption that the British Government would one day be liable for very large compensation payments, although no one had any idea what the size of the liability this might be.

Figures for Burma were plucked out of the air. One oft-quoted guess was £100m – a gross *under*estimation. Some MPs demanded that as the damage was inflicted *in* Burma, compensation should be paid out of Burmese revenues – regardless of the fact that the damage had been inflicted *on* Burma. More realistically the Cabinet was aware that Burmese public opinion would be inflamed if the colony was required to pay for the costs of war damage and especially if Burmese taxes were used to pay for war damage to European firms who had destroyed their property at the instigation of HMG.

Therefore the question of war damage compensation refused to go away The losses suffered by British firms were expected to be huge Some thought that BOC's losses alone might be in the order of £50m – an enormous sum and the equivalent of almost £2 billion at today's values.[2] It was a terrifying prospect, in view of the fact that BOC was only one of several large companies that had sustained huge losses during the war. Others included the Irrawaddy Flotilla Company (IFC), Steels, the BBTC, the British Burma Petroleum Company, the Yunan Mines Company, the Burma Cement Company, the CNAC and the BISNCo Ltd., and the list went on.[3]

Estimates crept up. Soon it was thought that total claims in Burma might be in the region of £165m, and that this sum might include British losses of £67m, of which 'denial' damage might account for £60m.[4] It was all complete guesswork. In any case the parameters changed after independence in January 1948, when the new Burmese Government disclaimed all responsibility for the payment of war damages.

The new Labour Government acknowledged that it had a moral obligation to assist those who had lost assets in Burma during the war. It was aware that the Conservative Opposition was keen to pounce if British commercial interests were not protected. It did two things. First it put £10m into a War Damages pot to which British firms and individuals could apply for compensation. Second it set up an independent committee chaired by Mr Walter Carter to assess the claims and disburse money equitably. It soon became clear that the Carter Committee had an impossible task and that £10m was completely inadequate. For the most part it was possible to make only minimal ex gratia payments.

The Conservative Opposition latched on to the Government's difficulties when the British Assets, Burma (Compensation) Bill was debated in the House of Commons on 8 December 1948, and the Burma compensation issue exposed sharp philosophical and political fault-lines between the two parties.

Colonel Crosthwaite-Eyre MP spoke on behalf of the Opposition.[5] He was horrified that the new Government of Burma had refused to honour its obligations under 'Article Seven' of the Burmese Independence Treaty, which supposedly *guaranteed* British concessions, contracts and rights of property. U Nu (the Burmese Prime Minister) explained that the Union of Burma had adopted a policy of 'state socialism' and was therefore likely to expropriate British assets. Nevertheless, he had given his word that equitable compensation would be paid for any expropriated properties. Crosthwaite-Eyre accused U Nu of breaking his promise, and he gave the example of treatment recently meted out to the IFC (about which more will be said later in this chapter).

Moreover, he complained that the Labour Government had failed to ensure that no British individual or company should 'suffer because of unilateral action by a foreign power'. He accused labour politicians of 'taking a rather impish delight in seeing British assets destroyed [and taking] the view that every time a British interest abroad is expropriated, a little more of wicked capitalism is destroyed'.[6]

***

The experiences of three major British companies –BOC, IFC and Steels – will be described in this section. They all suffered war damages as a result of the British Government's denial programme and fought long and hard for compensation.

***

Of all the companies, the BOC's struggles had the most far-reaching implications. It was a legal and constitutional cause célèbre.[7] On 3 February 1942, the General Officer in Command (Burma) ordered the destruction of all installations and stocks that might be of use to the enemy. This was in accordance with the British Government's instructions. Indeed, Mr W. L. Forster – a government official and an acknowledged expert on denial procedures – was sent out from Britain to supervise the programme. On 6 March the order was posted to evacuate Rangoon. This was the signal for the destruction of installations in and around Rangoon (including oil wells, pipe lines, refineries and other buildings and stocks of petroleum and other goods). The order was carried out on 7 March. Japanese forces occupied Rangoon on 8 March. Between 8 March and 19 April industrial installations north of Rangoon were destroyed at regular intervals. The last British forces left Burma on 20 May. By this time the denial programme had been completed. The destruction of the oil installations was particularly important as it was intended to assist the defence of India. It was beyond dispute that the demolitions had been carried out lawfully under the terms of the Defence of Burma Act, 1940.

Almost immediately the BOC lodged a compensation claim for £31 million. It issued a warning that the capital amount would gather interest at a rate of 5 per cent per annum. It will not go unnoticed that £31m was three times the amount that the Government had put in its contingency pot. Understandably the Government decided to take no further action on the BOC claim – or any claim – until procedures had been worked out and an independent war damage commission had been established.

One of the first acts of the War Damages Commission was to examine the BOC case. It dismissed the original £31m claim, adjudging instead that BOC had a valid claim for £17m. The Government took the Carter Committee's judgment to the Court of Sessions under the presidency of Lord Kilbrandon. The court upheld the Carter Committee's assessment of damages at £17m. The Government then lodged an appeal against Lord Kilbrandon's judgment in a Scottish Appeal Court. It upheld the appeal and reduced Lord Kilbrandon's award from £17m to £4,600,000. This was considerably less than the Carter Committee's recommendation of £17m but represented almost 50 per cent of the total amount in the War Damages Fund.

The BOC appealed against the Scottish court's judgment, and took the case to the House of Lords. By a 3–2 majority the Law Lords upheld BOC's appeal and judged that the £17 million recommended by the Carter Committee and awarded by Lord Kilbrandon should stand. The Law Lords' opinion was based on the argument that the scorched earth damage inflicted on BOC installations in 1942 was equivalent to requisitioning the property. In other words, it had been done for the public good, but at the expense of an individual proprietor. The Lords therefore held that the individual proprietor should be compensated from public funds.

Lord Radcliffe was one of the two Law Lords who dissented from the judgment. He maintained that courts of law were not competent to decide whether or not there were more urgent claims for reconstruction priorities on the public purse. 'War damage', he said, 'is beyond any exercisable or foreseeable control'. He argued that 'it is for those who fill and empty the public purse to decide when, by whom, on what conditions and within what limitations such compensation is to be made available, and that this was the case whether the damage is self-inflicted through the medium of a "scorched earth" policy or inflicted by the enemy'. Lord Radcliffe added prophetically that the House of Lords' judgment was likely to encourage other companies to stake claims, which if similarly upheld in courts of law, would require the Exchequer to find an additional £100m to £160m.[8]

The judgment prompted a furious political row, which continued to run on and on until 25 March 1965, when the Conservative peer, Lord Shepherd, argued that the then Labour Government had been wrong in 1946 to take the BOC compensation case through the courts of law rather than through Parliament. He complained that the House of Lords' judgment was in conflict with common law in that the BOC's demolitions were adjudged to be due *not* to battle damage but to the Government's denial policy.[9] Lord Shepherd argued that common law maintained that claims for war damage compensation was not permissible against the Crown, as by definition, it was carried out for 'the general defence of the realm' and therefore should be borne by the nation as a whole. Compensation could only be determined by the nation's ability to pay. He reminded the House of Lords that on 3 May 1920 the Attorney General had asked rhetorically: 'Are we to have two classes of persons in this country – one class that has given up, voluntarily or involuntarily, its property for the Defence and Safety of the Realm, and the other class, which has eagerly taken its compensation from the Losses Commission?' To which he answered, 'there must be one weight and one measure'.[10]

Lord Shepherd argued that Common Law should be restored to its rightful place and that the House of Lords' judgment on the BOC case should be rendered impermissible. He repeated that the guiding principle was that the burden of compensation must be borne by the nation as a whole. Therefore, the Government had a moral responsibility to compensate *equitably* for war damage *within their economic ability*. By way of illustration, he posited the example of a mythical factory that had been destroyed in the war. No claim could be made if it was regarded as an obstacle like a tank; a claim could be made if commanders had ordered it to be destroyed for denial purposes; however, it was uncertain whether or not a claim could be made if it had been mined in readiness for enemy occupation. He also complained that the House of Lords had imposed no strings in its BOC judgment so the company had been at liberty to spend the money in whatever way it wished. He pointed out that many thousands of companies and individuals had already received and accepted ex gratia payments that were a tiny proportion of the actual war damage they had suffered. It would be unacceptable, he suggested, if 23 years later, a small group of individuals and companies emerged to claim benefit from the privileged position of hindsight.[11]

The War Damage Act (1965) reversed the BOC case. It stated that no person was entitled at Common Law to receive from the Crown compensation for damage to or destruction of property that was caused by acts lawfully done by the Crown during a war.

In 1948, a new set of circumstances overtook the original proposition. The Burma Government nationalized the BOC's remaining assets to further complicate an already complex situation. The problem was that oil drilled in Burma was unsuitable for the international market because of its high wax content. This necessitated special refining and could only be traded because of BOC's links with Anglo-Iranian Oil Company.[12] But that is another story!

***

The IFC was one of the biggest and most iconic British enterprises in colonial Burma. The Irrawaddy and the Chindwin rivers provided *the* most important lines of communication along the length of the country from north to south. The Irrawaddy is a notoriously shallow river. It reaches its high-water mark in August, and the low-water mark in February is 11 metres lower than in August. The river is up to 4 miles wide at Hinthada and in the last 1,100 miles to the sea it drops only 500 ft. A vast amount of alluvial silt is carried down the Irrawaddy and it ends up in the delta, which has nine branches. The river is unnavigable above Bhamo during the dry season. Today the Irrawaddy is still the most important transport artery in Burma and in 2002 about 44 per cent of Burma's domestic freight was carried on the river.

Managing a huge commercial river fleet of the sort that navigated these waters demanded organizational and technical skills. The IFC was incorporated in Glasgow in 1865 as an offshoot of the Paddy Henderson Line. It was administered from its iconic headquarters at 50 Phayre Street (now Pansodan Street) and the former IFC General Manager's house is now the British Ambassador's Residence At its zenith in 1938, the company operated a fleet of 600 vessels – ranging from 326ft paddle steamers to small buoying launches – and had over 11,000 employees (200 of whom were British). They included engineers, crew, dockyard workers and office staff. William Denny and Brothers Limited built three-quarters of the IFC vessels and A. and J. Inglis Limited, Robert Duncan and Yarrow of Scotstoun constructed the others. The IFC's main shipyard was at Dalla (opposite Rangoon), and it had a smaller repair yard in Mandalay.

Before 1942, IFC vessels carried over 8 million passengers and 1.25 million tons of cargo annually. The company prospectus published in the 1930s described the diversity of its carrying trade that included 'great bales of cotton, bags of rice, blocks of jade, lacquer ware, silk, tamarind, elephants sometimes, woven mats, maize, jaggery, bullocks, marble Buddhas, oil cake, tobacco, timber'.[13] IFC vessels carried imports from Europe up-river, including 'motor cars, corrugated iron, condensed milk, matches, aluminium ware, sewing machines, piece goods, soap, cigarettes, cement and whisky'.[14]

During the Japanese invasion, IFC vessels were used to evacuate British and Indian troops and civilians up the Irrawaddy and the Chindwin rivers until the waters were too shallow for safe navigation. In accordance with the British Government's most of the IFC fleet was scuttled, bombed by the RAF or sunk by the Royal Navy in 1942. Including the cargo steamers *Ananda, Punjab, Panthay, Talifoo* and *Ceylon*, 112 vessels were scuttled at Mandalay, and 96 vessels at Katha. They included the prestigious mail steamers *Siam* and *Mysore* (both of which had been used as hospital ships) *Japan and Nepaul.* Also eight Sternwheelers were scuttled at Sittaung on the Chindwin, including the *Saga, Sarak, Soma, Sind, Sythet, Namta*, and *Popa.*[15] On 3 May 1942, a manager wrote, 'Katha is a sight, vessels anchored ten abreast and all deserted ... parties are ordered to sink every vessel'.[16]

After the war, the British Army commandeered the remaining IFC vessels most of which had been salvaged by Japanese engineers. However, on 1 June 1948 the entire fleet and other IFC assets passed into the hands of the new Burmese Government. In its place was established the Burmese state-owned enterprise the Inland Water Transport Board.[17]

The affairs of the IFC came under the spotlight during a debate on war damages in the House of Commons on 8 December 1948. The Conservative MP, Colonel Crosthwaite-Eyre expressed deep concern.[18] He had followed an exchange of letters between Attlee and U Nu in which Attlee had reminded the Government of Burma of its undertaking to honour all existing British concessions, contracts and property rights in Burma. Attlee had expressed the hope 'that the Provisional Government in Burma will not during this interim period take action which will prejudicially affect existing UK interests in Burma', to which U Nu had replied that State Socialism had been embedded in the Burmese Constitution so the expropriation of British assets was highly likely. Nevertheless, U Nu promised that he would ensure that compensation was paid equitably.[19]

Crosthwaite-Eyre was not at all convinced. He noted that a bill nationalizing the IFC had been introduced in the Burmese Legislature on 19 April 1948 and had been rushed through all its stages in a single day. The IFC was not represented in the debate, so was unable to contest the takeover. The bill became law with immediate effect even though it contained very few details. It was simply stated that IFC's assets would be hired by the Burmese Government on terms that would be settled at some future date. In the meantime, a three-man committee was set up to hammer out the arrangements. It consisted of a Burmese High Court judge, a representative of the Burmese Government and an IFC representative. The Burmese Government insisted that the transfer should be completed in six weeks – by 1 June 1948. The committee failed to complete its work in the time available and no agreement was reached on the amount of compensation to be paid.

Long after the company's assets were expropriated on 1 June the IFC remained in limbo. The three-man committee was dissolved in July and in its place a new committee was appointed. The same judge remained as president of the committee, but two *additional* members – the Secretary of the Burmese Government Planning Department and a member of the BOC – were drafted in. By this time the IFC had submitted a detailed compensation claim for £1.12m. The Burmese Government would agree to no more than £200,000 payable in *non-negotiable bonds*. Crosthwaite-Eyre was puzzled as to how the British Government could square this position with the statement it had made on 21 June, when it had claimed to 'have made it plain from the beginning that the Burmese Government must be able to meet in an acceptable currency the legitimate claims of British subjects'.[20]

Crosthwaite-Eyre also reminded ministers of the Burma Government's 1941 War Risks Insurance Scheme by which any company owning goods to the value of more than Rs. 15,000 was insured. In 1942 the British Government had requested British companies to deny the Japanese the use of their materials or stocks. The IFC had responded by destroying its shipping fleet, just as other companies had destroyed their crops of rubber and other commodities.

Immediately after independence the new Government of Burma had repudiated all these claims, insisting that Burma had had no interest in the war.

Indeed it was a victim of war rather than a participant in it. On 9 November 1948 the Chancellor of the Exchequer claimed that he had received no request from any company requesting assistance. Crosthwaite-Eyre questioned this. He presented evidence that in April 1942 the IFC and Messrs Foucar had both asked for assistance. The Chancellor of the Exchequer back pedalled and explained that 'he had not been involved in any *detailed* discussions between the firms and the Burmese Government' and that 'no *specific* claims had been put forward by the firms'.

Crosthwaite-Eyre accused Labour MPs of taking 'a rather impish delight in seeing British assets destroyed and seemed to take the view that every time a British interest abroad is expropriated, a little more of wicked capitalism is destroyed' He reminded the Government that

> every time a British asset is expropriated without compensation it affects not only our balance of payments, but also our ability to buy food and raw materials… . Our position has worsened and our resources for gaining foreign currency have depreciated. Burma has obviously flouted its agreements and repudiated that to which it set its name only a few months ago. On the other hand, we have given Burma the right to acquire £2 million of hard currency against sterling.[21]

Douglas Jay (Economic Secretary to the Treasury) put IFC's situation in the context of wider difficulties 'The Burmese Government have been engaged in allaying disorders [that have] affected their rice exports and foreign exchange resources. If compensation is to be paid, and paid in convertible currency, two things are obviously necessary – first the co-operation of the Burmese Government in the whole transaction, and secondly the recovery of Burma's economic fortunes' (see note 20). Douglas Jay pointed out that as far as the £2 million of hard currency was concerned, all countries in the sterling area (including Burma) were free to draw down hard currency.[22]

So it was that the nationalization issue had developed into a very long-running dispute over compensation between the Union of Burma and the IFC in Glasgow. The dispute was not resolved until May 1950. Even then it was not very satisfactory. The IFC shareholders received compensation for 105 salvaged vessels (only 19 of which were powered craft) plus a few buildings and a little equipment. The military fleet was not included in the settlement and nor were any vessels that had been built since the war. The total of £300,000 paid in compensation fell very far short of the company's expectations.[23] The IFC was forced into voluntary liquidation on 26 June 1950. After that, William Denny and Brothers Limited and the Yarrow Shipyard of Scotstoun each received orders to build four new 200ft paddle steamers for the Union of Burma Inland Water Transport Board and in 1956 the Yarrow Shipyard received its very last order from Burma for five quarter-wheeler steamers.

***

Steels was also a large British company that was involved both in the denial programme and the evacuation. It suffered huge losses at the hands of the Japanese and, after Independence, many of its operations were nationalized.

In its heyday before the war Steels was a vast, diverse organization with fingers in many pies. Unlike the BOC and the IFC, it was not a monolithic organization specialising in one product or service.[24]

Steels initial interest was in rice, and the company opened its first rice mill in 1871. In the 1890s it began to export teak, and in 1900 it purchased its first teak forest and elephant herd. It acquired a number of forest concessions over the next few years.[25] Steels also took over the Indo-Burma Petroleum Co., the second largest oil company in Burma.[26] The company had many other irons in the fire, including mining and cement interests. The Thayetmyo Cement works was opened in 1936 and, by 1940, a very large number of enterprises operated under the Steels' umbrella, including Consolidated Cotton & Oil Mills Ltd., Burma Company Ltd., and Steel's Lassio Agency Ltd. Many of Steels' own departments were effectively companies in their own right. They included the Rice Department, Timber Department, Imports Department, Sundry Produce Department, General Department, Forest Department, Jungle Buying Department, China Produce Department, Mining Department, and Ships Department. Latterly, Steels had also acquired significant interests in the significant companies like the BBTC and the RETSCo.

In 1942, Steels and its subsidiary organizations played a vital role in the evacuation and military retreat. During the fighting from 1942 to 1945, the company suffered enormous losses. Such was the extent, complexity and substance of Steels' trading activities, that it is impossible here to offer more than a few snapshots of the issues that faced the company and its subsidiaries.

The size and spread of Steels' business operations meant that evacuees and troops were never far from a Steels unit. Its huge workforce had many useful skills ranging from animal husbandry to water management. Steels was involved in transport services of all sorts – including elephants, lorries, buses and river craft. It meant that the company was in a position to move large numbers of evacuees and troops towards India in 1942 – often at the drop of a hat. One of the other major virtues of the company was that it had developed excellent administrative structures, which became especially valuable after the war when the company submitted a very complicated war damage claim.

Steels' reputation was based in part on its ability to manage large numbers of working elephants. Elephants were vital in many of its heavy-lifting activities – they cleared jungles, loaded huge teak logs, moved the Steels workforce from one place to another and performed all manner of other tasks. Elephants were especially valuable because they were able to operate in terrain where motor vehicles were of no use.

The Steels Forest Department: Elephants Claims Register No. 247 of 1949 is very illuminating. We learn, for instance that the total Steels Herd on 1 June 1941 consisted of 653 elephants and large numbers of elephant calves. Sixteen elephants had died or had to be 'written off' between 1 June 1941 and April 1942 (just before the evacuation through northern Burma began in 1942). This was a normal casualty rate in peacetime conditions. It meant that Steels had a total herd of 637 elephants at the beginning of May 1942. For obvious reasons, this number dwindled sharply during the course of the war. By 23 February 1949, when the final audit was carried out, only 264 elephants had been recovered.

Working out the wartime losses in all Steels' cost centres proved to be a very difficult job. Elephants were more problematic than most. The Finance Department had to work overtime, calculating depreciation, which was normally a standard accountancy procedure. It was not straightforward in the case of elephants. We are given some inkling of the difficulties in the correspondence of J. T. Nelson of Steels, Myitkyina. He wrote to an accountant in the Army HQ in, 28 April 1942, and referred to the fact that Steels had just 'hired' a number of elephants to the Army. Nelson added, 'It is of course understood in the event of the elephants being returned to us after hostilities that we would take them back at the price stated, less a reasonable allowance for hire and depreciation'.[27] In the margin the Army accountant had scribbled, 'How *does* one calculate depreciation of an elephant?'

The Steels Finance Department also had to translate losses of elephants into monetary values. It was calculated that the value of the herd in 1941 was Rs. 28,66,500, and that the total value of the elephants recovered by 1949 was Rs.11, 88,000. Therefore the total loss since 1942 was calculated at Rs. 16,78,500. This calculation was signed-off by the independent auditors in Rangoon on 24 February 1949. As a matter of interest, according to Army estimates, the value of a working elephant was Rs. 3,000. According to Steels it was Rs. 4,500. Such differences of opinion led to the passage of dozens of letters between F. D. Edmeades (who was in charge of Steels' elephants) and General Wakeley (who was in charge of the military retreat). Wakeley asked Edmeades to send 100 Steels' elephants to the west bank of the Upper Chindwin to assist in the retreat. The request was urgent and immediate. Edmeades was not keen. He said that it was too risky because it was an almost track-less area that was covered in very dense jungle, in which large numbers of wild elephants wandered around. He pointed out that Steels had already lost its Thanggyin, Prome and Pyinmana herds and did not wish to lose more elephants. In any case it was difficult in the Upper Chindwin to obtain fodder for the elephants or cash to pay the mahouts. Edmeades pointed out that forty Steels elephants were already working on the Hukawng Road Project, and that many more had been working on the Bhamo–Myitkyina Road. General Wakeley was not deterred by Edmeades's reservations. He made sure that he got his elephants, but not before a long running dispute opened up between Steels and the Army over losses of elephants, hire charges and unit prices.

The problem of absentee elephants was not the only issue to occupy the attention of Steels. Another matter involving Steels' subsidiary, the BBTC, which was equally difficult. Once again, the Army and the Government were involved – this time over a dispute about five of its vessels (the *Chindwin, Mongmit, Myitson, Drift* and *Dragon*). The dispute revolved around whether the BBTC had handed over the vessels to the Army, or whether they had been requisitioned. After much toing and froing, it was agreed that they had not been requisitioned.[28] A similar dispute rumbled on and on between the RETSCo and the Government over the seizure of thirty-two Bedford-Dorman buses that were used during the evacuation in 1942. The question was whether they had been requisitioned, bought or hired. The problem was exacerbated because all the paperwork had been lost. RETSCo insisted that the buses had been hired in the first place and had subsequently been destroyed in the evacuation. The imponderable question remained unresolved. Was the Government liable for the loss?

Several other units also appeared on Steels' 'worry list' – the Yebukan Mine was one. At the mine, 18 of the 28 most substantial items had been looted. They included corrugated iron sheets, oil pumps, air compressor, pressure gauges, exhaust fans, root-blowers, water pumps, oiling cups, generator crankshafts, Drysdale pumps, Ruston engines, bulldozer power pumps as well as the entire contents of a number of bungalows, offices and laboratories. Also on the list were the luxurious 'Glenside' manager's house in Rangoon, which had suffered extensive bomb damage, and the clerk's house at Dawbong and the Duneedaw Saw Mill, both of which had also been bombed. The Puzoondaung Rice Mill had first been looted and then deliberately set ablaze. The Burma Co. Ltd. Kanaungtoe Rice Mill had suffered a similar fate. These examples represented the tip of the iceberg. They were merely a cross section of the trail of destruction that had afflicted Steels' sites across Burma.[29]

The Steels claim for war damages in 1949 was a master class in responsible accountancy. Nothing was left to chance and nothing was fiddled. Every nut, bolt, machine, window, elephant, building, kitchen, bus, lorry, boat, teak log, mine, godown and pound of rice had to be accounted for, checked and recorded in each of the separate units operated by Steels and its subsidiaries all over Burma. There were exactly 264 separate units, each of which was a cost and profit centre and for each of which unique claims registers had to be produced. The units were scattered throughout the country, many of them in unheard of places like Yonzingyi, Ywathitgyi, Mahlaing, Kyauktalone, Mounggan, Shwedaung and Lower Kanoutngtoe. In addition, there were the more recognizable Steels properties of Glenside, Runnymede and Duneedaw.

The ledger items in the register ran to over 120 pages, packed with facts and figures. This truly monumental task was carried out with meticulous care by scores of Steels clerks. The data was carefully checked and audited before it was gathered into a huge company-wide matrix. An army of accounts clerks then grappled with variables based on three key dates – 1 June 1941 (the date of the Steels' *last* pre-war stocktaking), May–December 1942 (the date of the evacuation though northern Burma, and 24 February 1949 (the date of the Steels final claim).[30]

The company accountants' first step was to calculate the value of Steels' assets on 1 June 1941, the second step was to deduct the value of the losses and damages incurred up to May 1942. The third step was to factor in the standard rate of depreciation for the period up to 1949. The fourth step was to subtract the cost of all the destroyed, lost, or war-damaged items (see Table 10.1).

Table 10.1 summarizes the final claim that was submitted by Steels to the War Damage Commission in February 1949.

What happened next was interesting. Almost exactly one year after the claim was submitted to the Board of Trade in London, Steels received a letter from the assistant secretary of the Board of Trade, Insurance and Companies Department. Attached to the letter was a cheque for £477,940. 15. 4d. It was explained that this was Steels share of the Government's £10m War Damages Fund. It was roughly the equivalent of 26 per cent of Steels assessed losses. There was general relief in the company. On 23 March 1953 the Board of Trade contacted Steels again, this time with a final ex gratia payment of £6372.10.0. The assistant secretary referred to the Chancellor of the Exchequer's statement on 24 June 1949 in which he had explained that the payments were 'primarily for the purpose of assisting [companies] to overcome their capital handicaps in the task of rehabilitation'.[31]

***

The travails of the larger British companies might have been well documented. Also, in most cases, they were able to persuade powerful advocates to speak on their behalf in Westminster. This was not always the case for the thousands of small and medium sized claimants that proliferated in Burma. Very few records survive of their struggles.

One is constantly reminded that the £10m War Damages Fund Claim Fund set up by Labour Government was grossly inadequate. It was *supposed* to compensate every British citizen and every British company great or small. It is almost certain that many smaller companies and individuals gave up the ghost and resigned themselves to losing everything.

Records of efforts to obtain compensation dating back to 1945 suggest that it was extremely difficult for any small company to gain redress. The

Table 10.1 Steel Bros & Co Ltd: Summary of losses, 24 February 1949

Company/ Dept.	Building[e]	Factories[f]	Stock[g]	Timber	Livestock	River-craft	Vehicle	Total (Rupees)
C.C.&OM[a]	–	55,69,765	31,39,955	–	900	4,500	15,000	**87.71,605**
BCL[b]	2,500	46,57,800	–	–	–	–	–	**46,60,300**
Lassio[c]	63,300	–	2,23,914	–	–	–	5,000	**2,92,214**
Steel Bros[d]								
Rice	89,650	35,96,990	33,90,490			39,44,543	45,000	**1,10,66,673**
Timber	2,000	15,01,520	–	53,99,780	18,000	2,15,950	–	**71,37,250**
Imports	2,000	–	30,17,245	–	–	–	30,000	**30,49,245**
Produce	–	1,49,010	27,626	–	–	–	12,000	**2,82,932**
General[j]	2,59,584	–	–	–	–	–	–	**6,10,084**
Forest[k]	2,36,700	43,500	–	26,03,778	17,46,000	1,41,000	32,000	**50,17,249**
Jungle	–	47,300	90,900	–	–	–	–	**1,38,200**
China	–	–	3,34,400	–	–	–	–	**3,34,400**
Mining	–	6,990	65,037	–	–	–	–	**72,027,**
Ships	–	–	–	–	–	22,300	–	**22,300**
Rupees[i]	6,55,734	1,55,72,875	1,02,89,567	80,03,558	17,64,900	43,28,293	1,39,000	**4,14,54,479**

Source: National Archives, BT/228/63, Steel Brother & Co Ltd, Compensation Claims.

Notes

a Consolidated Cotton & Oil Mills Ltd
b Burma Company Ltd
c Steels Lashio Agency Ltd
d Steel Bros & Co Ltd, Departments
e Dwellings Accommodation, etc.
f Factories and other undertakings
g Stock in Trade & Produce in Store Additional categories not listed above
h Cash: Consolidated Cotton & Oil Mills Ltd – Rs. 34,265 and Steel's Forest Department, Rs. 13, 171: Total: Rs. 47, 436
i Commercial Offices: Steel Bros & Co, General Department – Rs. 3,5,500
j Business Equipment: Steel Bros & Co, Forest Department: Rs. 2,01,100
k Plantation Growths: Steel Bros & Co, Produce Department: Rs. 94,295

Thabawleik Tin Dredging Company Ltd provides some insights. The company was incorporated in 1923 and registered in Taiping in the Federated Malay States. Its declared capital was £200,000 divided into £1 shares. Its operations were in Malaya and Siam, but in addition it controlled tin mines at Thabawleik in the Mergui District of Burma. In 1939 it established a dredging operation to recover minerals from alluvial deposits. Thabawleik became the largest single tin producer in Burma and the company invested heavily in new equipment to produce 1,495 tons of premium quality tin (assayed at 72 per cent) in 1940–1941. During the war the Japanese seized some of its mines and dredging operation, which continued to produce tin throughout the war.

After the war the Thabawleik Tin Dredging Company was taken over by the Austral Malay Tin Company. Extensive (and expensive) repairs had to be carried out to the dredges and mine plants in Malaya and Siam before operations could resume. By 1946, Thabawleik produced 1,380 tons of tin ore. The directors were at pains to point out that this assisted the UK's sterling's balance of payments deficit. In 1946 the company lodged claims for war damage compensation against the British Government and the governments of Siam, Burma and Malaya. The claims included £88,000 for war damage incurred in the Thabawleik operations. The claims were sympathetically received in Malaya and Siam, but not in Burma.

In 1949, the directors learned that the claim had been rejected. No reason was given but there was clarification on 24 June 1949 when the terms of reference relating to the £10m War Damage Fund were announced in the House of Commons. The Chancellor of the Exchequer made clear that only companies owned, managed or controlled by British subjects domiciled in the UK were eligible for compensation. None of the Austral Malay Tin Company's directors and a few of its shareholders were domiciled in the UK.

During the next five years a furious flurry of letters passed back and forth between the British Government and the Austral Malay Tin Company. The list of correspondents included Walter Fletcher CBE, MP; L. R. Davies Private Secretary to the Secretary for Overseas Trade, Lord Pethick-Lawrence Secretary of State for the Colonies; the High Commissioner of the Federation of Malaya, Mrs Brinton, Board of Trade, Insurance and Companies Department; Commonwealth Relations Office; J. J. Emberton; S. Barker, Far East Section, Board of Trade, W.G. Head, Commonwealth Relation Office; E. L. Mercier,

Board of Trade, A. N. Goode, Director of Austral Malay Tin Ltd.; A. G. T. Chaplin, Under Secretary of State for the Colonies, Colonial Office; W. A. Freeman, Chairman of Directors, Thabawleik Tin Dredging Company Ltd; J. S. Brittain, Turquand, Youngs, McAuliffe & Co (Solicitors).[32]

The first of the letters (dated 14 March 1950) was from the directors of the Austral Malay Tin Company to the Chief Secretary of the Malaya Federation. They pointed out that the company had been operating in Malaya, Siam and Burma for the past thirty years, and that during that time the company had been profitable mines. Indeed, the mining operations were a rich source of revenue for shareholders. It was also claimed (almost as an afterthought) that they benefited local economies too. The last letter, dated 26 June 1955 was from E. L. Mercier at the Board of Trade in London. He wrote to the Austral Malay Tin Company (one senses with a sigh of relief) to say that under no circumstances could the company be regarded as a British-owned and British-controlled company. Mercier suggested that the directors should direct their energies to seeking help from the Australian Government.

The Thabawleik Tin Dredging Company Ltd. file remained open until 1981, but it gathered no more correspondence. However, there was a twist in the tale. Insurgent factions armed with automatic weapons attacked the Thabawleik Tin Dredging Company installations in December 1949 and in February 1950 'communist terrorists' finally brought tin dredging to a complete stop in the Tavoy area of Burma.[33]

***

At this point it is important to square the circle. This book started with accounts of the evacuation from Burma and it is with evacuees – or at least with hundreds of *British* evacuees – that the account must finish. As they arrived in India from February 1942 onwards, many of the evacuees began to draw up lists of personal items they had lost in the previous few weeks. Everyone had lost something, and many people had lost everything.[34] Only 32lbs of luggage – or sometimes only 16lbs – was allowed on evacuation flights. Even less luggage could be carried on the backs of the evacuees who walked out along muddy tracks to northern Assam. One can guess that every European house in Burma was full of precious things – wedding-presents, household gadgets, furniture, family photographs, silverware, clothes, books, knick-knacks and personal papers, expensive cars parked on the drives.

The Carter Committee, which received individual applications amounting to £70m, did not *start* work until 1950. By this time many evacuees had given up all hope of compensation. Very few *individual* claims seem to have survived, so it is impossible to give an overview. However, two contrasting applications are appended below. One was submitted by the Oxford educated, M. A. Maybury, ICS. He was a Sub-Divisional Officer and the son of wealthy parents. The other claim was from Rev. and Mrs Kinchin. They were Methodist missionaries. Like most Methodist missionaries of the day Kinchin came from a respectable lower middle-class family. He left school at fifteen and went to work for the Port of London Authority. He went out to Burma as a missionary in 1933 where he served in the Chin State. Maybury and Kinchin's respective claims reflect the disparities in their personal wealth and lifestyles. For example, the most expensive items in Kinchin's schedule were a woman's winter coat valued at £15 and a string of cultured pearls valued at £10. Only five of his items were valued at more than £5. It is not clear whether Maybury's inventory is valued in rupees or pounds, but whichever it was, not a single item was valued at *less* than £10 and his prize possession was a brand new Austin-12 valued at £1,250 (almost ten times more than Kinchin's *total* claim). It is possible that the two samples below are illustrative of the range of claims submitted between 1942 and 1950. No doubt, the War Damage Commission had great difficulty in deciding how to disburse the pitifully small ex gratia payments involved.

The instructions issued to young men before they sailed from England to take up appointments in the ICS are revealing. It was very clear that they were not expected to travel light. The list includes the following (see Table 10.2).

No doubt many of the young men had been used to going off to expensive boarding schools with tuck boxes each term. They would have taken the list in their stride. On the other hand, the list of items would have filled Methodist Missionaries with horror. The Missionary Society clearly provided severely pared-down lists for its men and women

Not a single colonial servant was immune from the indignity of arriving in Burma with huge amounts of expensive kit, and leaving with absolutely nothing. Lady Dorman-Smith noted in her diary that she and her husband had arrived at Government House in Rangoon on 23 February 1941 with

Table 10.2 Instructions to new Indian Civil Servants sailing from England in the 1930s

1 set of Black dress clothes, to include long and short coats, and white waistcoats; 1 Dark lounge suit; 2 Very thin lounge suits; 1 Plus-Four suit, 1 Thick overcoat; 1 Burberry plus possibly one light overcoat; 1 Loose flannel suit or blazer; 1 Sweater; 3 pairs grey flannel trousers; 3 pairs white flannel trousers; 4 Tennis shorts; 12 Evening collars; 12 Stiff linen collars; 12 Soft collars; 9 White dress shirts; 12 Thin soft shirts, 3 Flannel shirts without collars; 6 Thin vests; 6 Pairs thin pants; 2 Pairs thick pants; 6 Pairs lisle or silk black evening socks; 12 Pairs thin socks (of which 6 might be white); 3 Pairs thick stockings; 6 Suits Pyjamas; 1 Dressing gown; 3 Pairs of braces; 3 doz. Handkerchiefs; 1 Pair cloth riding breeches; 1 Pair well-made white cord riding breeches (as pattern for local tailors); 1 Pair leather gaiters; 1 Pair black boots; 1 or 2 Pairs brown boots; 2 Pairs of shoes; 1 Pair white tennis boots or shoes; 1 Pair of thick, strong shooting boots; 1 Pair of patent leather shoes; 1 Pair of Patent leather boots; 1 Pair bedroom slippers; NB. Riding boots are not necessary, except for polo; 1 Felt hat; 1 White 'sola' topi; 1 Umbrella; 4 Pairs of sheets; 4 Blankets; 2 Pillows; 1 Saddle (made to measure by a good saddler); 1 Set of harnesses; 1 Shot gun; 1 Rug; 6 Tablecloths; 12 Face towels; 12 Pillowcases; 12 Table napkins; 6 Bath towels; 1 Deckchair (for use on voyage and kept for subsequent use).
Articles to be bought on arrival in Burma: 1 Mosquito net; 1 Brown Shikar Topi; 4 Suits of thin, Holland silk (white drill suits are not normally worn); 3 Pairs of khaki shorts; 6 Khaki twill shirts with turndown collars; 6 White twill tennis shirts, 6 Thin gauze vests; 6 Pairs thin gauze pants; 1 Folding camp bed; 2 Pillows; 1 Mattress; 3 Suits of white dress clothes (short coats)
The following will be necessary within a year: 1 Folding dining table; 1 Folding camp table; 1 Folding camp table; 1 Camp wash stand with enamel basin; 1 Camp commode; 1 Zinc bath tub; 2 Folding camp dining chairs; A Glass canteen for 6 persons including: 6 one pint tumblers, 4 Port glasses, 4 Sherry glasses, 4 Liqueur glasses, 4 Finger bowls, 4 Glass salt cellars; Crockery and Cutlery from Army & Navy Stores.

Source: Memorandum A: Bengal, Assam, Madras, Bombay and Burma S&G 3001/1927, Kit (Indian Civil Service) S&G 3001/1927.

Note: Leather trunks are not so suitable as cane. It is convenient to have a large, strong wooden box with a removable inner shell of tin. The lids of the wooden box and inner tin box should open on hinges: A convenient size is 36" X 18" X 20". It will last forever, and besides performing the function of a safe, it will be useful for keeping warm clothes in during the rains; and if books or clothes are not required for long periods of time, the inner box can be soldered and rendered secure against damp and insects.

forty-five cases packed full of clothes and personal belongings.[35] Sir Reginald Dorman-Smith recalled that he left Government House before dawn on Sunday 1 March 1942 carrying one small attaché case in which was packed all his worldly goods.[36]

M. A. Maybury, ICS (Class 1), MA, Sub-divisional Officer at Kawkareik submitted two claims when he reached Simla. As Kawkereik was on the Burma–Thai frontier he was one of the first officials to be affected by the Japanese invasion. On 30 January 1942 he wrote to the Secretary to the Government of Burma (Home Department) explaining that it had been a very

Table 10.3 M. A. Maybury: Monthly income and expenditure account

Monthly Income: Basic Pay Rs.600 + Overseas Pay – Rs.150 + Special Pay – Rs.150 = Total Rs.666*
Monthly Expenditure: Deductions (tax etc.) – Rs.235, + Rent – Rs.154, + Servants (½ cook, ½ sweeper, dhobi), food etc., Rs.395 = Total Expenditure Rs.784 Monthly Deficit: Rs.118/- On the face of it the income figures do not seem to add up. Monthly income should be Rs.900, but according to Maybury his total monthly income was Rs.666. But in any case the claim was turned down in September 1943.

Source: IOR/MSS/EUR/D1080/7/7: Maybury papers: Income and Expenditure Accounts.

fraught time not least because their first son had been born just before the invasion on 8 January 1942. Mrs Maybury had taken the baby upcountry and they had been evacuated to India by air on 10 March 1942. Because of the rapid enemy advance from Myawaddy to Kawkareik Maybury had been forced to abandon his house and possessions on the morning of 21 January 1942. He explained that he had destroyed his car – an Austin 12 Tourer (RB 3927) – in accordance with denial procedures and had then evacuated with retreating British troops.[37]

His first claim was submitted on 8 April 1943 – it requested compensation for expenses and loss of income. To add gravitas to the claim he attached a note of support from Lionel Salt, Bursar of Pembroke College, Oxford (see Tables 10.3 and 10.4).

It is almost impossible now to determine how many such claims the Carter Committee received – and even more difficult to discover how much was shelled out to individual claimants in ex gratia payments. It was just one of the many causes of sadness and frustration that lingered long after the war had ended.

Table 10.4 M. A. Maybury: Inventory of possessions, 30 January 1942

Item	Value	Item	Value
Lounge suit	£100	2 Single Beds	£30
Square Table	£10	2 Commodes	£30
Bureau	£50	Medicine Chest	£50
Round Table	£15	Bath	£15
Chest	£50	Enamelware	£30
Book Case	£15	Long Mirror	£25
2 Reading Lamps	£20	Chest of Drawers	£20
2 Candlesticks	£15	Travelling Rug	£15
Peg Tables	£10	Blanket	£25
Bookcase & books	£120	Sheets	£15
Books[a]	£200	Pillowslips	£15
Wireless	£377	Table linen	£50
Care Suite	£250	Towels	£40
Dining table & chairs	£100	Cushions	£20
Lamp	£75	Curtains	£50
Valor Stove	£130	Mosquito nets	£30
Safe	£15	Kitchen utensils	£50
Camp Beds	£75	Wireless batteries	50
Stores	£250	Crockery and glass	250
Tilley Lamp	£38	Motor Car[b]	1250
Petromax Lamp	20	Etceteras[c]	250
Bedding Roll	£60	Clothes and shoes[d]	1060
TOTAL			**£5365**[e]

Source: IOR/MSS/EUR/D1080/7/7: Maybury papers: Inventory of War Losses for Compensation Claim.

Notes

a List of Books
Volume of Keat's poems, 2 volumes of Shelley's poems, Burns' poems, Halevy, Pages Choisies by Anatole France, Horace's Odes, Henry Newbolt's poems, Rosemary's Letter Book, Golden Treasury, Saunders' Buddhism, Shway Yoe, Stephen Hall, 'Our Times', Webster's History of the Ancient World, Rhyming Dictionary, Wordsworth's poems, Reade, 'Never too Late to Mend', Speeches on Indian Policy, Volumes 1 and 2, Collected Works of Shakespeare, Indian Friends and Acquaintances, Anatole France, 'Les Dieux Ont Soif', Zimmern's League of Nations and Rules of Law, Shway Yoe, Joad's Outline of Modern Philosophy, Book of Ballads, 1 Cookery book, Kipling, Just So Stories, Burmese Bird Life, 2 Albums of photographs.

b Motor Car: Austin 12 Tourer (RB 3927).

c Etceteras: Including, Singer sewing machine, trouser press, tie press, cash box, oil can.

d Clothes and shoes: Including, 2 pairs of boots, 1 pair of shoes (£10), 2 pairs of shoes (£5), 1 pair of evening shoes (£10), 1 pair of tennis shoes (£5).

e Values
Once again there is a mystery. Maybury indicates that the total value is £4530. The reason for the mathematical disparity is unclear (see Table 10.5).[38]

Table 10.5 Rev. F. A. Kinchin's compensation claim for loss of personal effects

	Qty	Description	Value		Qty	Description	Value
1	1	Winter Coat	£15.0.0	27	3	Light Blankets	£2.10.0
2	1	Tweed Skirt	£3.3.0	28	1	Flannel Sheets	£0.10.6
3	4	Velvet Coatee	£0.15.0	29	2	Guest Towels	£0.6.0
4	1	Evening Gown	£3.0.0	30	2	Dinner Napkins	£0.13.0
5	1	Dressing Gown	£1.11.6	31	2	Linen tea cloths	£3.10.0
6	1	Leather Handbag	£1.2.6	32	6	Tea Napkins	£0.15.0
7	1	Pr. Suede Gloves	£1.2.6	33	1	Bedspread	£1.0.0
8	1	String Pearls	£10.10.0	34	1	Lace Tablecloth	£1.10.0
9	1	Silver Hairbrush	£6.0.0	35	1	Lace centre	£0.15.0
10	1	Nail Brush	£0.6.6	36	12yds	Mosquito nets	£3.12.0
11	4lbs.	Wool	£3.4.0	37	12yds	Net edging	£0.18.0
12	2	Tooth Brushes	£0.5.0	38	12yds	Poplin	£3.12.0
13	1	Shan Silver Belt	£2.5.0	39	1	Tankhul Blanket	£2.5.0
14	4yds	Cotton Material	£0.15.0	40	1	Shan Tablecloth	£0.9.0
15	1	Dinner Suit	£4.10.0	41	4yds	Cotton Curtains	£1.13.0
16	1	Wool Bathing Trunks	£0.15.0	42	3	Shan Runners	£0.9.0
17	2 pr.	Men's Shoes	£7.10.0	43	1	Ducheuse Set	£0.7.6.
18	3 pr.	Silk Half Hose	£0.15.0	44	2	Bath Mats	£0.15.0
19	1	Shaving Brush	£0.7.6	45	1	Cutlery Canteen	£2.10.0
20	1 pr.	Serge Shorts	£3.7.6.	46	2	Egg Cups	£0.13.0
21	1pr.	White Drill Shorts	£1.19.0	47	1	Pastry Board	£0.13.6
22	1 pr.	Grey Drill Shorts	£1.2.6	48	1pr	Bookends	£0.15.0
23	1	Wool Blanket	£5.0.0	49	2	Inkstands	£1.11.6
24	1 pr.	Cotton Sheets	£5.12.0	50	1	Original Etching	£2.5.0
25	4	Towels	0.15.0	**51**	2	Damaged cases	£2.4.8
26	3	Embroidered Towels	1.0.0				
TOTAL						**£117.11.2.**	

Source: SOAS Folder 1(e) Kinchin Diaries Claim for compensation.

11

Epilogue

I find my zenith doth depend upon a most conspicuous star

Shakespeare: *Tempest*, Act 1. Scene 2,

Burma regained its freedom at 4.20 am on 4 January 1948. Astrologers chose the date and the time. The eminent Burmese lawyer, Dr Maung Maung, captured the mood perfectly. He described how this final severance from Britain was done almost in sadness. It was, he said, a bloodless revolution and a voluntary abdication of power and not a shot was fired in anger against the British ruler. However independence was won at a heavy price. It was a story of huge sacrifice.[1]

It is time to square the circle. Five years had passed between May 1942 and January 1948. During that time many sacrifices had been made on all sides. Of course there were different sets of rules and different objectives, but *both* British colonials *and* Burmese nationalists played deadly games of push and pull. In the end the games led to the demise of colonial rule.

The exploits of Cornelius William North in Shingbwiyang, William McAdam in the Chindwin Valley, Alexander Beattie in Dimapur, David Brown in Sittang, Percy Salkeld in the Hukawng Valley, Gyles Mackrell on the Dapha River and many others were still fresh in the memory. They had risked life and limb as they pulled exhausted evacuees out of jungles and pushed them into India. There was no going back from such a humiliation. It marked the de facto end of colonial rule

At the same time Burmese nationalists sought to seize the day. They knew they would never have a better opportunity to gain independence. The Government of Burma had fled, so they also played deadly games of push and pull – pulling Burmans towards independence and pushing the British out of Burma. Aung San was the main man. He blossomed in the latter stage of his life, risking all – courting one side and then the other – facing imprisonment, being reviled, exposed to danger on the battlefield and fending off the slings and arrows of his political opponents.

Nineteen momentous months elapsed between January 1945 and July 1947. Hopes were high, emotions were raw, and rumours circulated. Aung San occupied centre stage.[2] The jury was out on him. Senior British figures were divided. Sir Reginald Dorman-Smith and General Pearce were in one camp.[3] They considered Aung San and his followers to be terrorists. Lord Mountbatten and his senior officers were in another camp. They believed that Aung San and the Burma National Army (BNA) could be trusted. As Mountbatten was the force majeure, he was able to insist that his orders were obeyed.

Initially, not even Aung San's supporters were convinced. General Slim accused Aung San of switching to the Allied side merely because they were winning. Aung San retorted that 'it wouldn't have made much sense if you weren't winning'. On 20 April 1945, Lieutenant General F. A. M. Browning warned Aung San and his colleagues that their offences had not been forgotten and there was no general amnesty. At the same time General Pearce urged Mountbatten to treat Aung San as a war criminal (which Mountbatten refused to do), and Brigadier Lindop and Air Marshal Sir Philip Joubert made it their business to look out for any signs of BNA misbehaviour.

Mountbatten stuck to his guns and on 15 May 1945 he incorporated the BNA into a joint Allied–Burmese Army. Slim softened, acknowledging that Aung San was not ambitious, unscrupulous or a guerrilla leader, and that he seemed to be a genuine patriot. For his part, Aung San indicated his willingness to cooperate with the British. Slim believed that he would keep his word.[4]

Later Mountbatten took Aung San to one side and advised him that 'it was not possible to be a soldier and a political leader at the same time'.[5] These friendly words paid dividends. In September 1945, Aung San wrote to Mountbatten explaining that he was giving up his military career to concentrate on politics, adding, 'I should have liked to serve even if only to oblige you who have helped in so many ways and who will forever retain an affectionate place in my heart. . . . Whatever the future may be, I hope to retain the happy relations that bind you and us now'.[6]

On 30 January 1945, Aung San set out his political agenda. *The Defence of Burma* became the blueprint for his future political ideas.[7] He insisted that all ethnic groups should have equal political, economic and social rights, and that there should be no religious or racial discrimination. The Burma Army should be a microcosm of Burmese society as a whole. The Army would be organized into *class* battalions each formed exclusively of one ethnic group and officered by men from the same ethnic communities. Indians and Chinese would only be accommodated if they agreed to join 'the people of Burma in creating a new state'.[8] Capitalism must be controlled and restricted, essential industries nationalized and the rights of workers protected. The size of land holding should be restricted, and land should be put in the hands of farmers. Burma would form alliances with friendly nations and be a member of the United Nations.[9] The Government would be based on the consent of all people.[10] Burma would avoid the type of economic union deprecated by Lenin, in which the constituent parts contradicted the whole.

Aung San spent the next few months travelling through the country and testing his ideas, listening carefully to other people, noting their comments, moderating his views and developing key themes. He trod a tightrope, but his popularity increased day by day and he received plaudits from all sides. Tom Driberg, MP, described him as 'absolutely incorruptible – fanatical, perhaps, and ardently nationalist, but honest … the Tito of Burma. He represented a break from 'the petty sectionalism and jealousy of Burma's past'.[11] Rev George Appleton joined a crowd of 20,000 people at the Shwedagon Pagoda in January 1946. Aung San, who was the only speaker, passed almost unobserved onto the platform and then quietly began his speech – no ostentation and no rehearsed ovation. He spoke for three and a half hours. It was electrifying, and the crowd hung on his every word.[12]

It was difficult to believe that Aung San was still only thirty years of age. During the next few months, he grappled with a number of weighty political issues. For example, he was uncertain whether Burma should remain in the British Commonwealth, and he was concerned about the limitations of nationalism in the post-independence world. However, he had no doubt about some things. He condemned imperialism in all its forms, and contended that no nation had the right to rule another.[13]

By November 1946, Aung San's mind was made up. He wrote to Attlee demanding that Burma be given full independence within one year, and insisting that it would remain *outside* the commonwealth. Attlee immediate immediately invited Aung San to a conference in London.

The London Conference that opened in January 1947 was one of those rare, epoch-changing occasions.[14] U Tin Tut described the scene.

> It was snowing hard outside on that winter's day in London, Monday 27 January 1947, but the Cabinet Room at number 10 Downing Street was pleasantly warm.... The long council table occupied most of the room and there had sat ... many great personages of state. In more recent history, the War Cabinets of two great wars had frequently sat in that room and the decisions they had reached had affected the course of human history. This was a particularly auspicious occasion ... the British representatives sat on one side, with Mr Attlee in the centre. The Burmese representatives faced them with U Aung San in the centre.... There was a tense silence as Mr Attlee and U Aung San inscribed their signatures with firm hands to both copies. We had made history; a new era of Anglo-Burmese friendship and cooperation had begun.[15]

U Saw was one of two members of the Burmese delegation who refused to sign it – Atlee described him as a villain who smiled and smiled.[16]

Aung San returned from London on the crest of a wave. He broadcast to the nation reminding listeners, that 'freedom does not fall from the sky ... [and] freedom is not here yet'. He explained that elections would be held for a Constituent Assembly. It would draft a new constitution and decide whether Burma should remain in the Commonwealth. He concluded in a surprising way: 'Whatever the decision might be,' he said, 'we should remain friends with the British. These are days when nations cannot stand alone'.[17]

Two most pressing issues demanded Aung San's urgent attention – national unity and the new constitution. The two issues were inextricably bound together, but national unity was top of the agenda.

Early in February 1947, Aung San convened a conference in the village of Panglong in the Shan States.[18] Arthur Bottomley, British Undersecretary of State for Dominion Affairs was the principal guest. Leading Chins, Kachins and Shans attended as representatives, and Karens were there as observers. From the outset Aung San emphasized the need for national unity and for the next few days he worked tirelessly – pressing the flesh, visiting each delegation in turn, discussing late into the night, listening to demands and discussing representation on the Executive Council. He promised to invest in their roads and schools and won the support of the most important minority leaders, including U Vum Ko Hau (Chin), Mongpawn Sawbwa Sao Sam Htun (Shan) and Duwa Sinwa Naung (Kachin).

The Panglong Agreement was signed on 12 February 1947. Its main provisions were as follows. Representative of the hill peoples would be elected to the Executive Council to be responsible for frontier area matters. Two deputies would represent the other races of Burma. The frontier areas would be fully autonomous in internal affairs and Central Government would provide them with financial assistance. Bottomley was very impressed by the conference in general and by Aung San in particular. He promised to advise the British Government to accept the Panglong Agreement in full. It was such an important milestone that in future February 12th was celebrated as 'Union Day'. It is still a national holiday in Myanmar.

The chief Chin representative was fulsome in his praise of Aung San, describing him as 'the one strong unifying factor'. Most of the delegates were similarly impressed. 'He was not free with promises, did not use sweet flattery or cunning diplomacy but when he gave his word it was obvious that he meant it.' U Vum Ko Hau recalled the night when Aung San strode over to the hut where the Chin delegation was staying. For several hours he discussed affairs of state informally over cups of tea. When they asked him if the Union Government would assist the Chins with much-needed roads and schools, he unhesitatingly said yes. The Chins fell under his spell and decided there and then that to join the Union, only because of 'Aung San, who personified the spirit of Panglong'.[19]

The next few weeks were extremely busy. Elections for the Constituent Assembly were due to be held 9 April 1947. In the meantime, Aung San met with Rance on 21 February 1947 to discuss electoral procedures. Then he travelled endlessly around the country, campaigning for the AFPFL. Wherever he went he attracted large crowds. He had become something of a superstar. At the same time, he had become the real power in the Executive Council, so much so that Rance was unwilling to take decisions without Aung San's say-so. Philip Nash, Private Secretary to the Governor noticed that nothing was done without Aung San's personal approval.[20]

In the midst of all these affairs of state, Aung San had to deal with some annoying diversions. At the end of February, for example, Burmese soldiers mutinied against their British officers. Aung San instructed them to obey orders as Burma would soon be free. Such was their respect for Aung San that they did as they were told. On 25 February 1947, he had to meet a Karen delegation. They intended to boycott the forthcoming elections. The Karen leadership was divided. Aung San persuaded them to stay on board. He also had difficult meetings with U Saw, Thakin Ba Sein, Dr Ba Maw and the 'Red Flag' communists. Each one of them opposed Aung San and intended to boycott the forthcoming elections. Aung San pointed out that the AFPFL would achieve independence within a year, but it cut no ice.

Elections for the Constituent Assembly were held on 9 April 1947. Of the 255 seats in Ministerial Burma, AFPFL won 172, the communists 7 seats and independents 3 seats. Of the minorities the Karen community won 24 seats, the Anglo-Burman community 4 seats and the frontier areas 45 seats. The vast majority of the elected delegates were young men and women from Aung San's People's Volunteer Organisation. As expected, U Saw's Myochit Party and Dr Ba Maw's *Mahabama* Party boycotted the elections. Dr Ba Maw warned ominously that, 'It is not elections that are going to decide the future of Burma, but the gun. All you want in Burmese politics is to start on the winning side and to have plenty of guns'.[21] The Communist Party did take part and won seven seats in the Assembly.

Eight hundred AFPFL members met between 18 and 23 May 1946 in the Jubilee Hall in Rangoon. The purpose of the meeting was to discuss Aung San's draft of the constitution before the forthcoming Constituent Assembly. Aung San reminded the delegates that he would tolerate no form of monarchy in Burma and that it was essential to base the government on the principles of socialism and democracy. The AFPFL Supreme Council quickly endorsed Aung San's economic agenda, which included the nationalization of basic industries, the abolition of landlordism and the encouragement of cooperative societies. He was concerned for the welfare of workers, peasants and national minorities and stressed that workers must serve the people, not bosses. The delegates spent a lot of time discussing whether or not Burma should stay in the British Commonwealth. In the end, they were persuaded that only complete independence was acceptable and on 23 May Aung San read out aloud the following words: ' The Supreme Council declares its firm and solemn resolve to proclaim Burma an independent Sovereign Republic'. The Draft Constitution was ratified at the AFPFL pre-constituent assembly convention on 23 May 1947. The die was now cast.

Two developments took place at this time. In June 1947, Thakin Nu led a delegation to London to persuade Attlee to transfer power before 31 January 1947. Attlee readily agreed. Second, at a conference held in the Sorrento Villa in Rangoon on 6 June, Aung San urged the attendees not to blame imperialism for everything, but instead to work tirelessly for national unity among the different races, tribes and nationalities in Burma. On 7 June he wrote to Rance proposing that the Frontier Districts and Ministerial Burma should be treated as one unit.

The Constituent Assembly began on 16 June 1947.[22] Aung San opened proceedings in his capacity of president of the Executive Council. He introduced the draft constitution. He was firmly in control. Aung San was supported by 172 out of the 182 delegates from Ministerial Burma and all 45 delegates from the frontier areas. One or two of the frontier area delegates wavered, so Aung San urged them not 'to return to darkness … after we showed you the light'. The Shan and Karenni representatives agreed not to exercise their right to secede within the next ten years. The leaders of the minority groups confirmed once again their *personal* allegiance to Aung San. It was another personal triumph. Aung San's friend, Thakin Nu was elected as the Speaker. Aung San explained that citizenship in Burma would be based on birth or naturalisation and that all citizens would be citizens of Burma rather than citizens of one or other of the constituent areas. The state would own the means of production, land and natural resources. 'Landlordism' would be ended. Every tiller in Burma would own his own land. Aung San condemned peasants who withheld their rents and revenues and refused to repay government agricultural loans. It was, he said, the duty of free people everywhere to pay taxes to their democratically elected governments. Tenants who failed to pay rents made it impossible for the owners of the land to pay their taxes. He announced that if necessary government officials would use force to collect the money.[23] There was general approval when Aung San confirmed that the Union of Burma would be an independent sovereign republic outside the Commonwealth, and that it would *not* recognize the British monarch.

On 13 July, Aung San gave a public speech in Rangoon. He warned that independence had not yet been won. Some said that he seemed tired, and that it sounded like a farewell speech.

In the meantime, dark rumours swirled around Rangoon. One story claimed that guns had been stolen from the garrison armoury and another suggested that political parties were planning a coup. Some of his supporters were concerned that Aung San's life might be in danger. The rumours continued day after day. On 18 July it was reported that automatic weapons and ammunition had been issued from an army base on forged papers.

A meeting of the Executive Council had been scheduled for Saturday 19 July 1947. The meetings were always held in the Secretariat Building. Aung San would be in the chair as usual. That morning he had decided to wear his favourite gold-material *longyi*. He left his home in Tower Lane at about 9.00 am. Members of the Council began to assemble soon after 10.15 am. Gunmen burst into the chamber at about 10.30 am. Aung San rose from his seat at the head of the table as if to stop them. It was a final gesture of command. It failed. Aung San was felled in a hail of bullets from automatic weapons wielded by the gunmen. Eight Council members were also killed along with several guards. At a stroke 'Burma had lost the one man who held the nation's confidence and who might have led the people through a peaceful transition from colonial to independent rule'.[24] It was a tragedy of monumental proportions.

When the terrible news filtered out, the whole nation was stunned. People from all walks of life in Burma came to Rangoon pay their respects. World leaders – including King George VI, Nehru and the US Secretary of State – sent messages of sympathy. In Burma itself the newspapers were filled with messages of sympathy, and even the Communist Party of Burma condemned the murders. There was genuine sadness, even despair.

Aung San was only 32 years of age. He had dominated Burmese politics since 1936.[25] It was a watershed moment. The country was on the brink of independence and Aung San had been at the peak of his powers. There were signs of civil unrest and accusations were hurled around. British agents and communists were among those suspected of the murder. His old friend Nu was called upon to step into the breach. U Nu's calming influence was invaluable.

The day of 26 July was designated as a day of national mourning. Tributes were paid to Aung San in the Constituent Assembly on 29 July 1947. U Nu described him as the embodiment of the people's will and aspirations; the people and their chosen leader were one. His integrity, humility, dedication, patriotism and courage were legendary. He was *the* national hero, a man of few words, cold and odd, but uninterested in personal gain. After the war, his material wealth consisted of two suits of worn and threadbare uniform. When he took off his military jacket he had nothing underneath, not even a vest. He displayed moral and physical courage and was the unanimous choice as leader. U Nu had also heard many stories of the courage he showed in combat.

U Kyaw Nyein said that leadership was not given to Aung San. He had earned it by his many qualities. He unified Burma, her people, young and old, the political parties and organizations. His dream was a free and united Burma and he made the dream come true. Saw San Po – a Karen activist – described Aung San's natural flair for turning bitter enemies into stout friends'. For example, he (Saw San Po), had planned to boycott the Constituent Assembly elections until Aung San 'told me I must decide whether as a leader I would lead'. Sama Duwa Sinwa Nawng said that Bogyoke Aung San was not only the leader of the Burmese but also of the Kachins. He was one of the people. The frontier peoples trusted Aung San. He brought them together, made them one family again. He was humble and unassuming. Power did not turn his head. The gates of Bogyoke's house were never shut. There were no guards. People could walk in and see him any time.[26]

Distinguished people from all walks of life queued up to pay their respects. For example, F. S. Donnison described how Aung San fired the imagination of the Burmese, gained their support and restored self-respect to a proud people. There was about him, Donnison wrote, a Spartan air, a certain ruthless idealism and integrity that appealed to the youth of the country. His crudity and forthrightness came like a breath of fresh air into the atmosphere of corruption and intrigue, and he had won the respect of the British administrators. 'His assassination deprived his country of the one man who might have been able to enforce discipline on his followers in the lawless years that lay ahead. He alone was able to unite his people, speak for them, and give expression to their spirit as no one else had done since the days of Alaungpaya two hundred years ago'.[27]

Maurice Collis described the assassination of Aung San as a cruel blow. Because of him, the British and the Burmese had parted as friends 123 years after the British had annexed the maritime provinces of Arakan and Tenasserim and 62 years since they had taken Mandalay and banished King Thibaw. It is often the case with great men, that they appear when the moment is ripe. Fortunately, the historical process that had produced so many would-be liberators finally had Aung San as its central figure.[28]

A lengthy criminal trial followed in due course. There was really only one suspect. U Saw was executed on 8 May1948 at Insein Jail. He wore his usual jacket and a silk longyi and shook hands with his executioners. His accomplices Maung Soe, Thet Hnin and Hmon Gyi were executed at the same time. Sein Gyi and Yan Gyi Aung were hanged at Rangoon Central Jail. Thu Kha was spared at the last moment. For years after the event, U Saw was reviled as a villain and traitor.

This marks a fitting end to this rambling story. Through the jungles and dusty plains of Burma, bands of brave adversaries battled against odds between 1942 and 1947. They fought against the elements, well-armed foes, and fled from evil forces. A rich fellowship of integrity and common purpose might have bound them together, but it did not.

Burma was the victim and loser. The series of events that unravelled between 1942 and 1947 revealed an awful symmetry. In May 1942, columns of young British engineers, teachers, administrators, lawyers, timber experts and businessmen streamed out of the far north of the country into India. In July 1947, the 32-year-old Aung San, the greatest leader of his generation, lay dead on the floor of the Secretariat Building together with eight of his ablest young lieutenants. What might these young people have achieved together? It was not to be. Within one year, Burma had descended into a vicious civil war from which, to this day, it has never fully recovered.

Glossary of Terms

Place names: Throughout the book colonial-era words and spellings have been used. They were often anglicized to assist English speakers. Thus Burma is used, not Myanmar, Rangoon, not Yangon, Arakan, not Rakhine State, Maymyo, not Pyin-oo-Lwin, and so on

Adipadi leader or prime minister. E. G. Dr Ba Maw was given the title 'Adipadi' during the Japanese occupation

Bancor artificial currency proposed by J. M. Keynes

Bogyoke senior general (i.e. a Burmese military term)

Burma Road road completed in 1938 to transport supplies and materials (landed in Rangoon) to Kunming (China)

chaprasis junior Indian office worker

chowkidar watchman or gatekeeper

Chettiar Indian landowning caste

dacoit robber, brigand

dak A road stage along which a postman or *dakwala* would run. The Government of Burma erected *dak-bungalows* for travellers or officials

Dakota The C-47, the military version of the DC-3 airliner, which first flew in 1935.

Dharamsingh term applied to soldiers serving in the Dogra Regiment

Dobama Asiayone Nationalist Organisation *meaning* Burma ourselves

doolies litters slung between coolies to carry evacuees

durwan Indian porter or doorkeeper

Ga Jingpaw (Kachin) term for settlement

godown warehouse

Havildar Indian soldier equivalent to the rank of sergeant

Hka Jingpaw (Kachin) term for river

Jhum Naga term for arable plot or clearing in jungle

Jingpaw (or Jingpo) largest ethnic group of Kachin peoples

khadi Indian material

khalasis Indian dock worker

khud A deep ravine or chasm

longyi A garment consisting of large piece of cloth knotted around the waist and running to the feet. It is worn by both men and women

Lysol cleaning and disinfecting product

Mahabama Party 'Greater Burma' Party, founded by Dr Ba Maw
mahout Elephant man or boy
Myochit Party 'Patriot' Party, founded by U Saw in 1938
Naik Military rank (equivalent to a corporal) in the British Indian Army;
paniwallah Indian water bearer
Phenyle A dark brown liquid manufactured as a powerful disinfectant and often used in military hospitals.
pongyi Buddhist monk
punkah revolving or manually manipulated fan
Satyagraha Anti salt-tax campaign in India in 1930
Sepoy Indian soldier serving under British orders
Sinyetha party led by Dr Ba Maw
Sirdar Sikh term for NCO
skilly thin broth
Swaraj campaign for the use of Indian product
Subedar Punjabi term for NCO
Thakin 'Master' (the chosen form of address of members of the *Dobama Asiayone*)
Tonga Indian light horse-drawn carriage or rickshaw.
Tuk tuk A three-wheeled motorized cycle or motorbike

Notes

Foreword

1 He was born in Myitkyina in 1931 and grew up in the town. After the war, he became a Supplies manager in a shipping company.
2 Michael D. Leigh, *The Evacuation of Civilians from Burma: Analysing the 1942 Colonial Disaster*, London: Bloomsbury, 2014.
3 The airstrip ceased to operate on 6 May when Japanese planes bombed Myitkyina.
4 PRO: FO 643/66 (51/GSO/47), Hugh Tinker (ed.), *Burma, the Struggle for Independence 1944–1948*, Volume II, London: Her Majesty's Stationery Office, 1984, pp. 109 and 110.
5 On 28 April 1942, General Goddard ordered the full retreat of all British forces from Burma.
6 See Philip Woods, *Reporting the Retreat: War Correspondents in Burma*, London: Hurst and Company, 2016, pp. 23–36. Woods is one of very few contemporary historians willing to set the record straight. His chapter entitled 'The Governor of Burma and His Critics' is fair-minded and long overdue. It provides a robust defence of Sir Reginald Dorman-Smith.

Chapter 1

1 Fine studies of the World War II Burma military campaigns have been written by Christopher Bayly and Tim Harper, Graham Dunlop, Alan Warren, Louis Allen and others.
2 There were seventy-one bombing raids on London alone. To sustain its population Britain needed to import over 1m tons of supplies per week. Between 1940 and 1943, 3,500 merchant ships and 175 Allied warships and 783 U-boats were sunk.
3 Japan invaded Malaya on 8 December 1941 (local time). The attack on Pearl Harbor took place on 7 December (US time).The dates were one and the same. General Yamashita's 25th Army landed at Kota Bharu in Malaya.
4 Winston S. Churchill, *The Grand Alliance*, London: Cassell, 1950, p. 551.

5 General Sugawara Michio (1888–1983) commanded air operations. He had at his disposal eighty Mitsubishi bombers and thirty Nakajima fighters for the raids on Rangoon.

6 Alan Warren, *Burma 1942: The Road from Mandalay*, London: Continuum, 2011, p. 39 and pp. 56–62. General McLeod stationed the 53rd Brigade of the 18th Indian Infantry Division, 45th Brigade of the 17th Indian Infantry Division, and the Burma Army 1st Division.

7 General Sir D. K. McLeod (1885–1958) joined the British Indian Army in 1903. He was GOC Burma, 1939–1941. Later he was head of the British Red Cross in Southern Europe 1944–1945.

8 General Shojiro Iida (1888–1980) commanded the 15th Army in 1941. He oversaw the occupation of Thailand and masterminded the invasion of Burma in January 1942. He drove the British forces out of Burma in mid-May 1942. He was captured in Manchuria in July 1945 and was imprisoned until 1950. General Shōzō Sakurai (1889–1985) commanded the 33rd Army Division and ordered the attacks on India. As commander of the 28th Army he organized the Japanese retreat to Moulmein in July 1945.

9 Major-General Smyth (17th Indian Division) was entrusted with the defence of the Sittang Bridge. Realizing that he could not repel Takeuchi's 55th Army, he withdrew his men to the west bank and ordered the destruction of the bridge. Two-thirds of Smyth's men and the division's entire stock of guns, ammunition and equipment were left on the *other* side. A few managed to swim to safety. Japanese ground forces were now able to advance through Burma.

10 Field Marshal Archibald Percival Wavell, Viscount and 1st Earl, GCB, GCSI, GCIE, CMG, MC, K. St. J., PC, (1883–1950); Educated at Winchester College and Sandhurst. C-I-C India. When Wavell arrived in Burma in February 1942, he disciplined the commanders responsible for the Sittang Bridge fiasco. Wavell later became Governor General and Viceroy of India, where he had to deal with the Bengal Famine, the Quit India campaign and demands for a separate Muslim State.

11 Tsuji, Masanobu, *Singapore: The Japanese Version*, London: Constable, 1962 p. 263.

12 Christopher Bayly and Tim Harper, *Forgotten Armies: The Fall of British Asia 1941–1945*, London: Allen Lane, Penguin Books, 2004, p.116.

13 Bayly and Harper, *Forgotten Armies*, p. 116. Six thousand tough, heavily armed, Japanese troops in each division *cycled* silently through Malaya and took defending forces off guard. Nakane, '*My Diary 1942*', B.A.M. Collection, RHO explains that they had to cycle along byroads for up to 20 hours per day.

14 Wavell's full title was Commander in Chief of American-British-Dutch-Australian Command (ABDACOM) Southeast Asia.

15 Field Marshal Alanbrooke, *War Diaries 1939–45*, ed. Alex Danchev and Daniel Todman, London: Wiedenfeld and Nicolson, 2001, 23 January 1942, p. 227. Alanbrooke criticized the 'parochially-minded' Dr H. V. Evatt, Australian Minister for External Affairs, while privately admitting that he (Alanbrooke) was at fault for sending Commonwealth reinforcements to Singapore instead of Rangoon.
16 Wavell had lost an eye at Ypres in World War I and on 10 February 1942 he fell off a pier, when boarding a flying boat in Singapore.
17 Lieutenant-General Sir T. J. Hutton KCB, KCIE, MC (1890–1981): Educated at Rossall and Royal Military Academy, Woolwich; 1909; appointed General Officer Commanding Burma in January 1942, but demoted in February 1942. General Alexander was appointed over his head. Hutton then served as Alexander's Chief of Staff. Wavell and several other senior officers pronounced Hutton unfit to command in the field. He retired in 1944.
18 Sir John George 'Jackie' Smyth, 1st Baronet, VC, MC, PC (1893–1983); educated at Repton and Sandhurst; commissioned into the British Indian Army in August 1912; awarded the Victoria Cross in 1915; evacuated from Dunkirk n 1940; commanded 17th Indian Infantry Division in March 1941; retired in 1942; elected MP for Norwood in 1950.
19 Hutton was GOC British forces in Burma, so had overall responsibility. Major-General Smyth, as CO of the 17th Indian Division was responsible for military forces in southeast Burma. In his memoirs, *Milestones*, London: Sidgwick & Jackson, 1979, Smyth claimed that, shortly before the Sittang Bridge debacle, Hutton had turned down his request to withdraw his troops to the west bank of the river.
20 BL/MSS/EUR/E215/32 (a), Dorman-Smith, Unpublished draft Memoirs, p.156.f, describes Wavell's frequent visits to Government House in Rangoon (Wavell described it as 'the best hotel in town'). Each time Wavell arrived he reminded Dorman-Smith of 'a Harley Street specialist [come] to see a very sick patient'.
21 Nicholas Tarling, *A Sudden Rampage: The Japanese Occupation of Southeast Asia 1941–45*, London: Hurst & Company, 2001, p. 257.
22 Joyce C. Lebra, *Japanese-trained Armies in Southeast Asia*, New York: Columbia University Press, 1977, p.181.
23 Ienaga Saburo, *Japan's Last War*, Oxford: Blackwell, 1979, pp. 179–180.
24 Britain annexed Arakan and Tenasserim after the First Anglo-Burmese War (1824–1826). The Burmese were forced to pay an indemnity of £1,000,000.
25 Bal Gangadhar Tilak was suspected of having orchestrated a wave of looting, train robberies, bomb incidents and attacks on European clubs. William Curzon a British MP was assassinated in July 1909, and during World War I German arms and ammunition were distributed to nationalist groups. Moderates like Naoroji and Gokhale forced Tilak out of the Congress Party.

26 Gandhi's followers protested against the 1915 Defence of India Act, which prohibited anti-colonial activities. The Rowlatt Commission proposed extending the Act, by imposing press censorship and detaining political activists without trial. The *Swaraj* Movement campaigned for the use of only *khadi* (Indian material), the boycott of British schools and law courts and the non-payment of taxes. The *Satyagraha* marchers in 1930 manufactured salt illegally from seawater, but the march ended violently in April 1930 and, as a result, 100,000 people (including Gandhi) were imprisoned.

27 He reduced membership fees, removed distinctions of caste, ethnicity, religion and sex, adopted Hindustani for use in the All India Congress Committee and introduced leadership elections. During the 1920s, thousands of Congress volunteers went out to address social problems – such as alcoholism, lack of sanitation, medical aid, the oppression of women and illiteracy – and to set up small-scale cottage industries for the production of *kadhi* cloth.

28 See Michael D. Leigh, *Conflict, Politics and Proselytism Methodist Missionaries in Colonial and Postcolonial Upper Burma, 1887–1966*, Manchester: Manchester University Press, 2011, pp. 47–54 and pp. 101–106.

29 The YMBA launched a militant campaign against the wearing of shoes in pagodas.

30 The boycotters claimed that the University of Rangoon would become an elitist institution as a result of the Act.

31 Scholars such as Jan Becka, Michael Charney, D. K. Fieldhouse, Patricia Herbert, Daw Khin Yi, Andrew Porter, Anthony Stockwell, Donald Eugene Smith, Robert H. Taylor, John H. Badgley, Dr Ba Maw, Parimal Ghose, Mikael Gravers, Gustaaf Houtman, Lu Pe Win, Maitri Aung Thwin, U Maung Maung, U Myint-U Thant, E. Sarkisyanz, U Thein Pe Myint, provide fascinating insights into Burmese nationalist movements during the 1920s and 1930s.

32 Loosely translated the title *Thakin* meant 'master'. Burmese servants used the term *Thakin* when addressing European employers.

33 This point must not be overstated for, as was the case elsewhere in the Empire, Burmans were often ambivalent to British rule. Many had benefited from British education, courses of study in India or Britain, and periods of gainful employment in British companies. Close and respectful relationships were often formed between Burmese house servants and British families, Burmese pupils and British teachers and Burmese employees and British managers.

34 The mountains were reported to rise to 12,000 feet and the streams were tributaries of the Brahmaputra and Surma rivers.

35 Anthony Powell, *The Ledo Road* Issue 6, *Mai Hsoong*, pp. 44–47. Military equipment and materials destined for China had to be flown over 'the Hump' from India after the Burma Road was closed. The Ledo road cost $150,000

($2,208,653 in today's money), and 15,000 US soldiers and 35,000 local labourers were employed to build it. More than 1,100 Americans and countless indigenous workers died. Almost all the US soldiers were black. Churchill famously described the Ledo Road as 'an immense, laborious task, unlikely to be finished until the need for it has passed'. The Allies were able to send supply planes directly to China, after they recaptured the Myitkyina airstrip on 17 May 1944. 650,000 tons of military equipment had been *flown* to China by the end of the war. The first convoy of 113 vehicles left Ledo on 12 January 1945 and reached Kunming on 4 February 1945. The jungle reclaimed much of the road after the war.

36 See, Bérénice Guyot-Réchard, *When Legions Thunder Past: The Second World War and India's Northeast Frontier* (2016) War in History, Kings College London Research Portal. 51 British Army units and 47 US air squadrons were based in Assam and Manipur, including 340,000 Indian, 100,000 British, 90,000 West African, 65,000 Chinese, and 10,000 American troops.

37 Alistair Rose warned that 'conditions make miles a poor measure', but Rowland boasted that he had walked '450 miles' from Sumprabum to Margherita, Langham-Carter that he had walked '300 miles in 30 days'. He derided those who had walked 'only 150 miles' (BL/IOR/MSS EUR D975/4, Langham-Carter: *Account of my Trek from Burma*). Alistair Rose was upset when he discovered that another evacuee had taken only 18 days to reach Assam, whereas it had taken him 38 days to complete the same journey. Apedaile says he lost two stones in a month, Langham-Carter's weight fell from 10.25 to 8.5 stones while Rose's weight fell below 8 stones (see IOR/MSS EUR D975/4, Langham-Carter: *Account of My Trek from Burma*).

38 Vorley insisted that he 'could have done *no* more in such volatile circumstances' and that 'only a dictator' could have prevented 'the suicidal migration' in the Taungup Pass. Gordon Apedaile blamed the porters in a letter written from a hospital bed in Calcutta (IOR EUR MSS F260/4, Apedaile Papers, Letter to 'Uncle Fred').

39 For an account of the disagreements between Dorman-Smith, Vorley and de Graaf Hunter, see Michael D. Leigh, *The Evacuation of Civilians: Analysing the 1942 Colonial Disaster*, London: Bloomsbury, 2014, pp. 39–50.

40 Cornelius North stayed at his post in Shingbwiyang until October 1942.

41 See Geoffrey Tyson, *Forgotten Frontier*, Calcutta: W. H. Targett & Co. Ltd., 1945, chapter II,'Enter the Planter', p. 51

42 B. R. Pearn, was professor of history at Rangoon University before the war and head of the Government in Exile's Publicity Department 1942–1945. He was one of the few who had predicted that junior Burmese civil servants would be capable of filling the shoes of their British predecessors.

43 For example, there are accounts of loyal Burmese servants being abandoned on quaysides in March 1942 as their former employers sailed off to safety. Gifts of cash did little to soften the blow. In some cases, Burmese servants readily joined anti-British nationalist movements.
44 The United Nations Relief and Rehabilitation Administration (UNRRA) Report for 1947 lists 13 million Chinese, 15 million Germans, 11 million Soviets, 2 million Poles, 450,000 Ukrainian civilians and at least 650,000 Jews. The United Nations Refugee Agency (UNHCR) Global Trends Report for 2016 indicates that 65.3 million refugees had been displaced by war and persecution. The main contributors included Columbia (6.9m); Syria (6.6m); Iraq (4.4m.) and one-tenth of the total population of Yemen.
45 Severe refugee crises were reported in Afghanistan, Colombia, Iraq and Syria, South Sudan, Burundi, Yemen, Central African Republic, Myanmar and Ukraine.
46 Ian Brown, *A Colonial Economy in Crisis: Burma's Rice Cultivators and the World Depression of the 1930s*, London: Routledge Curzon, 2005. Brown provides an authoritative account of the rice frontier in Burma during the economic boom years of the 1920s and the Depression of the 1930s.

Chapter 2

1 Ships stopped sailing from the Port of Rangoon to Calcutta at the end of February; the Taungup Pass route was closed in March. Able-bodied males were not allowed to fly to Chittagong from Shwebo, which was bombed at the end of April. The airstrip at Myitkyina was bombed on 6 May.
2 In many cases, the evacuees' wives and children had already flown from Shwebo to unknown destinations in India.
3 The last trains ran on 7 March and the journey by road was very slow.
4 This is an extract from a letter written by one of the corporation wives to her father. She probably made light of the trip, which David Brown pointed out was 100 per cent worse than she suggests (Alistair Brown, private collection).
5 Letter dated 2 October 1942 from David Brown (BBTC) from Central Hotel, Cochin State, South India (Alistair Brown, private collection).
6 Ibid.
7 Wallace wrote large numbers of testimonials for colleagues and subordinate staff. He noted, for example, that D. J. W. Bartlett had stayed at his post in Kawkereik and that Saw Sein Mone and A. L. Brownlow were the last police officer and civil officer to leave Moulmein. On the other hand, he noted that G. H. Reilly had left against orders.

8 Walter Ian James Wallace, OBE, CMG. b.1905 Sandgate, Kent, d.1993; educated Bedford Modern School and St Catharine's College Cambridge; entered Indian Civil Service 1928 and posted to Burma. Deputy Commissioner (1933), Settlement Officer (1934–1938), Deputy Commissioner (1939–1942) and Defence Secretary (1942–1944); Colonel and Deputy Director of Civil Affairs (1944–1945); Assistant Secretary Colonial Office (1949–1962) and Assistant Under-Secretary of State (1962–1966); m. Olive Mary Spriggs of Southsea in 1940 (she d.1973).

9 S. R. Rippon, director of Veterinary Service, was one of those in the group. Wallace wrote his account in 1976.

10 A few excellent photographs accompanied Wallace's brief, matter-of-fact account of his journey. One can only guess that they could have been the work of an anonymous professional photographer who happened to be travelling in Wallace's party.

11 Low water levels at the end of dry season presented serious navigational hazards.

12 The pilots had been ordered not to fire at Indian refugees for political reasons. Wallace and the other Europeans took no chances. Although they were dirty and sunburned, they lay face down on the deck to conceal any vestiges of whiteness.

13 Dr. Archie McAdam and Dr. Helen McAdam (son and daughter-in-law of Dr. William McAdam) edited William McAdam's extensive wartime papers. I am indebted to their work. Dr William McAdam had previously held positions in Shwebo, Toungoo, Taunggyi and Tavoy civil hospitals.

14 McAdam wrote the citation for Taylor's OBE (dated 29 July 1942) in which he generously acknowledged the debt he owed to Taylor.

15 The practice of dispatching un-inoculated evacuees continued right up to 28 April.

16 In the midst of death, corpses, cholera cases and destruction, McAdam managed to record some intriguing snippets in his diary. For example, we know that he broke his watch glass on 16 March; on 20 March he had a haircut – a 'proper prison crop' – and on 24 March he saw a black partridge, a hare and a wild cat.

17 His diary entry for 16 April read, 'attempted dacoity on deck passengers sleeping on shore … alarm raised'.

18 Major W. McAdam, diary entry 20 April 1942.

19 Taylor's citation dated 29 July 1942.

20 Major W. McAdam to L. M. Lees, ICS, dated 29 July 1942.

21 *The London Gazette* of 29 January 1943 recorded that Major William McAdam, IMS was awarded the OBE for bravery and distinguished services in the evacuation of Burma. He contributed to 'the success with which disease along this route was kept to a minimum … between Kalewa and Tamu … he

encouraged the medical staff and remedied deficiencies in medical stores and treated emergencies'.

22 It was estimated that about 37,500 evacuees took the Bishenpur–Silchar route.

23 These tracks were on the Burmese side of the border, and were therefore vulnerable to Japanese attack.

24 Christopher Gimson, CIE (1986–1975); educated Oundle and Emmanuel College Cambridge; Political Agent, Manipur (1933–1946). Gimson was fifty-six in 1942.

25 A huge recruitment drive got underway immediately in the garden estates. It is worth noting that ITA policy demanded that anyone employed on the evacuation project had to be a *volunteer*. The following figures give an idea of the numbers of labourers provided: to Aijal Road – The Dooars Tea Circle sent 4,000; to the Manipur Road – The Nowgong Circle sent 1,100; North Bank Circle sent 2,000; Lakhimpur and Sibsagur Circles sent 6,000 and the Recruiting Districts (TDLA) sent 3,000.

26 Dak bungalows originally built to accommodate mail-runners.

27 In March there were only six days on which *more* than 1,000 refugees arrived, whereas in April 1942 there were only twelve days on which *fewer* than 1,000 arrived.

28 In fact, 'issuing a railway ticket' sounds simpler than it really was because so many different South Indian languages had to be used, and group tickets both simplified and complicated things.

29 Most injuries on the trek could be attributed to natural causes, but there were also several instances of lorries (driven by inexperienced drivers) rolling off the road.

30 Geoffrey Tyson, *Forgotten Frontier*, Calcutta: W. H. Targett, 1945, p. 42, Tyson compared the dynamism of these voluntary activities with the Government's relief activities, which he suggested lacked urgency and imagination.

31 See Tyson, *Forgotten Frontier*, chapter 3, 'Mud and Miracles at Dimapur'.

32 See Tyson, *Forgotten Frontier*, chapter 1V, 'The first Hundred and Fifty Thousand'.

33 Tyson, *Forgotten Frontier*, p. 44

34 For example, the wife of a scientific officer at the ITA Station in Tocklai volunteered to cook for the evacuees.

35 Mrs Shaw, the iconic camp commandant of the so-called European ITA Camp was killed in the first raid on Imphal on 10 May 1942. It was a seminal moment in that it gave the impression that the Japanese were approaching India itself. The second bombing raid of Imphal occurred on 16 May. It created panic among the town's population.

36 This was due to the sterling work of Colonel Taylor and Major McAdam.

37 Tyson, *Forgotten Frontier*, p. 40, Tyson is quoting from a letter written by Mr Justice Braund to a friend. Braund was the Refugee Administrator in Shillong.

38 J. S. and H. M. Vorley, *Road to Mandalay*, Wilton, Wilton 65, 2002, chapter 12.

39 All their rice was stolen while they slept in the village of Thanan on 16 May.

40 They averaged seventeen miles per day and the longest single day's walk was twenty-three miles.

41 He described them as 'two disinterested and bored … little worms without manners'. Vorley was critical of both military and Indian Government officials. For example, he described how the Army had unwisely commandeered a European refugee camp at Imphal, which had been very well run by a tea planter named Blenerhasset.

42 Vorley, *Road to Mandalay*, chapter 13. Little is known about Ricketts's epic expedition. It certainly merits much more than a mere footnote. The party appears to have included seven Europeans, five infants and thirty-four children and for some reason they followed a route into Manipur via Hopin, Tamanthelayshi and Somra. They used elephants for first 80 miles and covered it between 6 and14 May. The next stretch of 190 miles was much slower. They all suffered from dysentery and malaria and nine of their number died on the way. The rest did not arrive in Dimapur until 21 June and they all had to be hospitalized.

43 BL/MSS/EUR/1028, Alwyn Henry Seppings: Memoir 1932–1946: Alwyn Henry was the last of three generations of Seppings in Burma. His grandfather, Edmund Henry Seppings was born in 1864. He went out to Burma in 1890 and in 1893, married Ma San Mi. Alwyn's father, Henry Lockyer Seppings was born on 24 December 1895. He became an engineer and worked for Burma Railways before transferring to the PWD. In 1942 he was the superintending engineer in Shwebo (the most senior district rank in PWD). He married Edna May Blazey. Alwyn Henry Seppings, their second son was born in 1924. In 1942 he was eighteen years of age.

44 Claude Blazey was Mrs Seppings's brother. They met by chance in Myitkyina. He had driven up in a very smart and distinctive black Ford Sedan.

45 It was so called because of the very high incidence of malaria.

46 Alwyn Seppings later handed over a firearms certificate and the gun was returned.

Chapter 3

1 IOR/MSS/EUR/C554, R. S. Wilkie, ICS, Commissioner for Sagaing Division: Diary of a Journey from Myitkyina to Margherita.

2 IOR/EUR/MSS /F260/4, Gordon Apedaile, ICS, Defence Secretary in the pre-war Burma Government. He had evacuated to Maymyo with other senior government

officials in April and to Myitkyina on 3 May. Apedaile's wife flew out on one of the last planes but Apedaile refused to go although he had bacillary dysentery and a medical certificate permitting his evacuation. Apedaile was responsible for rice dumps along evacuation routes and for the Myitkyina–Mogaung trains. He maintained that colonial officials had been ordered to leave Myitkyina on the last plane but had chosen to ignore the instruction.

3 IOR/ EUR/ MSS/ F/260/4, Apedaile Papers: Letter to 'Uncle Fred'.

4 1942/ MSS/ EUR/ D/975/4, Reginald Langham-Carter, *Account of my Trek from Burma to India.*

5 IOR/ EUR/ MSS/ F/260/4, Apedaile Papers: Letter to 'Uncle Fred'.

6 IOR/MSS/EUR/ D/975/4, Reginald Langham-Carter: *Account of my Trek* ,1 November 1942.

7 U Ba Aye and his wife were unable to get to the rendezvous in Myitkyina on time because their daughter was one of those killed at the Myitkyina airfield.

8 Langham-Carter said the cook and the corporal were invaluable, getting fires lit, food cooked and bullocks loaded. The whole party had to act as coolies.

9 Several refugees were injured in the attack. U Than Tun Kaing (Assistant Superintendent of Police in Myitkyina) was particularly valiant. On 8 May the Japanese landed two troop carriers and occupied the town.

10 Maihtaung is at mile 103 on the Myitkyina–Sumprabum road.

11 IOR/MSS/EUR/C554, Wilkie's diary account became increasingly illegible, but Langham-Carter wrote his *Account of my Trek from Burma to India* very neatly and legibly on Hotel Cecil notepaper while recuperating there.

12 Chinese troops reportedly took most of the rice before setting fire to the town.

13 Extract from P.G.G. Salkeld, *A Letter to My Mother*, from Calcutta, 20 August 1942, giving an account of life on his way out from Burma via the Hukawng Valley, April/May 1942.

14 Salkeld, *A Letter to My Mother*, 20 August 1942.

15 Salkeld, *A Letter to My Mother*, 20 August 1942.

16 Estimated by Brigadier Whitworth at an address given to the Royal Central Asian Society, 14 July 1943.

17 North had arrived in Burma in 1939 at the age of twenty-two. He was responsible for administering Kachin and Naga tribesmen in this Godforsaken part of the world. in was twenty-three years of age.

18 Geoffrey Tyson, *Forgotten Frontier*, Calcutta: W. H. Targett & Co. Ltd., p. 57.

19 Cornelius William North was only twenty-five years old in 1942. He had joined the BFF in1939 and continued to serve in it until1947; 1948–1950 Colonial Service, Tanganyika; 1950–1952 A.D.C. and acting D.C., Yei, Equatoria; 1952–1955 Local Government Inspector, Darfur; 1977–1981 Secretary, Middle East Association.

20 Stephen Brookes, *Through the Jungles of Death: A Boy's Escape from Wartime Burma*, London: John Murray, 2000.
21 Brookes, *Through the Jungles of Death*, p. 128.
22 Brookes, *Through the Jungles of Death*, pp.154–156.
23 Brookes, *Through the Jungles of Death*, pp.160–161.
24 Brookes, *Through the Jungles of Death*, p. 93. The title was a reference to an episode in 1941 when Naga headhunters reportedly killed 150 people.
25 Brookes, *Through the Jungles of Death*, p.179.
26 Stephen Brookes wondered whether North had slighted his Burmese mother and whether his father had accused North of racism.
27 It seems a very exact figure, and one that is almost certainly exaggerated.
28 Salkeld, *A Letter to My Mother*, 20 August 1942.
29 Salkeld, *A Letter to My Mother*, 20 August 1942.
30 Salkeld, *A Letter to My Mother*, 20 August 1942.
31 Wilkie opted to stay behind in Burma to help other evacuees. The Anglo-Indian with the septic foot followed later on a stretcher.
32 Rose, who was a senior partner in T. D. Findlay & Son Ltd., had been working on the company's annual accounts in Moulmein when the Japanese forces invaded Tenasserim. He dropped what he was doing and drove straight up to Mandalay.
33 OIR/MSS/EUR /C581, Alistair Rose, *A Short History of T D Findlay & Son Ltd: East India Merchants 1839–5*: Account of the evacuation from Burma January–June 1942.
34 At the same time, Wilkie had completed ten miles along the Sumprabum Road. Rose seems to have confused the exact chronology of the events of 6 and 7 May. Government House was occupied until the morning of 7 May and Battersby (the only known 'aide') had already left in Wilkie's party. Interestingly Rose described how two transport aircraft were destroyed on the runway while they were waiting to take off and Japanese planes strafing a ferry on the Irrawaddy. Presumably he was referring to 7 May when he wrote that 'it was quite clear that the town of Myitkyina was ripe for bombing the next day', and that the evacuees in Myitkyina had been advised to set off as quickly as possible for Mogaung and the Hukawng Valley route into Assam.
35 The story of the Bishop Strachan pupils was most mysterious and tragic. Rose blamed their subsequent demise on the leadership of two inexperienced army men.
36 Tyson, *Forgotten Frontier*, p. 59, for example, on one occasion a group of twelve Gurkhas had volunteered to get a rope across the Namyang River, but only seven of the twelve survived the attempt.
37 Tyson, *Forgotten Frontier*, p. 61.
38 A treatment that was supposed to stop the loss of blood.

Chapter 4

1 At one point, a party of Burma Rifles soldiers had helped the ITA party. They had spent the last six days marching 133 miles in the opposite direction from Shingbwiyang.
2 S. Farrant Russell, *Muddy Exodus: A Story of the Evacuation of Burma, May 1942*, London: Epworth Press, 1943, pp. 28–29.
3 For the record, Maggie weighed 6,000 lbs. and stood 7.5 feet high at the shoulder.
4 He was determined to return to his home village in the Hukawng Valley.
5 Russell, *Muddy Exodus*, pp. 41–42.
6 In 1942 it had rained incessantly from 12–28 May, again from 3–10 June, and from 14–21 June.
7 *Jhums* were plots cleared by Nagas for seasonal agricultural purposes. The area was normally teeming with birds, bison, elephant and rhino.
8 Russell, *Muddy Exodus*, pp. 49–50.
9 Geoffrey Tyson, *Forgotten Frontier*, Calcutta: W. H. Targett, 1945, chapter 7.
10 On 1 June *exactly* 1,355 evacuees arrived at the Nampong Camp and then the numbers began to fall. 145 evacuees arrived on 5th June, 780 on 6th June, 811 on 7th June and 530 on 8th June.
11 Tyson, *Forgotten Frontier*, chapter 7,
12 A treatment that was supposed to stop the loss of blood.
13 Later Rose joined the Burma Intelligence Corps of the Indian Army 17th Division.
14 Stephen Brookes, *Through the Jungles of Death: A Boy's Escape from Wartime Burma*, London: John Murray, 2000, p. 128.
15 Imperial War Museum, Oral History Unit, 03413, Lecture 16 January 1978, Rev Wilfred Crittle, recorded by Gordon Bowerman.
16 Russell, *Muddy Exodus*, p. 47.
17 Tyson, *Forgotten Frontier*, p. 80. The investigating officer reported that the jungle had quickly covered the skeletons.
18 BL/IOR/EUR/MSS/Folio 27/930, Lecture given by Brigadier Dysart Whitworth (Officer in Command, Upper Assam) on 14 July 1943. '*The evacuation of refugees and the Chinese Fifth Army from the Hukawng Valley into Assam, Summer 1942*'. Published in the Royal Central Asian Society Magazine. Whitworth cites Mr Jarman.
19 R. S. Wilkie, Diary of a Journey from Myitkyina to Margherita, MSS/EUR/E/215/60.
20 Russell, *Muddy Exodus*, p. 27.
21 Imperial War Museum, Oral History Unit, 03413, Lecture 16 January 1978, Rev Wilfred Crittle, recorded by Gordon Bowerman.

22 Imperial War Museum, Oral History Unit, 03413, Lecture 16 January 1978, Rev Wilfred Crittle, recorded by Gordon Bowerman. The young couple's 'back-story' was equally sad. They had been booked onto a plane and were about to fly. However, their five-year-old son was ill and had to be taken off. He died in hospital. The whole family therefore missed the flight.

23 Imperial War Museum, Oral History Unit, 03413, Lecture 16 January 1978, Rev Wilfred Crittle, recorded by Gordon Bowerman.

24 BL/IOR/M/41/3/955-B270/4, an undated letter from Miss Z. N. Gilbert to Miss Lou Beale referring a letter from Mrs Oakley (Lon/14243/43), quoted in Michael D. Leigh, *The Evacuation of Civilians from Burma: Analysing the 1942 Colonial Disaster*, London: Bloomsbury, 2014, p. 225, the elderly gentlemen were Fred Thompson and Mr Davidson.

25 Tyson, *Forgotten Frontier*, p. 75.

26 Tyson, *Forgotten Frontier*, p. 75.

27 Tyson, *Forgotten Frontier*, p. 76, at the Namyang Hka the Steels' elephants carried many women and children across the river, but they caused a lot of damage to the track on the supply route between Nampong and Namgoi.

28 HRH Prince of Wales, Tyne Cot Cemetery, Centenary Service for the Battle of Passchendaele, 31 July 2017.

29 Tyson, *Forgotten Frontier*, p. 59.

30 Tyson, *Forgotten Frontier*, p. 74.

31 See John Ebenezer Marks, *Forty Years in Burma*, London: Hutchinson, 1917, chapter X: 'The Diocesan Orphanage'. The home had been established in Rangoon during the late nineteenth century for the orphan children of European fathers and Burmese mothers.

32 J. S. and H. M. Vorley, *The Road from Mandalay*, Wilton: Wilton 65, 2001, p. 69

33 Vorley, *The Road from Mandalay*, p. 79, Vorley blamed the overcrowding on the Principal Medical Officer at the Thabyetkyin District Hospital who had commandeered all the available space to evacuate his patients and staff. Mrs Vorley was actually on the steamer. She claimed to have prevented the pupils from boarding – one of the most difficult decisions of her life, she said – although she did permit the wife, baby and young sister-in-law of one of the evacuation officers to board.

34 Vorley also suggested that Miss Lilian Bald had been given 'almost criminally bad advice'. He insisted that the tragedy would not have happened if he and his lieutenants, Ricketts and Booth-Russell had been in charge at Myitkyina.

35 Two American Baptist Missionaries looked after the younger children while they were in Sumprabum. When it fell into Japanese hands a Japanese officer (who happened to be a Christian) took the children under his wing.

36 The list of references in the Evacuation Registers is as follows: *Arrivals in India*: 23 March 1942 Timothy Knight (11 yrs); 26 May 1942 Eileen Henderson; 20 October 1942, Harry and Robert Prosser; 26 October 1942 Betty Davis (6 yrs) and Lloyd Davis (9 yrs); 28 October 1942, Molly Bott, Shirley Bowen, Elspeth Campbell (8½ years) and Annie Campbell (6 yrs), Monica Lancaster (8 yrs), Jeanette, June and Peter MacDonald, Florence Williams, Greta, Gloria and Heather Htoon; 16 November 1942, Hazel Bennett. *Deaths*: The following all died at Yawbang before the end of August 1942: Miss Lilian Bald, Principal of Bishop Strachan's Home; Poppy Bennett (12 yrs); June Grant (12 yrs); Laura Lancaster (17 yrs); Zena Prosser (18 yrs), Pat Prosser (15 yrs) and Kitty Prosser (13 yrs); Ethel Soliday (12 yrs); Betty Swan (15 yrs) and John Swan (12 yrs); Iris Morris (17 yrs), Dixon Morris (12 yrs) and Kenneth Morris (11 yrs). The following all died at Sumprabum: Amy Johnston (8 yrs) ; Lavender Davis (7 yrs); Vivienne Mueller (6 yrs) and Maxine Mueller (7 yrs) died at Sumprabum; Dawn Rosario (8 yrs) on 26 October 1942. The following died at Taihpa in August 1942: Miss Dorothy Law (teacher at Bishop Strachan's Home) and Diana Doupe (13 yrs). Elizabeth Doupe (10 yrs) died at Margherita and Ruth Montgomery (13 years) died at Tapaung before the end of August 1942.

37 BL/IOR/EUR/MSS/Folio 27/930, Lecture given by Brigadier Dysart Whitworth (Officer in Command, Upper Assam) on 14 July 1943. '*The Evacuation of Refugees and the Chinese Fifth Army from the Hukawng Valley into Assam, Summer 1942*'. Published in the Royal Central Asian Society Magazine.

38 Tyson, *Forgotten Frontier*, p. 90, Early in June, General Lo and the HQ Staff of the Chinese Expeditionary Force had arrived in Dibrugarh. It was clear that the extrication of the Chinese Fifth Army was a pressing problem. It had disappeared for several weeks and was eventually traced to Dalu on the Chindwin River, where the RAF dropped several items of food they so desperately needed. It was now approaching Shingbwiyang and the leading regiment arrived just as the Pangsau Pass became impassable. Urgent talks took place between General Lo, Brigadier General Whitworth and Lambert (a frontier political officer) who proposed to bring out the Chinese Fifth Army by Naga footpaths to the southeast of the Pangsau. It was an audacious plan that succeeded. (Brig. Gen. Whitworth, address to the Royal Central Asian Society).

39 The scheme to link India, Burma and China had first been mooted in March 1942 and the first ITA gangs arrived on site between 5 and 10 May.

40 For further information on the ITA's role on the Hukawng Valley evacuation route, see Tyson, *Forgotten Frontier*, chapter V, 'Over the Pangsau'.

41 IOR MSS EUR F174/1309, Indian Tea Association Report: Commissioned by the Administrator General, *The Evacuation of Troops and Civilians from Burma by the Pangsau Route: Namyang River to Lekhapani, May to July 1942.*

42 Tyson, *Forgotten Frontier*, p. 56, Tyson quoted from the diary of an unnamed ITA officer on the reconnaissance expedition that left from Assam at the beginning of May 1942. The reports were submitted to Major-General Wood. Among other things, they contained detailed descriptions of the remote Naga village of Nongki and an account of the recruitment of seventy Naga porters in Nampong.
43 The ITA's responsibilities started at the Tagap Ga Camp. The next camp was eight miles further along the track at Namlip, where ITA engineers had built a bridge over Namlip Hka. The next camp was at Tagung Hka, which was another eight miles along the track and up a very steep gradient.
44 Shingbwiyang was a frontier village and HQ of a junior political officer.
45 For an excellent account of the issues facing General Wood and his colleagues, see Tyson, *Forgotten Frontier*, pp. 52–56.
46 Excluding the 'Burma-administered' camps at Taikham Zup, Yangson, Namlip, Ngalang Ga, the twelve camps were located at Tagung Hka, Nawngyang, Shamlung, Nampong, Namgoi, Namky, Namchick, Fuffalo [Ngokpi], Kumlao, Tirap, Tipong and Lekhpani.
47 Tyson, *Forgotten Frontier*, p. 71
48 Russell, *Muddy Exodus*, p. 50.
49 Russell, *Muddy Exodus*, p. 47. It should be mentioned that Maggie the elephant disappeared at Nampong and was never seen again.
50 The term 'liaison officer' was borrowed from road-building projects in which Royal Engineers (or Indian engineers) designed and supervised the construction of the roads, while planters (termed liaison officers) managed the labourers who carried out the work. In this case the work was carried out between Taikham Zup and Nampong.
51 Alasdair Ramsay Tainsh, MBE, (1913–1998), educated Elizabeth College Gurnsey and Jesus College Cambridge His obituary dubiously suggests that he helped to save 19,000 evacuees in Northern Burma of whom only 19 died. The gentian violet procedure is now widely adapted as an antidote to plural voting in elections.
52 BL/IOR/EUR/MSS/Folio 27/930, Lecture given by Brigadier Dysart Whitworth (Officer in Command, Upper Assam) on 14 July 1943. '*The Evacuation of Refugees and the Chinese Fifth Army from the Hukawng Valley into Assam, Summer 1942*'. Published in the Royal Central Asian Society Magazine.
53 It was curious that the clinics dispensed cigarettes as well as medicines.
54 The ITA subsequently withdrew from Dinjan, in order to concentrate its resources at the camp in Lekhpani.
55 The number of porters by ethnicity employed by the ITA on the Hukawng Valley route in 1942 were as follows: PCC, 200–300; Abors, 900–1,200; Khasis, 1,000; Pnars, 1,000; Garos, 2,250; Total, 5,350–5,750.

56 Tyson suggests that bandaging their perfectly healthy feet was a favourite ploy of the Pnars.
57 On a few rare occasions, evacuees were killed when packages dropped on their heads
58 It was recommended that every hundred Europeans should be allocated 20lbs. tinned meat, 65lbs. biscuits, 5 lbs. tea, 5lbs. sugar, 3lbs. tinned milk and 5 lbs. marmite, and every hundred Indians 70lbs. rice, 15lbs, dahl, 5lbs. salt, 5lbs. sugar, 3lbs. tinned milk and 5lbs. tea – that is, a total of 103lbs of rations for every one hundred Europeans or Indians.
59 Tyson, *Forgotten Frontier* , chapter V1, 'Early days on the Ledo Road' (The Jeep Road).
60 Lieutenant-General Irwin, Commander of the 4th Corps and Brigadier Whitworth, Commander of the Northern Area Brigade.
61 Tyson, *Forgotten Frontier*, chapter 1X, Withdrawal and the End.
62 In 1943, Brigadier Dysart Whitworth (Commanding Officer Upper Assam) pointed out that it was impossible to supply many camps from the air, so they were dependent on porters for all their food and medical stores. He went on to claim (dubiously) that nearly 700 porters had died by the end of July 1942.
63 IOR MSS EUR F174/1309, Indian Tea Association Report: Commissioned by the Administrator General, *The Evacuation of Troops and Civilians from Burma by the Pangsau Route: Namyang River to Lekhapani, May to July 1942.*
64 He retained a skeleton staff at Namlip to check-in and feed any stragglers. An average of thirty per day arrived between 1 and 5 June. 780 arrived on 6 June, 811 on 7 June and 530 on 8 June. Worryingly, a high proportion of the new arrivals were women and children.
65 Tyson, *Forgotten Frontier*, p. 97.

Chapter 5

1 See Geoffrey Tyson, *Forgotten Frontier*, Calcutta: W. H. Targett, 1945, pp. 9f.
2 BL/IOR/EUR/MSS/Folio 27/930, Lecture given by Brigadier Dysart Whitworth (Officer in Command, Upper Assam) on 14 July 1943, entitled '*The evacuation of refugees and the Chinese Fifth Army from the Hukawng Valley into Assam, Summer 1942*', Published in the Royal Central Asian Society Magazine.
3 Tyson, *Forgotten Frontier* p. 101.
4 For example, Rowland blamed N. Moses (a railway surveyor) whom he nicknamed 'the Dutch Jew'.
5 Tyson, *Forgotten Frontier*, p. 99.

6 The European adventurers were Errol Gray in 1892, Woodthorpe and MacGregor in 1894, and Prince Henry of Orleans in 1897, and Prichard (about whom little is known), somewhat later.

7 Footage of the real-time exploits of the elephants was captured on film that is held in the Cambridge Centre for South Asian Studies. It is one of the most astonishing pieces of film surviving from World War II.

8 Tyson, *Forgotten Frontier*, pp. 111 f.

9 The BCCC started (but did not complete) a railway line between Lashio and Kunming. The *San Francisco Chronicle* of 27 November 1941 compared it to the Panama Canal Construction project in that it would also win a 'victory over malaria ... plague and cholera'. Early in 1942, Rowland demanded (and received) from Dorman-Smith the 'dictator powers' necessary to keep the trains running.

10 After 22 April all men over the age of forty-five were permitted to board planes so Rowland within his rights to fly out at a time when young able-bodied men brazenly barged onto planes. Rowland had already earned his stripes on 27 April when Maymyo was bombed. He had 'hared' all over Burma and in twelve hours managed to evacuate to Myitkyina most of the 4000 Indian and Anglo-Indian railwaymen and their families.

11 Smaller groups also joined them at intervals.

12 See, Andrew Martin, *Flight by Elephant: The Untold Story of World War II's Most Daring Jungle Rescue*. London: Fourth Estate, 2013.

13 Eileen Rossiter was born in Kalimpong, Sikkim (India) on 12 December 1942.

14 Rossiter's family arrangements were complicated. He had had one daughter (Patricia Rossiter) with, Khin Nyein, a Burmese Buddhist woman, and another (Maureen Rossiter) with Khin Nyun, another Burmese Buddhist woman.

15 BL/IOR MSS EUR C816, Edward Wrixon Rossitter (c/o Grindlay & Co, Calcutta), letter written from India to his mother, 30 October 1942. The Government had withdrawn his wireless transmitter and receiving set and his own radio went out of order. He had decided on the route to China rather than to India because he understood that the paths lay through deep jungle on the India route, that it would take six weeks to complete the journey, that there were no villages and all food would have to be carried by coolies. How right he was. Rossiter's account was very egocentric. He made no reference to Rowland, and his facts and figures are very vague and questionable – for example, that they had 300 coolies and carried 2,000 lbs. of rice.

16 Fraser and Pratt had been captured by Japanese troops, who confiscated Fraser's spectacles and Pratt's boots. They escaped, although the former couldn't see and the latter couldn't walk.

17 Tyson, *Forgotten Frontier*, pp. 103–104, Ronald Jardine's diary: Jardine notes, for example that the large village of Kamku had been abandoned many years previously.

18 IOR/MSS/EUR/112 Letter, Rowland to wife. We do not know where he got the figures.
19 Rossiter claimed that he had received a wireless message in Sumprabum promising that they would be met here. It was vague and ultimately misleading.
20 They were under an Indian NCO, Rattan Singh.
21 Tyson, *Forgotten Frontier*, p. 124
22 Rowland blamed Rossiter for handing over a lot of the food to a party of sepoys.
23 See Tyson, *Forgotten Frontier*, pp. 122 ff.
24 Footage of the real-time exploits of the elephants was captured on film that is held in the Cambridge Centre for South Asian Studies. It is one of the most astonishing pieces of film surviving from World War II.
25 The Sikhs explained that fifteen of their number had died on the way. It was an indication of the treacherous conditions in the area.
26 The Dapha Camp was only two hours flying time from Dinjan.
27 Pratt and Fraser had been captured by the Japanese and had escaped together before joining the Chaukan expedition.
28 Edward Wixon Rossiter of the BFF was an Irish Protestant. He had four children. Patricia Rossiter was born to Khin Nyen, a Burmese Buddhist woman on 12 April 1931 in Mandalay; Maureen Rossiter was born on 18 April 1933 in Mongyai (Shan State) to Khin Nyun, also a Burmese Buddhist woman. John Michael Rossiter was born on 21 November to Nang Hmat, a Shan Buddhist woman, and Eileen Rossiter was born in Kalimpong, Sikkim (India) on 12 December 1942, also to Nang Hmat.
29 Tyson, *Forgotten Frontier*, chapter XIII, 'One more River'.
30 En route he had a useful briefing from Webster.
31 They met on 4 September.
32 The letter from Margherita was dated 3 September and was dropped by plane on the Dapha Camp on the instructions of the Refugee Administrator. A runner had brought it to Mackrell.
33 The 'striking party' was led by Naik Gyanbahadur, and included compounder Havildar Sanam Lama, Naik Manichand Rai, and Six 'Political Porters' – Santabir, Gungabahadur, Tami, Chintamani, Dilbahadur, Karnabahadur.
34 Brigadier Whitworth was one of those in the plane.
35 See Tyson, *Forgotten Frontier*, chapter VIII, 'Naga sores and dysentery'.
36 It must be remembered that the association had a policy of allowing only genuine volunteers to enlist. Hitherto it had encouraged all estates to produce labourers based on a formula of ten labourers per 100 acres of cultivated land. This was no longer producing enough volunteers.
37 BL/IOR/MSS/EUR/F174/633(b), Indian Tea Association: Report of the General Committee: For year ended December 1942, Calcutta 1943.

Chapter 6

1 Pioneer tea planters had hacked their original tea estates out of dense, evergreen jungles formed of giant bamboo and lianas trees. These were often 250 feet high and could have circumferences of 30 feet. When the area was cleared the tea was planted in 12-acre blocks. These were separated by shade trees that were planted 48 feet apart. It was very labour intensive. Naga and Jingpo tribesmen were employed to clear the land and elephants were used for the heavy work. By 1942 elephants – each of which weighed about 4.5 tons – were still widely used on the tea estates. Traditionally the planters would go on big game hunting expeditions in the cold season – so they grew up as jungle survival experts and as first-class shots. It was as if they were genetically prepared for the rigours that faced them in 1942

2 BL/IOR/MSS/EUR/F174/633(b), Indian Tea Association: Report of the General Committee: For year ended December 1942, Calcutta 1943. To give one example of the degree of intensity of the labour needed, 160 women were required to pluck the crop from every12 acres of planted tea.

3 Manipur was the largest and most southeasterly state in Assam, so the evacuation routes from Burma passed through it.

4 Geoffrey Tyson, *Forgotten Frontier*, Calcutta: W. H. Targett & Co. Ltd., 1945.

5 There were no fewer than 23 ITA Circles in Assam.

6 It had first been mooted in March 1942 after the Burma Road to Kunming was closed.

7 BL/IOR/MSS/EUR/F174/633(b), Indian Tea Association: Report of the General Committee: For year ended December 1942, Calcutta 1943, p. 59.

8 BL/IOR/ MSS EUR F174/1310. Notes of a meeting held in New Delhi between representatives of the ITA, Government of India, and Military High Command, dated, 23 September 1942. Present, for the I.T.A: J. Jones (Chairman), R.J. Nicholls (i/c, European Personnel and ITA Labour Contingents and, Member of the Roads, Sub-Committee) and, J.B. Morrison (Assistant Secretary): (For the Army) Lt.-Col. P.T. Harrison (Assistant-Director of Labour for Eastern Army), Brigadier H.A. Courtenay, and Maj.-Gen. C.M.P. Durnford (Deputy Quartermaster-General): For the Government) R.H. Hutchings (Additional Secretary, War Department).

9 BL/IOR/MSS/EUR/F174/633(b), Indian Tea Association: Report of the General Committee: For year ended December 1942, Calcutta 1943. A small proportion of this number was involved in constructing aerodromes or defence installations in Chittagong or supply roads to China – but the vast majority were working on evacuation routes.

10 BL/IOR/MSS/EUR/F174/633(b), Indian Tea Association: Report of the General Committee: For year ended December 1942, Calcutta 1943.

11 CCSAS: Indian Tea Association Papers, p. 61ff. Notes on the Official Government Report on the Evacuation of Refugees (Calcutta): Parliamentary Notice, 13 October 1943, London Session, 1942/1943 (3rd Sitting Day after October).
12 Tyson, *Forgotten Frontier*, pp. 145–146.
13 It must be remembered that the association had a policy of allowing only genuine volunteers to enlist. Hitherto it had encouraged all estates to produce labourers based on a formula of ten labourers per 100 acres of cultivated land. This was no longer producing enough volunteers.
14 BL/IOR/MSS/EUR/F174/633(b), Indian Tea Association: Report of the General Committee: For year ended December 1942, Calcutta 1943.
15 For example, it established pop-up clinics and cafes *between* camps. They were very popular with evacuees.

Chapter 7

1 Sealdah Station, Calcutta was designed by Glanville and built in 1869. It was the terminus for the Bengal–Assam Railway. Immediately outside the station concourse, on Bouzabar Street, passengers could catch trams to Rajabazar, Howrah Station, High Court, Dalhousie Square, Park Circus and Dharmatala.
2 The names of thousands of lower caste Indian refugees were recorded in the Register of Civilian Evacuees in 1942 but many thousands more chose not to register at the Indian border.
3 *Burma Nadu* Vol. 2, No. 3, January 1945, 'Evacuees in India'. The 'Burmese' evacuees included Anglo-Burmans, Indo-Burmans and Zerabadis.
4 Amitav Ghosh, *Exodus from Burma: A Personal Account*, 2011.
5 Dr Krishnan Gurumurthy's grandfather was originally from Madras. He went to Burma to make a living at the turn of the century. Dr Gurumurthy's father was born in Rangoon in 1902. He worked for Burma Railways. His mother came from a small village near Madras, and they had seven children (six boys and a girl) including Krishnan who was born in 1933. At the end of January 1942 Krishnan's father bought tickets for the steamer from Rangoon to Calcutta for the whole Gurumurthy family (consisting of Krishnan, his brothers, sister, grandmother, grandfather, mother and father). At the last moment they were not allowed to board because the British Government 'thought that only the lives of the British and Anglo-Indians were worth saving'. Instead, they evacuated to India via the Chindwin, Tamu and Dimapur.
6 I am grateful to Ms Lisa Oakley, Head of the English Department at Woodhouse Grove School, who introduced me to the obscure but apt term '*proleptic irony*'.

It is an irony that is not immediately apparent, but which is borne out by later events.

7 Among this number was also a clutch of Indian entrepreneurs who had monopolized urban taxi, motor truck, bus, and rickshaw businesses in Burma, and there were 303 Indian-owned factories, including seven engineering factories, fifty-one sawmills, 190 rice mills, three vegetable oil mills and twenty-four cotton-ginning factories. Indian firms owned the largest hosiery mills. The total value of these factories was estimated at £11.25m. Indian-owned property in Rangoon including multistoreyed residential quarters, mercantile houses, shopping centres, theatres and cinemas, was estimated to be worth in the region of Rs.160m., and in Burma as a whole Indian property was estimated to be worth Rs.250m.

8 J. Russell Andrus was professor of economics at Rangoon University and S. N. Haji and R. G. Ayengar were leading Indian businessmen in Burma.

9 The most recent anti-Indian rioting had broken out in Rangoon on 26 July 1938 and spread to Mandalay. It was over the publication of anti-Buddhist sentiments by a Burmese Muslim. By April 1939, the rioting had spread to rural areas where Burmese tenants rioted against Indian landlords. The unrest did not abate until September 1939.

10 B. R. Pearn, *The Indian in Burma: Racial Relations: Studies in Conflict and Cooperation*, p. 35, Ledbury: Le Play House Press, 1947.

11 Wealthy evacuees stayed at the Astoria, Grand, Great Eastern, Continental and Central Imperial hotels in Calcutta, or in one of the chain of Grand Hotels in Simla, Naini Tal and Patna. Others stayed in the Woodlands Hotel in Old Delhi.

12 Among the Roman Catholic institutions to provide accommodation were St Hilda's Mission in Lahore, St Xavier's Mission in Patna and Our Lady of Providence Convent in Calcutta and the Good Shepherd Convents in Mysore and Bellary and St Mary's Convent in Benares. Salvation army hostels, YMCA buildings, boy scouts and girl guides headquarters, secretariat camps, and the Jantar Mantar House also provided accommodation.

13 Evacuation camps were located at Agra, Alighar UP, Allahabad, Almora UP, Amritsar, Anandagiri (Ootacamund) SI, Bangalore, Bhandara, Bilaspur, Brook Hill (Naini Tal), Chunar UP, Coimbatore (the biggest of the camps), Dinapur, Fatehpur, Ghazipur, Gorakhpur, Jhansi UP, Lahore, Mullingar, Mussoorie, Nagpur CP, Partabgarh, Patna (where a Mr and Mrs Barbosa were assigned to Block 'R', Room 10, Road 6), Saharanpur, Saugor, Sialkot, and Sitapur.

14 BL/MSS/(390) 300, New Delhi Reuters press release (1751) 1942, Lady Dorman-Smith was approached to persuade employers to help with the scheme.

15 The first bomb fell on a police station 100 yards from the D'Mello's flat in 42nd Street. Ian D'Mello remembered a glass window being blown out and their pet dog running away never to be seen again.

16 Information kindly provided by Mr Ian D'Mello in correspondence with the author between 1 and 8 March 2012.

17 Michael D. Leigh, *Conflict, Politics and Proselytism: Methodist Missionaries in Colonial and Postcolonial Upper Burma, 1887–1966*, Manchester: Manchester University Press, 2011.

18 In Chittagong the women were taken to the European Club where they were fed and issued with large square gin bottles filled with boiled water. This was a source of considerable embarrassment for the Methodist women. Several of the Methodist missionaries (especially Rev Stanley Vincent, Rev Clement Chapman and Rev Eric Firth), played a leading role on the evacuation of civilians along the Chindwin Valley route.

19 The National Bank of Burma had liquidated the Mission account so the missionaries could draw out no money.

20 Six missionaries met in Benares. Six were on leave, one was away on military service, four were unable to attend and three had returned to England.

21 The British intelligence services were no better informed than the missionaries. See *Burma during the Japanese Occupation: Government of Burma Intelligence Bureau Report*, Simla, 1943.

22 For example, the scholarly Rev. H. C. Willans, lost all his books on Burmese literature and his collection of hand-coloured slides, which it had taken a lifetime to collect.

23 Some of the absentees were on furlough, others were elsewhere in India and some were on active service.

24 For example, Rev. J. L. Leigh had joined the X1V Army and Rev. W. A. Holden had joined the Burma Civil Affairs Service, CAS (B), with a military rank.

25 The missionaries in synod justified their views, pointing to the case of Tuahranga, a Chin Methodist minister, who was helping the Secret Service 'in addition to his mission work' and a 'Christian leader of the Karens' who had been shot by the Japanese.

26 So vivid was the experience that many years later, old men who had been children at the time, still felt compelled to write about it. To name but two, David Reed, *The Trek from Mandalay*, London: Minerva Press, 1996, and Stephen Brookes, *Through the Jungle of Death: A Boy's Escape from Wartime Burma*, London: John Murray, 2000.

27 For example, even the hugely respected Rev. Vincent Shepherd became something of an outsider because he was on furlough in England in 1942. He was Chapman's designated successor, but was unable to get to Calcutta until February 1944. In March 1945 he was diagnosed with leprosy and was invalided back to England. Rev. Eric Firth became the acting Chairman. He had the great advantage of having evacuated from Burma with the others.

28 I am indebted to Ian E. Scholey, *The 'Babylonian' Captivity of the Hongkong and Shanghai Banking Corporation and the return to Burma in 1945'*, SOAS, University of London, MA Dissertation, 2007, which provides a fascinating insight.

29 Sir Arthur Morse (1892–1967) became commissioner and general manager of the HSBC Bank in December 1941 just nine days before Japanese planes bombed Rangoon. In 1943 he became chairman and chief manager of the Bank

30 Sir Robert Bruce was manager of the Rangoon Branch of HSBC. He was understandably cautious because between 19 and 24 February 1942 the Rangoon-based exchange banks in Rangoon had already been evacuated once. Important ledgers and records were taken by train to Mandalay or sent by sea to Calcutta. The HSBC office in Mandalay was destroyed in the air raid of 3 April and ten days later the Bank ended its operations. On 15 April the staff were taken by car to Shwebo and flown to Calcutta. Initially Sir Robert had intended to transfer the bank to Lahore, but no premises were available.

31 King, Frank H. H., *The History of the Hong Kong and Shanghai Banking Corporation*, Vol. iii, Return from Grandeur, 1919–1945, and Vol. iv, From Regional Bank to International Group, 1941–1984 (1988–1991), Cambridge: Cambridge University Press, 1987. There were strong similarities between the problems facing the Hong Kong and Rangoon branches of the bank.

32 HSBC wanted to return to Burma at the earliest opportunity but, in any event, none of the exchange banks was able to return to Rangoon until December 1945, seven months after the city was reoccupied.

33 Reginald Clark believed that he stayed in The Rainsay Hospital in Naini Jal, Uttar Pradesh. Some of Clark's friends were worse off than him. Jim Grierson had arrived in Calcutta after a 365-mile walk and was rushed off to hospital with malaria and severe exhaustion. Peter Buchan and Peter Beechers were both suffering from amoebic dysentery. Jack Murphy had been killed in the air raid on Imphal. Jemma Wardlesworth had been killed in the bombing raid on Myitkyina and Mrs Childers had been severely wounded. Clark's lawyer colleague, North Surridge, had arrived in Calcutta weighing only 9 stones after he had walked nearly 500 miles to Kunming. The sister and three daughters of Clark's old Indian butler had all died on their way out of Burma. Mrs Oxbury and her child had been lost at sea, when their steamer was torpedoed on the way back to Britain, and Marie Lockley was very seriously ill in Calcutta.

34 The list of Clark's acquaintances included Nicky Hepburn, Tino Martin, Nicky Williams, Joan and James Robertson, Sam and Evelyn Weatherfield, Kenneth and Marie Lockley, Mrs Freddy Welch, the St John Clays, the York-Topps, Mollie and Rodney Blake, Ron and Elsie Atkins, Arnold and Vera Orr-Deans, Tim and Nora Healy, the Macconachie's, Heydl Petch, the Paynes, the Walfords, Eb Miller, Ian

Nelson, George Cheyne, Sir and Lady Dunkley, Sir John Wise, Sir John Francis Sheehy, Sir Robert and Lady Kathleen Bruce, Peggy Watson, Muriel Horrocks, Mrs Marsden-Ranger, Mrs MacWhite, Beryl Parry, James Forrest, Charlie Cowie, Harold Roper, Lady June Hobson, Jim and Doris Mabel Grierson, Cicely Atkins, Enid and Mardi Marden-Ranger, Maisie Bateman, Enid and North Surridge, Sir Lionel Leach, the Bostocks, the Browns, Margot Williams, Martin Gibbons, Alan Wright, Brush Taylor, Barbara Butler, Lieutenant General Sir Gordon Jolly), Curly Emery (Imperial Bank); H B Prior, Bruce Hay (Simla Bank), Gordon Innes (Steels), Ronnie MacRobert, 'Shorty' Marsh, Doris Cooke (wife of Bob Cooke, Military Police), Pakenham, the Walsh's, Pakenham, Brian Carey, Tom and Anne Cowie, 'Sippy' Wilkinson, Cyril and Eve Paget, Edmeades (Steels), Mrs MacLaren (Stewart Smith's and Allens), Norah and Cyril Walters, the MacDonalds (27 Windermere Park), Simla, he complained was 'simply lousy with Burma people'. He mentioned the Dunkleys, John Wise, Johnny Rowland, the Martin-Lees, the Foucars, Wilkes, the McLarens (Mandalay Brewery), Columbine, Toshi Stoneham, Bill Bush, Treston, 'Beaver' Bensley, the Buchanses, Hippy, Peter and Jimmie Poynton, the Witchers and the Weatherfields, the Horrockses, Peter and Daphne, Slade ICS (Customs Member on the Revenue Board), Wilfred and Gwen Packham-Walshe, Rodney and Mollie Blake and Mr Frane (Henderson's Marine Superintendent).

35 For this he was paid the princely sum of 4,000 Rs per month and given the substantive rank of Lieutenant Colonel (Grade 1).

36 The president was a 'decent little man – a Hindu Sessions Judge' and the other member was a Moslem lawyer.

37 The function was hosted by Sir Godfrey Davies the Chief Justice of the Court in Karachi

38 *Southport Guardian and Southwest Lancashire Chronicle, 29 March 1944*: Appointed Indian High Court Judge: Birkdale man's jungle trek to elude Japs. 'Three weeks of tortuous trekking through Burmese jungles ... and on one occasion being saved from almost certain death by an Indian peasant, Mr R Clark ... is waiting to take up an appointment in the Indian High Court.... Forty-nine years old Mr Clark was a barrister in Burma before the Japanese invasion.... With five companions he marched on foot to the Indian frontier.... Mr Clark's friends were all younger and more active men than he ... and at one point he was so exhausted that he begged them to go on and leave him.... Shortly afterwards he found himself waist deep in a treacherous swamp and would have perished but for an Indian peasant and his wife. With their help and the use of their bullock, Mr Clark was rescued from the swamp and the peasant insisted on sharing his scanty food stock.' Clark's journey from Myitkyina to Ledo, entitled 'Burma Journey', is also described in the National Review (June, July and August 1943).

39 His house is now the exquisite Linthwaite House Hotel, which is run expertly and charmingly by Reginald Clark's daughter and granddaughter.

40 Government House was more or less undamaged in the war. Much of the furniture was intact when the Dorman-Smiths returned to Rangoon in 1945.

41 Lady Dorman-Smith Diary, 4 May 1942.

42 Thomas Cook was married to Lady Dorman-Smith's daughter, Jacqueline. After he was killed in action. Jacqueline later married Captain Peter Homfray..

43 She flew on a China National Aviation Corporation plane and her son-in-law met her at the aerodrome.

44 Gallagher O'Dowd, *Retreat in the East*, London: Viking Press, 1942.

45 Wagg visited Lady Dorman-Smith on 18 December 1942. See Alfred Wagg, *A Million Died: A Story of the War in the Far East*, London: Nicholson and Watson, 1943.

46 For the saga of Richard de Graaf Hunter and J. S. Vorley, see Michael D. Leigh, *The Evacuation of Civilians from Burma: Analysing the 1942 Colonial Disaster*, London: Bloomsbury, 2014. Hunter came to lunch on 30 December.

47 MacDougall and Rossington accompanied Dorman-Smith on the flight from Myitkyina to Dum Dum. The circumstances of their escape from Myitkyina are described in, Leigh, *The Evacuation of Civilians from Burma*.

48 On 2 January 1944 the news came through that Lady Dorman-Smith's son-in-law, Captain Thomas Cook (Jacqueline's husband) had been killed in action.

49 IOR EUR MSS F260/4, Apedaile Papers: Summary of a letter written from Gordon Apedaile to his 'Uncle Fred' on 1 July 1942:

50 They had been members of the Burma War Comfort Association in Rangoon and had caused Lady Dorman-Smith much grief in the old days.

51 *Towards a Greater Burma*, Speeches on Burma Reconstruction at the Anglo-Burma Conference Dinner, given by H. E. the Rt. Hon. Sir Reginald Dorman-Smith, GBE, Governor of Burma, Simla, 1944 (Cambridge Centre for Asian Studies)

52 George Algernon West, (1893–1980); Went to Burma with SPG in 1921; served at St. Peter's Mission in Toungoo; His first wife, Helen Margaret Scott-Moncrieff died in 1925. West succeeded Norman Henry Tubbs as Bishop of Rangoon in December 1934. In June 1941 he was unconscious for three weeks after a motor accident. He was recuperating in India when the Japanese invaded Burma. In 1942 West went to the United States as Bishop of Atlanta. In April 1943 he married Grace Hay in North Carolina and they returned to India later that month. He returned to Burma on 9 July 1945 and continued as Bishop of Rangoon until 1954. In1965 he became Assistant Bishop of Durham.

53 Here Bishop West was quoting from Sir John Tait.

54 Mr Elliot (Anglo-Burman Member of the House of Representatives), Mr Campagnac, MBE, Mr Gibson, and Mr Kirkham were among the leading Anglo-Burmans exiled in India.

55 Robert Ely McGuire, ICS, b. 1901; Secretary Government of Burma 1942–5; Deputy Director Civil Affairs, 1945; Commissioner, Magwe Division, 1946–7; Secretary to the Governor of Burma, 1947.

56 Churchill had ordered Dorman-Smith to leave Burma immediately by plane rather than to risk capture.

57 J. S. Vorley was Dorman-Smith's main critic. He was a rival of Richard de Graaf Hunter. A Governor of Burma might normally expect to be included on the Honour's List. Lady Dorman-Smith was scathing when all Churchill gave her husband was a bouquet of flowers.

Chapter 8

1 The following account is based on the daily entries in Lady Dorman-Smith's *Diary* from 16 October 1945–5 August 1946.

2 Government House looked much the same as it had done from the outside, but it was a mess inside and the outlying buildings and gardens were in a terrible state.

3 The Surrender Ceremony took place in the 12th Army HQ. The Japanese generals lined up behind General Kimura. They stepped forward one by one and handed over their swords to General Stopford. Lady Dorman-Smith noted that they were all untidily dressed in dull green uniforms, crumpled white shirts and 'awful top boots'. The programme for the rest of the week read as follows: 17 October, Civic Reception; 18 October, afternoon tea with CAS (B) officers; 20 October, lunch aboard HMS *Cleopatra*, and a 'Welcome Dinner' hosted by Mr Justice Ba U and Sir Nya Bu at the Orient Club; 21 October, RAF service in the Methodist Church; 22 October, a tea party hosted by the Burma Muslims and Tyabyi & Co.

4 The glittering guest list included, Colonel Moffatt, Colonel Craddock, Lady Carlisle, Brigadier Wodehouse (Toc-H), Miss Hinden (UNRRA), Sir Hubert Rance, Sir Hugh Saunders, General Symes, General Wood, Brigadier Armstrong, Sir Soan Telfer-Smollett, Sir Paw Tun, Mr Justice Ba U, U Htoon Aung Kyaw, Lord Allanbroke, General Sykes, U Pu, Mr Schleiter (USA Consul), Sir Victor Sasson, Admund Angelieu (Governor of French Indo-China), Mrs Thomas (Burma Office), Brigadier Thomas, Air Chief Marshall Sir Keith, Lady Pack, Miss White (YMCA) Mr Owen (Indian Trade Commissioner), The Moderator of the Scots Kirk, and Isabelle Hutton (wife of General Hutton).

5 Major-General Sir Hubert Rance had taken over military control of Burma after the liberation of Rangoon in 1945. He had to give permission before Dorman-Smith could return as Governor in October 1945.

6 Donnison Papers, MSS/EUR/B357/f 374/OIOC; Jehu revealed this over a drink in a bar in India.

7 Aung San had allegedly killed the headman of Thebyugone village in front of a large crowd.

8 Excellent accounts of Aung San's life are provided in, Silverstein, Introductory Essay in Maung Maung's '*Political Legacy of Aung San*', p. 3; Aung San, undated mimeograph, '*Burma's Challenge*' and, Maurice Collis, *Last and First in Burma (1941–1948)*, London: Faber & Faber, 1956, p. 270. Aung San was born in Natmauk, educated at the Anglo-Vernacular National High School in Yenangyaung and University of Rangoon. He described how a love of politics as a student interrupted his 'brilliant academic career'. He failed his degree in 1938. He co-founded the All Burma Students Union and was a leader of the student strike in 1936. In 1938, he became Secretary General of *Dobama Asiayone.* He also served on the Committee of the *All Burma Cultivators' League* and co-organized the *Freedom-Bloc* (a coalition between *Dobama Asiayone* and Ba Maw's *Sinyetha).* In the 1930s Aung San flirted with communism, nationalism, socialism, Marxism, and the ideas of Nehru, Subhas Chandra Bose and Sun Yat Sen. He supported the idea of non-violent peasant socialism as advocated by Dr Ba Maw's *Sinyetha* Party and Thakin Mya's *All Burma Cultivator's League.*

9 Most of the recruits were Burmese exiles living in Thailand.

10 In July 1942 the BIA was reorganized as the BDA.

11 Ba Maw (1893–1977), born in Maubin; graduated from the University of Calcutta in 1924 and was then awarded a doctorate from the University of Bordeaux. He was a lawyer when he returned to Burma; he defended Saya San in 1931, and advocated Burmese independence. He was elected to the legislature and served as prime minister from 1937 to 1939. He was arrested and imprisoned for sedition in1940. In August 1943 the Japanese military authorities appointed him *Adipadi* (head of state) in the nominally independent Burmese Government. Ba Maw escaped to Japan in 1945 but was later imprisoned. He returned to Burma in 1947 and was arrested (but immediately released) on suspicion of complicity in the murder of Aung San. Under General Ne Win Ba Maw was imprisoned from 1963 to 1968. He founded the Mahabama (Greater Burma) Party and died in Rangoon.

12 After the war, the AFO was renamed the Anti-Fascist People's Freedom League (AFPFL)

13 In 1944 Thakin Soe had persuaded Aung San to join the Burmese Communist Party. He discovered it was bitterly divided by warring factions.

14 The distance from London to Rangoon by air was 5,573 miles and by sea, it was 9,000 miles.
15 Labour won by a massive majority of 146 seats.
16 See, P. H. Lindert, *Key Currencies and Gold 1900–1913*, Princeton Studies in International Finance No. 24, Princeton: Princeton University Press,1969, Finlo Roher, *What's a little debt between friends*, BBC, 10 May 2006. Some of the debts predated the Napoleonic wars and $4.4 billion-worth of debt dated from World War I.
17 This was on condition that any items still being used after the war would be purchased at 10 per cent of the production cost.
18 The transport infrastructure, power stations, public buildings and factories had to be rebuilt, five million houses had been destroyed during the war and 18 million tons of shipping had been lost.
19 The Ottawa Conference of 1932 gave preference to goods traded between colonies and dominions. It worked against Britain's interest. Between 1934 and 1938 exports to the dominions fell while imports from the dominions rose, increasing Britain's balance of trade deficit.
20 A Parliamentary question eventually revealed this secret agreement.
21 See, Heinlein, Frank; *British Government Policy and Decolonisation 1945–63: Scrutinising the Official Mind*, Abingdon: Routledge, 2002, pp. 5, 19 and footnotes 4 (p. 73), 36 and 37 (p. 75).
22 Even tiny shifts in the US economy tended to put the pound sterling under intense pressure.
23 The 'First Empire' was divided into two sections – a *formal* empire consisting of colonies (including Burma) inhabited by indigenous peoples, and an *informal* empire comprised of former Ottoman and German territories mandated to Britain in 1918 under Article 22 of the League of Nations Covenant. The 'Second Empire' consisted of the 'Dominions' (Canada, Australia, South Africa and New Zealand) acquired between 1760 and 1815 and settled by British emigrants. Dominion status was embodied in the Statute of Westminster of 1931, which created a two-tier structure with 'white' dominions at the top and 'indigenous' colonies at the bottom. By 1965 17 'non-white' former colonies had been admitted to the British Commonwealth.
24 Other undertakings included the liberalization of international trade, guarantees for freedom of the seas and international standards for labor
25 Roosevelt confirmed this at a press conference on 2 January 1942. F. D. R's son, Elliott Roosevelt also insisted that his father intended to eradicate *all* forms of colonialism and Wendell Willkie (Roosevelt's Special Envoy) assured Chinese leaders in Chunking in October 1942 that America would eliminate all forms of colonialism

26 Off the record, Roosevelt's son confirmed that his father was determined to eliminate colonialism after the war, and in Chunking in October 1942 Wendell Willkie (Roosevelt's Special Envoy) told Chiang Kai-shek that 'colonial days' and the age of 'the empire of nations over other nations' were gone forever. In private Churchill conceded that 'without America, the Empire will not stand'.

27 Churchill announced this in his Mansion House Speech of 10 November 1942. His stance explains why he was unwilling to discuss Burmese independence with U Saw during their bizarre meeting in London.

28 Ronald Robinson, 'The Eccentric Idea of Imperialism, with or without Empire', in W. J. Mommsen and J. Osterhammel (eds), *Imperialism and After: Continuities and Discontinuities*, London: Allen & Unwin, 1986, pp. 267–289.

29 Partha Sarathi Gupta, *Imperialism and the British Labour Movement 1914–1964.* London: Macmillan, Cambridge Commonwealth Series, 1975.

30 Heinlein, chapter 12, 'Conclusion', p. 387.

31 The Fabian Society was founded in 1884 and was instrumental in the setting up the Labour Party in 1900. Fabians preferred gradualism to revolution and were among the first to advocate a minimum wage, a universal healthcare system, the abolition of hereditary peerages, a national education system and a welfare state. On the other hand, in 1900 *Fabianism and the Empire* supported Britain's involvement in the Boer War.

32 Obafemi Awolowa later became premier of Western Nigeria. Lee Kuan Yew had nothing but disdain for the Fabians, blaming 'their' welfare state for undermining British society and ruining the economy.

33 In *Forgotten Armies: The Fall of British Asia 1941–1945*, London: Allen Lane, Penguin Books, 2004., p. 26.Christopher Bayly and Tim Harper point out that Field-Marshal Slim had warned Churchill that 90 per cent of troops in the XIV Army intended to vote Labour, and that there were several instances of small-scale mutinies among British troops serving in Southeast Asia.

34 Francis Wheen, *Tom Driberg: His Life and Indiscretions*, London: Chatto, 1990, p. 2.

35 Bayly and Harper, *Forgotten Armies*, pp. 95–96.

36 Bevin (General Secretary of the Transport and General Workers' Union) argued that the sale of British capital goods to India was more important than the conditions of workers in the Indian subcontinent. He expressed pride in the fact that Britain was 'at the centre of a great Empire and Commonwealth of Nations' and he wanted to retain Britain's great power status.

37 Most British skilled craft workers supported Bevin's stance. Heinlein claims that the predictions of both Lenin and Rhodes who were aware of the attraction of imperial profits and protectionism.

38 J. M. Keynes' theories were expounded in 1936 in *The General Theory of Employment, Interest, and Money*, London: Palgrave Macmillan, 1936. He advocated increased public spending to stave off a 1930s-style Depression.
39 The extraordinary range of measures included, the Family Allowance Act (1945), National Insurance Act (1945); Industrial Injuries Act (1946); National Assistance Act (1948) and the National Health Service Act (5 July 1948), the Children's Act (1948), R.A. Butler's Education Act (1944), the Town and Country Planning Act (1947) One and a quarter million council houses were built between 1945 and 1951. The New Towns Act (1946) authorized new towns in Stevenage, Basildon, Newton Aycliffe and Peterlee.
40 Arthur Attwood and D. C. Brayford were the high profile defendants
41 The men had just returned from a long tour of duty in Java.
42 Bayly and Harper, *Forgotten Armies*, p. 98, In the last pre-war census, in 1931, peninsular Malaya's population was 3.79 million of which 49 per cent were classified as Malays, 34 per cent Chinese and 15 per cent Indians. Singapore was already a major Chinese city. Had it been included in the statistics the proportion of Malays would have fallen to 44 per cent. Britain's sociopolitical plan was the unification of ten existing Malayan authorities into a single plural society under the British Crown.
43 One intended consequence was the rise of the Malaya Communist Party.
44 See Martin-Harvey/21/5 F.O. 371/31867. The issue was first mooted in 1943 in correspondence exchanged between Dorman-Smith, Leo Amery and Anthony Eden. It was agreed that Burma could be more easily be *re-conquered* if a ring of Western-controlled territories around it – hence the idea of a British protectorate in Thailand
45 Nicholas Tarling, *Britain, Southeast Asia and the onset of the Cold War, 1945–1950*, Cambridge: Cambridge University Press, 1998, pp. 22–36 and 108–128.
46 Bayly and Harper, *Forgotten Armies*, p.140.
47 Vichy France signed an armistice with the axis powers on 22 June 1940 shortly before Major-General Takuma Nishimura attacked Vichy Indochina where more than 100,000 French citizens were living. The Armistice Agreement allowed 6,000 Japanese troops to be permanently stationed in Indochina and 25,000 to be in transit at any one time. French settlers reported the whereabouts of British Special Forces and worked with the Japanese in suppressing local communist risings.
48 On 9 March 1945, the French started to disobey orders. Japanese forces carried out a major purge of Vichy supporters. Japan also established a quasi-independent government in Hanoi.
49 The 32nd Infantry Brigade under Brigadier E.C.V. Woodford and the Indian 16th Light Cavalry.

50 The reinforcements included the RAF 273rd Squadron, the British 14/13 Frontier Rifles, the 3rd Brigade of the 100th Division under Brigadier C.H.B. Rodham, and the 14/13th Indian infantry regiment under Lt.-Col. Gates.
51 Bayly and Harper, *Forgotten Armies*, p.159.
52 General Sir Alexander Frank Philip Christison, GBE, CB, DSO, MC (1893–1993) served with distinction during the Burma Campaign. In September 1945, he was called upon to deputize for Admiral Lord Louis Mountbatten as commander of SEAC. He took the surrender of the Japanese Seventh Area Army and the Japanese South Sea Fleet in Singapore on 3 September 1945. In 1946, Christison took up the appointment of Allied Commander of forces in the Dutch East Indies.
53 That is, men of the 29th Seaforth Highlanders and 23rd the Indian Division.
54 He had been Governor of East Java before the war.
55 It was estimated that up to 6000 Indian troops, 20,000 armed regulars and 120,000 civilians were involved in the skirmishes.
56 Christison estimated that there had been 10,000 casualties including the deaths of 600 Allied soldiers.
57 Nationalists who had collaborated with the Japanese fought against nationalists who had not collaborated.
58 Bayly and Harper, *Forgotten Armies*, pp. 217–223.

Chapter 9

1 War Cabinet W.M. (43) Minute 3 IOR: L/PO/9/6, 14 April 1943. W.M. (43) 54th Conclusions, Secret: Burma, Future Policy.
2 Leopold (Leo) S. Amery 1873–1955: born in India, son of Charles Frederick Amery, an Indian Forestry officer and Elisabeth Johanna Saphir, a Hungarian Jewess; educated at Harrow (contemporary of Winston Churchill), at Balliol College Oxford where he gained a First in Classics, and a fellow of All Souls College. During the Boer War, Amery was a *Times* correspondent; critical of Sir Redvers Henry Buller, an associate of Sidney and Beatrice Webb; Liberal Unionist MP for Birmingham South, 1911–1945; Parliamentary under-secretary in Lloyd George's wartime national government: helped draft the Balfour Declaration; critic of the League of Nations and the 'facile slogan of self-determination'; First Lord of the Admiralty 1922–1924; Colonial Secretary in1924: Critic of Appeasement; anti-communist; distrusted Franklin D Roosevelt's administration, famously attacked Chamberlain in 1940; quoting Oliver Cromwell, 'I say let us have done with you. In the name of God, go!' As Secretary of State for India, he complained that Churchill knew 'as much of the Indian problem as George III did of the American colonies'; lost his seat in the 1945 election.

3 L. S. Amery to Sir Reginald Dorman-Smith, IOR: L/PO/9/6.

4 L. S. Amery to Sir Reginald Dorman-Smith, IOR: L/PO/9/6, Burma Office 15 April 1943, p. 26.

5 IOR: l/PO/9/8, Conservative Party MPs Burma Sub-Committee, Report, 11 August 1944, pp. 69–70.

6 Sir Arthur Bruce, KBE: born in 1895, arrived in Burma in 1920; manager of the BBTC from 1926–1947; from1944–1945, Commercial Adviser to the Governor.

7 Hugh Tinker (ed.), *Burma the Struggle for Independence* 1944–1948, Vol. 1, HMSO, London: 1983: Narrative of Events, pp. 990–999.

8 Aung San claimed that project boards were nothing more 'than a device for re-establishing British companies at Burma's expense'.

9 IOR MSS EUR E 362/3.

10 Thomas Lewis Hughes (b 1897), Secretary to the Governor of Burma 1942–1946.

11 IOR: MSS EUR E 362/5, Thomas Lewis Hughes CBE, ICS (1897–1980). Burma 1923–1939, Governor's Private Secretary 1942–1946, pp. 1013–1014.

12 Sir John Wise, KCMG, ICS: born1890; Burma from1914–1947: Counsellor to the Governor, 1940–46: Adviser to the Secretary of State for Burma, 1946–1947.

13 BL/IOR/MSS/EUR/E 362/18, p.1032.

14 Sir Raibeart Maclntyre MacDougall, Esq, ICS, Secretary to the Government of Burma in the Department of Education.

15 Tinker (ed.), *Burma, Struggle for Independence*, Vol. 2, no.116, pp. 159–162, IB (46), PRO: CAB 134/342: India and Burma Committee, 26 November 1946.

16 Tinker (ed.), *Burma, Struggle for Independence*, Vol. 2, p. 224–5, no. 161, pp. 224–225: Extract from *Dawn* Newspaper on 6.1.47. IOL: SM 20, Report of General Aung San's broadcast from Delhi.

17 BL/IOR/M/4/2555, Letter from U Nu to Sir Stafford Cripps, 9. 9. 47, PRO: CAB 127/151.

18 Frederick William Pethick-Lawrence, 1st Baron Pethick-Lawrence PC (1871–1961): son of wealthy Unitarians and Liberals: educated Eton and Trinity College, Cambridge; barrister; married Emmeline Pethick, active socialist and women's suffrage campaigner in 1901; involved in the Labour Party and in the Women's Social and Political Union (WSPU); served a prison sentence in 1912 after Christabel Pankhurst's window-smashing campaign; a founding member of the Union of Democratic Control (UDC), an anti-war organization; 1918 – worked on a farm as a conscientious objector; 1923 MP for Leicester West; Financial Secretary to the Treasury 1929–1931; 1935, MP for Edinburgh East; 1942 Leader of the Opposition; 1945: Baron Pethick-Lawrence; 1945–1947, Secretary of State for India and Burma; 1947 involved in negotiations leading to India's independence in 1947.

19 Tinker (ed.) *Burma: The Struggle for Independence* 1944–1948 Vol.1 211 Burma Conversations: B.UK. (47) 21 January 47. PRO: CAB.

20 BL/IOR/M/4/2554, Minutes of Governor's Executive Council Meeting 6January 1947.

21 BL/IOR/MSS/EUR/M/4/2554159, Minutes of the Executive Council Meeting, 6 January 1947, the mysterious net loan of £8.5M (or was it £22M) was discussed. HMG had supposedly given it in 1945–1946. The telegram emphasized that it was not a gift and that it must be repaid within a year. It was also reported that the Burma Government had asked if it could approach the US Government for a loan. The reply was that HMG would not object.

22 Sir Arthur Bruce, Report, December 1945. Nb. in 1945 £1 was worth about £40.80 in 2017 values.

23 Tinker (ed.), *Burma, Struggle for Independence*, Vol. 1, p. 998, Lord Pethick-Lawrence to Sir Reginald Dorman Smith, 18 December 1945.

24 Sir Richard Stafford Cripps (1889–1952); wealthy barrister; entered Parliament as a Labour MP in 1931. He advocated cooperation with the communists and was expelled from the Labour Party in 1939; Ambassador to the USSR, 1940–1942; member of Churchill's War Cabinet in 1942 and was later Minister of Aircraft Production. He rejoined the Labour Party in 1945; president of the Board of Trade (1945–1947); Chancellor of the Exchequer (1947–1950) in Attlee's Government. He was credited with laying the foundations of post-war prosperity. Cripps presided over the so-called age of austerity, keeping rationing in place and maintaining full employment with static wages.

25 Tinker (ed.), *Burma, Struggle for Independence*, Volume II, 165, PRO: CAB 127/95, 8 Jan 1947 Chancellor of the Exchequer to Secretary of State for Burma.

26 Tinker (ed.), *Burma, Struggle for Independence*, Volume II, 211 Burma Conversations: B.UK. (47) 21 January 47. PRO: CAB 133/3

27 Some subtexts underlay the discussions. One was that Burmese leaders were aware that £30million for the purposes of rehabilitation had been granted to Malta. However, although Burmese leaders may disagree with the following analysis, the committee agreed that Burma and Malta were not analogous. Malta was a 'vital strategic point in the Empire' whereas Burma was not, and Malta was administered as a colony whereas Burma was not. It was also noted that Burmese politicians were over-optimistic about the chances of getting loans from India and the United States.

28 For example, the debts related to the separation railway rolling stock.

29 These are described in Chapter 9.

30 The Viceroy of India, Lord Wavell, had met General Aung San on 4 January. On 8 January 1947 he wrote privately to Lord Pethick-Lawrence, describing Aung San as 'an interesting personality and a strong character, though unattractive and I doubt how much wisdom he has got'. On 14 January 1947 he wrote again, saying, 'your conversations with Aung San will be difficult. He struck me as a suspicious, ignorant, but determined little tough'.

31 Tinker (ed.), *Burma, Struggle for Independence*, 220, Burma Conversations: B. (UKR) (47), 22. 1. 47, PRO: CAB 133/3.
32 Tinker (ed.), *Burma, Struggle for Independence*, 235, Burma Conversations: United Kingdom Papers, B.U.K. (47), PRO: CAB 133/3, 24 January 1947, Financial Questions.
33 Tinker (ed.), *Burma, Struggle for Independence* Burma Conversations; B.C. (47) 10th Meeting, Record PRO: Cab 133/3, p. 376.
34 AFPFL won 173 of the 210 seats, the Communist Party won 7 and the Karen Youth Organisation won 19.
35 BL/IOR/MSS/EUR/M/4/2677337, Telegram from Sir Gilbert Laithwaite to P.G.E. Nash, 25 April 47The fall in rice output was despite anticipated rice export of 900,000 tons in 1947 and an increase of 7,760M acres under cultivation in1946–1947, representing a total increase of 1,150,000 over 1945–1946.
36 IOR/ MSS/EUR/L/PO/9/4, Burma Treaty, Hugh Dalton to Clement Attlee, 11 October 1947.
37 William Francis Hare, 5th Earl of Listowell, GCMG, PC, (1906–1997); educated at Eton College, Balliol College, Oxford, Magdalene College, Cambridge and King's College, London (awarded a PhD in 1932); member of the London County Council for East Lewisham1937–1946, and for Battersea North, 1952–1957. He entered the House of Lords in November 1931; Labour Party Whip in House of Lords from 1941 to 1944; Under-Secretary of State for India 1944–47; Postmaster-General, 1945–1947; Secretary of State for India 1947 and Secretary of State for Burma 1947–1948; Minister of State for Colonial affairs 1948–50; Governor General of Ghana 1957–1960. He spoke for the last time in the House of Lords in July 1995 aged 88.
38 BL/IOR/MSS/EUR/M/4/2677, Telegram from Earl of Listowel to Sir Hubert Rance, 30 May 1947.
39 BL/MSS/EUR/IOR/M/4/2590, Cabinet: India and Burma Committee (chaired by Clement Attlee), IB (47), 9 January 1947.
40 IOR: MSS/EUR/R/8/13, Dorman-Smith to U Tin Tut, 17 April 1943. U Tin Tut, CBE was minister of finance and deputy prime Minister in Aung San's pre-independence government and was instrumental in the Panglong negotiations. He was not present at the fateful cabinet meeting on 19 July 1947, which claimed the lives of Aung San and six other cabinet ministers. After independence in 1948, he became minister of foreign affairs. He was educated at Dulwich and Queen's College, Cambridge and was the first Burman to become an ICS officer. U Tin Tut was killed by an assassin's bomb in Sparks Street on 18 September 1948.
41 BL/MSS/IOR: R/8/13, U Tin Tut to Dorman-Smith, 18 April 1943.

42 Tinker (ed.), *Burma, Struggle for Independence* 365 Sir Hubert Rance to the Earl of Listowell, 29 May 47, Top Secret p.p. 365–366
43 Tinker (ed.), *Burma, Struggle for Independence*, Listowell, telegram 1218, 30 May 47, on future Indian policy.
44 Tinker (ed.), *Burma, Struggle for Independence*, 442, Speech by Bogyoke Aung San, 13 July 1947, pp. 442–443.

Chapter 10

1 Losses in Borneo and Sarawak (excluding oil damage) were estimated to be £8 million.
2 £1 in 1947 was worth roughly £38.50 in today's values. Hence the BOC claim was just under £2.0bn.
3 Michael D. Leigh, *The Evacuation of Civilians from Burma: Analysing the 1942 Colonial Disaster*, London: Bloomsbury, 2014, pp. 211–225 and pp. 126–132.
4 Losses in Borneo and Sarawak (excluding oil damage) were estimated to be £8 million.
5 Hansard, House of Commons Debate 8 December 1948, Volume 459 sections 474–83, Colonel Crosthwaite-Eyre (New Forest and Christchurch).
6 Hansard, House of Commons Debate 8 December 1948, Volume 459, §479].
7 The BOC had four associated companies – Burmah Oil Co. (Burma Trading) Ltd., Burmah Oil Co. (Burma Concessions) Ltd., Burmah Oil Co. (Overseas) Ltd. and Burmah Oil Co. (Pipe Lines) Ltd.
8 Lord Shepherd pointed out that the Anglo-Saxon Company in Malaya was also destroyed under contract. The total figure of its losses were estimated at £12.5 million of which the Government contributed £2.5 million – that is, 20 per cent of the total estimate Both BOC and Anglo-Saxon were destroyed for the same economic and military purposes. Anglo-Saxon received 20 per cent, and was satisfied; while the BOC received 27 per cent and was dissatisfied.
9 Hugh Tinker (ed.), *Burma: The Struggle for Independence*, 1944–48, Volumes 1 and II, London, Her Majesty's Stationery Office, 1984; 211 Burma Conversations: B.UK. (47) 21 January 47. PRO: CAB 133/3.
10 Hansard, Volume 264, c.c. 730–44, House of Lords Debate, Second Reading, 25 March 1965. Appeals from the First Division of the Court of Session, April 21: Lord Reid.
11 Hansard, Volume 264, c.c. 730–44, House of Lords Debate, Second Reading, 25 March 1965.
12 Tinker (ed.), *Burma: The Struggle for Independence*; 216 Cabinet: India and Burma Committee IB (47) 22. I. 47, PRO: CAB 134/343, p. 315.

13 H. J. Chubb and C. L. D Duckworth, *The Irrawaddy Flotilla Company Limited 1865–1950*, National Maritime Museum: Maritime Monographs and Reports, No. 7, 1973, p. 18.
14 Irrawaddy Flotilla Company Prospectus, 1930.
15 H. J. Chubb and C. L. D Duckworth, *The Irrawaddy Flotilla Company Limited 1865–1950*, National Maritime Museum: Maritime Monographs and Reports, No. 7, 1973, pp. 13–18, and 75–76.
16 Captain Watts, Trek from Katha to Imphal, Diary entry for 3 May 1942.
17 Long after the war the Inland Water Transport Board still operated 400 vessels and employed 4,000 staff.
18 Colonel Crosthwaite-Eyre (1913–1978), son of Major John Symons Crosthwaite and Dorothy Muriel Eyre; educated Downside and Trinity College, Cambridge; married Baroness Maria Alexandra, daughter of Baron Heinrich von Puthon, of Schloss Mirabel, Salzburg in 1939; colonel in the Royal Marines in 1945; elected as Conservative MP for New Forest and Christchurch in 1945 until his resignation in 1968.
19 Hansard, Volume 459, c.c. 474–83, House of Commons Debate, British Assets, Burma (Compensation), 8 December 1948.
20 Colonel Crossthwaite-Eyre cited two other examples – first, was a small private rice-producing company, Kyautaga Estates, which owned 40,000 acres. It was unable to operate after the Burmese Government encouraged banditry and dacoity in the area and then expropriated the estate without compensation. Second, was Messrs. Foucar and Company, Limited, Teak Estates, whose assets were seized, also without compensation.
21 Hansard, House of Commons, Volume 459, British Assets Debate, §479]].
22 Hansard, House of Commons, Volume 459, British Assets Debate, 474–483, Paragraph, 482; Colonel Crosthwaite-Eyre.
23 Matthew Foley, *The New Cold War and National Assertions in Southeast Asia: Britain, the United States and Burma, 1948–1962*, London: Routledge: Studies in the Modern History of Asia, Abingdon, 2012, p. 65.
24 William Strang Steel founded the company in 1870. He was a successful Glasgow merchant who moved to London in 1873. He took over the commercial interests of James Finlay & Co Ltd. Finlay became a leading shareholder in Steels.
25 Their earliest forest concessions were Saing Yane, Indawgyi Valley and Yonbin Forest. The Burmese Government nationalized the teak forests in 1948.
26 Indo-Burma Petroleum Co. merged with the BOC in 1954.
27 National Archives, BT/228/63, Steel Brother & Co Ltd., Compensation Claims. J. T. Nelson to Army HQ, 28 April 1942.

28 National Archives, Letter from K. W. Foster, Secretary to the Government of Burma, to Under Secretary of State for Burma, Burma Office, 8 March 1945.
29 National Archives, BT/228/63, Steel Brother & Co Ltd, Compensation Claims.
30 National Archives, T & 6c, 102 62/139, Burma Scorched Earth Policy, Steel Brothers & Co Ltd v Lord Advocate.
31 National Archives, Compensation for War Damage Losses in Burma, Files BT 228/63, TS 58/612 andT296/131, Letters from the Assistant Secretary of the Board of Trade Insurance and Companies Department: 'Summary of Losses due to War Damage Sustained by Consolidated Cotton & Oil Mills Ltd, Burma, Company Ltd, Steels Lashio Agency Ltd and Steel Brothers & Company Ltd', dated 24 February 1950, 23 March 1953.
32 National Archives C0825/80/7. The file contains thirty-nine lengthy letters relating to this one dispute.
33 Tin Dredges, 'Stop: Terrorism in Burma', *Sydney Morning Herald*, 8 February 1950.
34 For example, the author, the son of evacuees, has no birth certificate – it was lost in the rush out of Burma. After sixteen years in Burma, his parents had only a few odds and ends and a couple of photographs proving that they had once been there.
35 BL/IOR/MSS/EUR/215/40: *Lady Dorman Smith's Diary*, 23 February 1941.
36 BL/IOR/MSS/EUR/E/215/326: Dorman-Smith, *Unpublished Memoirs* pp. 11–12.
37 IOR/MSS/EUR/D1080/7/7 Maybury Papers: Letter to Secretary to the Government of Burma, Home Department, 30 January 42.
38 IOR/MSS/EUR/D1080/7/7 Maybury Papers Inventory of possessions.

Chapter 11

1 Dr. Maung Maung, *A Trial in Burma: The Assassination of Aung San*, The Hague: Martinus Nijhoff Publishers, 1962 (Second Edition: Yangon: Unity Publishing House, 2012).
2 See Angelene Naw, *Aung San and the Struggle for Burmese Independence*, Bangkok: Nordic Institute of Asian Studies, Silkworm Books, 2001.
3 Others in this camp included Brigadier Prescott (Deputy Director of CAS (B) and formerly Inspector General of Police), Brigadier Lindop (Deputy CAS (B) officer in the X1V Army), and Air Chief Marshal Sir Philip Joubert (Head of the Civil Affairs Organisation and former RAF C-I-C, Coastal Command).
4 Field Marshal Sir William Slim. *Defeat into Victory*, London: Cassell, 1956.
5 U Tin Tut, *U Aung San: A Memoir*, Burmese Review, 25 August 1947.

6 Letter from Aung San to Mountbatten, 25 September 1945.
7 *Defence of Burma*, 30 January 1945.
8 *Problems of Burma's Freedom*': op cit.
9 *Defence of Burma*, 30 January 1945.
10 *Bogyoke Aung San's Address*, Aung San, op cit.
11 Tom Driberg, MP, Speech in the House of Commons, 2 November 1945 (HANSARD Vol.415, columns 800–803).
12 Rev. G. Appleton, 'The Burmese Viewpoint', *Asiatic Review*, London, July 1948.
13 Aung San's address to the supreme council of the AFPFL, August 1946.
14 British Representatives: Mr C. R. Attlee, (Prime Minister); Mr A.V. Alexander (Minister of Defence); Sir Stafford Cripps (President of the Board of Trade); Earl of Listowel, (Postmaster General); Mr C. P. Mayhew, (Under Secretary of State for Foreign Affairs); and Mr A. G. Bottomley, (Under Secretary of State for the Dominions). Burma Representatives: U Aung San, (Deputy Chairman of the Executive Council); Thakin Mya; U Ba Pe; Thakin Ba Sein; U Saw; U Tin Tut; U Kyaw Nyein; U Aung Than; Thakin Chit; and U Ba Yin. Advisers and officials: Sir David Monteath (Permanent Under Secretary of State for Burma); Sir Gilbert Laithwaite, (Deputy Under Secretary of State for Burma; Sir Raibeart MacDougall (Counsellor to the Governor); U Shwe Baw (Secretary to the Burmese Delegation); Mr C.G. Eastwood, Senior Officer of the Secretariat of the Conference).
15 U Tin Tut, 'It was a Historic Moment', *Burmese Review*, 24 February 1947.
16 Clement Attlee, *As It Happened*, London: Heineman, 1954, p.188.
17 Bogyoke Aung San's broadcast of 4 February 1947 on Burma Radio.
18 It was held from 7 to12 February.
19 U Vum Ko Hau, The Spirit of Panglong,
20 P. G. E. Nash, *Memoirs*, IOR MSS EUR E/362/7.
21 *London Times*, 12 April 1947.
22 '*Fourteen Points*', *Burma's Fight for Freedom*.
23 *The Burman*, 23 March 1947, 'U Aung San's appeal to pay lands revenue, rent and agricultural loans'.
24 Josef Silverstein, *The Political Legacy* of Aung San: Introductory Essay, Data Paper 86, Southeast Asia Program, Department of Asian Studies, Cornell University, Ithaca, New York, 1972, p. 3.
25 Silverstein, *The Political Legacy of Aung San*.
26 Speeches in the Constituent Assembly, 29 July 1947.
27 F. S. Donnison, *British Military Administration in the Far East, 1943–46*, London: H. M Stationery Office, 1956.
28 Maurice Collis, *First and Last in Burma (1941–1948)*, London: Faber & Faber, 1956.

Bibliography

Private Papers

Brown, David, Papers (courtesy of Mr Alastair Brown).

Clark, Reginald, Papers (courtesy of Mrs Diana Kennedy).

Darlington, Papers (courtesy of Ms Lois Knight).

McAdam, Major William, Papers (courtesy of Dr Archie McAdam and Dr Helen McAdam).

Salkeld, P. G. G. Papers (courtesy of Mr John Salkeld).

Unpublished correspondence, diaries and memoirs, India Office Records, British Library

BL/IOR/MSS/EUR/E362/7: P. G. E. Nash, '*Recollection of events leading up to the handover of powers*'.

BL/IOR/MSS/EUR/E/362/7: P.G.E Nash, *Memoirs.*

BL/IOR/MSS/EUR/MSS/F/260/4: Gordon Apedaile, ICS, Defence Secretary, Burma Government.

BL/ IOR/ MSS/ EUR/ F/260/4: Gordon Apedaile, Letter to 'Uncle Fred'.

BL/ IOR/ MSS/ EUR/ D/975/4: Reginald Langham-Carter: *Account of my Trek from Burma to India.*

BL/ IOR/ MSS/ EUR/ D/975/4: Reginald Langham-Carter Hotel Cecil, Calcutta Letter to his Mother from Calcutta, 20 August 1942.

BL/ IOR /MSS/EUR/1028: Alwyn Henry Seppings: Memoir 1932–46.

BL/ IOR/MSS/EUR/C/554: R. S. Wilkie, ICS, Commissioner, Sagaing Division: *Diary of a Journey from Myitkyina to Margherita.*

BL/OIR/MSS/EUR /C/581: Alister Rose, *A Short History of T D Findlay & Son Ltd: East India Merchants 1839–5.*

BL/IOR/MSS/EUR/DIO/80/7/7: Maybury Papers.

BL/IOR/MSS/EUR/Folio/27/930: Lecture given by Brigadier Dysart Whitworth (Officer in Command, Upper Assam) on 14 July 1943. 'The Evacuation of Refugees and the Chinese Fifth Army from the Hukawng Valley into Assam, Summer 1942'. Published in the Royal Central Asian Society Magazine.

BL/IOR/MSS/EUR/F174/1309: Indian Tea Association Report: Commissioned by the Administrator General, *The Evacuation of Troops and Civilians from Burma by the Pangsau Route: Namyang River to Lekhapani, May to July 1942.*

BL/IOR/MSS/EUR/M/41/3/955-B/270/4: undated letter from Miss Z. N. Gilbert to Miss Lou Beale referring to a letter from Mrs Oakley (Lon/14243/43).

BL/IOR/MSS/EUR/ C/816: Edward Wrixon Rossitter (c/o Grindlay & Co, Calcutta), letter to his Mother, 30 October 1942.

BL/IOR/MSS/EUR/F174/633(b): Indian Tea Association: Report for year ended December 1942, the General Committee Calcutta 1943.

BL/IOR/MSS/EUR/112: Letter from Sir John Rowland to wife, August 1942.

BL/IOR/MSS/EUR/F174/1310: Notes of a meeting held in New Delhi between representatives of the Indian Tea Association, the Government of India and the Military High Command, 23 September 1942.

BL/IOR/MSS/EUR/(390) 300: B. R. Pearn, *The Indian in Burma: Racial Relations: Studies in Conflict and Cooperation*, Ledbury: Le Play House Press, 1947.

BL/IOR/MSS/EUR/F/260/4: Apedaile Papers: Letter from Gordon Apedaile to his 'Uncle Fred', 1 July 1942.

BL/IOR/MSS/EUR/B357/f 374/OIOC: Donnison Papers.

BL/IOR/MSS/EUR/215/40: Lady Dorman-Smith's Diary.

BL/IOR/MSS/EUR/E/215: Papers of Sir Reginald Dorman-Smith.

BL/IOR/MSS/EUR/E215/32: Dorman-Smith, Unpublished Memoirs.

BL/IOR/MSS/EUR/L/PO/9/6: War Cabinet Minutes.

BL/IOR/MSS/EUR/L/PO/9/6: Telegram, L. S. Amery to Dorman-Smith, 15 April 43; Telegram no. 1218, Listowell to Dorman-Smith, 30 May 47, and Telegram Laithwaite to Nash, 25 April 47.

BL/IOR/MSS/EUR/E/362/5: T. L. Hughes, Personal Recollections.

Other archival sources

National Archives: BT/228/63: Steel Brothers & Co Ltd, Consolidated Cotton and Oil Mills Ltd, and Steels Lashio Agency Ltd, Compensation.

National Archives: T96/131: Compensation for War Damages Losses in Burma: Steel Brothers & Co Ltd and Indo-Burma Petroleum.

National Archives: TS 58/540–543: Steel Bros & Co Ltd v Lord Advocate, Claim for Compensation.

Imperial War Museum, Oral History Unit, 03413: Lecture 16 January 1978, Rev. Wilfred Crittle, recorded by Gordon Bowerman.

Cambridge Centre for South Asian Studies (CCSAS): Film, *Elephant Man.*
Cambridge Centre for South Asian Studies: Indian Tea Association Papers, Notes on the Official Government Report on the Evacuation of Refugees (Calcutta): Parliamentary Notice, 13 October 1943, London Session, 1942/1943.
Cambridge Centre for South Asian Studies: *Towards a Greater Burma*, Speeches on Burma Reconstruction at the Anglo-Burma Conference Dinner, by H.E. the Rt. Hon. Sir Reginald Dorman-Smith, GBE, Governor of Burma, Simla, 1944.
Durham University Library, Special Collections: 815/5/1–17, C. W. North Papers.
School of African and Oriental Studies, Special Collections: Folder 1(e), Kinchin Papers.

Published primary and secondary sources

Alanbrooke, Field Marshal, *War Diaries 1939–45*, ed. Alex Danchev and Daniel Todman, London: Wiedenfeld and Nicolson, 2001.
Attlee, Clement, *As It Happened*, London: Heineman, 1954.
Badgley, John H. *Politics among the Burmans: A Study of Intermediary Leaders*, Athens: Ohio University Center for International Studies, 1970.
Ba Maw, Dr, *Breakthrough in Burma: Memoirs of a Revolution, 1939–46*, New Haven, CT: Yale University Press, 1968.
Bayly, Christopher, and Harper, Tim, *Forgotten Armies: The Fall of British Asia 1941–1945*, London: Allen Lane, Penguin Books, 2004.
Becka, Jan, *The National Liberation Movement in Burma during the Japanese Occupation Period (1941–1945)*, Prague: Oriental Institute in Academia, 1983.
Brookes, Stephen, *Through the Jungles of Death: A Boy's Escape from Wartime Burma*, London: John Murray, 2000.
Brown, Ian, *A Colonial Economy in Crisis: Burma's Rice Cultivators and the World Depression of the 1930s*, London: Routledge Curzon, 2005.
Charney, M. W., *A History of Modern Burma*, Cambridge: Cambridge University Press, 2009.
Churchill, Winston S., *The Grand Alliance*, London: Cassell, 1950.
Cobain, Ian, *The History Thieves: Secrets, Lies and the Shaping of a Modern Nation*, London: Portobello Books, 2016.
Collis, Maurice, *Last and First in Burma (1941–1948)*, London: Faber & Faber, 1956.
Donnison, F. S., *British Military Administration in the Far East, 1943–46*, London: H. M Stationery Office, 1956.

Foley, Matthew, *The New Cold War and National Assertion in Southeast Asia: Britain, the United States and Burma, 1948–1962*, Studies in the Modern History of Asia, London: Routledge, 2010.

Gallagher, O'Dowd, *Retreat in the East*, London: Viking Press, 1942.

Ghose, Parimal, *Brave Men of the Hills: Resistance and Rebellion in Burma 1825–1932*, Honolulu: University of Hawai'i Press, 2000.

Gravers, Mikael, *Nationalism as Political Paranoia in Burma*, Richmond: Curzon, 1999.

Gupta, Partha Sarathi, *Imperialism and the British Labour Movement 1914–1964.*, New York: Holmes & Meier, 1975.

Guyot-Réchard, Bérénice, *When Legions Thunder Past: The Second World War and India's Northeast Frontier*. (2016) War in History, Kings College London Research Portal.

Heinlein, Frank, *British Government Policy and Decolonisation, 1945–63: Scrutinising the Official Mind*, Abingdon: Routledge, 2002.

Hyam, Ronald, and Martin, Ged. Reappraisals in British Imperial History, London: Macmillan, Cambridge Commonwealth Series, 1975.

Ienaga Saburo, *Japan's Last War*, Oxford: Blackwell, 1979.

Keynes, John Maynard, *The General Theory of Employment, Interest, and Money*, Palgrave: Macmillan, 1936.

Keynes, John Maynard, *How to Pay for the War: A Radical Plan for the Chancellor of the Exchequer*, London: Macmillan, 1940.

King, Frank H. H., *The History of the Hong Kong and Shanghai Banking Corporation*, Vols. III & IV, Cambridge: Cambridge University Press, 1987.

Lebra, Joyce C., *Japanese-trained Armies in Southeast Asia*: New York: Columbia University Press, 1977.

Leigh, Michael D., *Conflict, Politics and Proselytism: Methodist Missionaries in Colonial and Postcolonial Upper Burma, 1887–1966*, Manchester University Press, 2011.

Leigh, Michael D., *The Evacuation of Civilians from Burma: Analysing the 1942 Colonial Disaster*, London: Bloomsbury, 2014.

Lindert, P. H., *Key Currencies and Gold 1900–1913*, Princeton Studies in International Finance No. 24, Princeton: Princeton University Press, 1969.

Lu Pe Win, U, *History of the 1920 University Boycott*, Rangoon, 1970

Marks, John Ebenezer, *Forty Years in Burma*, London: Hutchinson & Co., 1917.

Martin, Andrew, *Flight by Elephant: The Untold Story of World War II's Most Daring Jungle Rescue*. London: Fourth Estate, 2013.

Maung Maung, *A Trial in Burma: The Assassination of Aung San*, The Hague: Springer, 1962.

Maung Maung, *A Trial in Burma: The Assassination of Aung San*, The Hague, 1962, 2nd edn (Yangon: Unity Publishing House, 2012)

Maung, Maung, *From Sangha to Laity, Nationalist Movements of Burma 1920–1940*, New Delhi: South Asia Books, 1980.

Maybury, Maurice, *Heaven-Born in Burma: Flight of the Heaven-Born*, Castle Carey: Folio Hadspen, 1984.

Myint-U Thant, *The Making of Modern Burma*, Cambridge: Cambridge University Press, 2001.

Naw, Angelene, *Aung San and the Struggle for Burmese Independence*, Bangkok: Nordic Institute of Asian Studies, Silkworm Books, 2001.

Pearn, B. R., *The Indian in Burma: Racial Relations: Studies in Conflict and Cooperation*, p. 35, Ledbury: Le Play House Press, 1947

Porter, Andrew N. and Stockwell, Anthony, J., *British Imperial Policy and Decolonisation 1938–64*, London: Palgrave Macmillan, 1987.

Reed, David, *The Trek from Mandalay*, London: Minerva Press, 1996.

Robinson, Ronald, 'The Eccentric Idea of Imperialism, with or without Empire', ed. By W. J. Mommsen and J. Osterhammel, *Imperialism and After: Continuities and Discontinuities*, London: Allen & Unwin, 1986. pp. 290–314.

Russell, S. Farrant, FRCS, *Muddy Exodus: A Story of the Evacuation of Burma, May 1942*, London: Epworth Press, 1943.

Sarkisyanz, E. *Buddhist Backgrounds of the Burmese Revolution*, The Hague: Martinus Nijhoff, 1965.

Shaw, Bernard, *Fabianism and the Empire: A Manifesto by the Fabian Society*, London: G. Richards, 1900.

Silverstein, Josef, *The Political Legacy of Aung San: Introductory Essay*, Data Paper 86, Southeast Asia Program, Department of Asian Studies, Ithaca, New York, Cornell University, 1972.

Slim, Field Marshal Sir William. *Defeat into Victory*, London: Cassell, 1956.

Smith, Donald Eugene, *Religion and Politics in Burma*, New Jersey: Princeton University Press, 1965.

Smyth, Major-General J., *Milestones*, London: Sidgwick & Jackson, 1979.

Tarling, Nicholas, *A Sudden Rampage: The Japanese Occupation of Southeast Asia 1941–45*, London: Hurst & Company, 2001.

Tarling, Nicholas, *Britain, Southeast Asia and the onset of the Cold War, 1945–1950*, Cambridge: Cambridge University Press, 1998.

Taylor, Robert H., *The State of Burma*, London: C. Hurst, 1987.

Taylor, Robert H., *Marxism and Resistance in Burma, 1942–1945: Thein Pe Myint's Wartime Traveler*, Southeast Asia Translation Series, volume 4, Cornell University, Ithaca: Southeast Asia Program, 1994.

Tinker, Hugh (ed.), *Burma, The Struggle for Independence, 1944–48*, Volumes 1 and II, London: Her Majesty's Stationery Office, 1983.

Tsuji, Masanobu, *Singapore: The Japanese version*, London: Constable, 1962.

Tyson, Geoffrey, *Forgotten Frontier*, Calcutta: W. H. Targett, 1945.

Vorley, J. S. and H. M., *The Road from Mandalay*, Wilton: Wilton65, 2002.

Wagg, Alfred, *A Million Died: A Story of the War in the Far East*, London: Nicholson and Watson, 1943.

Warren, Alan, *Burma, 1942: The Road from Mandalay*, London: Continuum, 2011.

Wheen, Francis, *Tom Driberg: His Life and Indiscretions*, London: Chatto, 1990.

Woods, Philip, *Reporting the Retreat: War Correspondents in Burma*, London: Hurst, 2016.

Newspapers

The London Gazette, 29 January 1943.

London Times, 12 April 1947.

The Observer, 25 June 2017.

Reuters, New Delhi (1751) 1942.

The San Francisco Chronicle, 27 November 1941.

Reports

Conservative Party MPs, Burma Sub-Committee: Report, 11 August 1944.

Report: *Burma during the Japanese Occupation: Government of Burma Intelligence Bureau*, Simla, 1943.

The *United Nations Refugee Agency (UNHCR) Global Trends Report for 2016.*

The United Nations Relief and Rehabilitation Administration (UNRRA) Report for 1947.

Unpublished Dissertation

Ian E Scholey, 'The "Babylonian" Captivity of the Hongkong and Shanghai Banking Corporation and the return to Burma in 1945', SOAS, London University, MA Dissertation, 2007.

Speeches

Aung San, Address to the Supreme Council of the AFPFL, August 1946.

Aung San, Speeches in the Constituent Assembly, 29 July 1947.

Churchill's Mansion House Speech of 10 November 1942.

Driberg, Tom, MP, Speech in the House of Commons, 2 November 1945 (Hansard Vol.415, columns 800–803).

HRH Prince of Wales, Tyne Cot Cemetery, Centenary Service for the Battle of Passchendaele, 31 July 2017.

Sir Reginald Dorman-Smith: After Dinner Speech given at the, *Towards a Greater Burma Conference*, 1944, Cambridge Centre for South Asian Studies.

Journal Articles

Appleton, G., 'The Burmese Viewpoint', *Asiatic Review*, London, July 1948.

Aung-Thwin, Maitri, 'Introduction: Communities of Interpretation and the Construction of Modern Burma', *Journal of Southeast Asian Studies*, 39:2 (2008): 187–192.

Clark, Reginald, 'Burma Journey', *National Review*, June–August 1943.

Powell, Anthony, 'The Ledo Road', Mai Hsoong, Air KBZ, in-flight magazine, Issue 6, 2016.

Taylor, Robert H., 'Politics in Late Colonial Burma: The Case of U Saw', *Modern Asian Studies*, 10.2 (1976): 161–193.

Tinker, Hugh, 'A Forgotten Long March: The Indian Exodus from Burma 1941', *Journal of South East Asian Studies*, 7/1, March 1975.

U Tin Tut, 'U Aung San, a Memoir', *Burmese Review*, 25 August 1947.

'U Aung San's Appeal to Pay Lands Revenue, Rent and Agricultural Loans', *The Burman*, 23 March 1947.

U Tin Tut, 'It Was a Historic Moment', *Burmese Review*, 24 February 1947.

Registers

Register of Evacuees from Burma: Volume 1, European, Anglo-Burman, Anglo-Indian and Other Non-Indian Evacuees: Volume 2: Indians, A-L, Volume 3, Indians M-Z, Evacuee Enquiry Bureau, Government of India (Department of Indians Overseas), July 1943.

Burma Nadu, Vol. 2, No. 3, January 1945, *Evacuees in India*.

Miscellaneous Sources

Aung San, *Defence of Burma*, Introduction to Data Paper 86, Southeast Asia Programme, Ithaca Cornell University Press, 1972, 30 January 1945.

Aung San, '*Fourteen Points*', *Burma's Fight for Freedom*. Introduction to Data Paper 86, Southeast Asia Programme, Ithaca Cornell University Press, 1972.

Aung San, undated mimeograph, '*Burma's Challenge*'.

Ghosh, Amitav, *Exodus from Burma: A Personal Account*, June 21, 2011 (internet article).

Harvey Martin, 21/5 F.O. 371/31867 (quoted in Tarling, *A Sudden Rampage*).

Nakane, '*My Diary 1942*', BAM Collection, (quoted in Bayly and Harper, *Forgotten Armies*).

Powell, Anthony, *The Ledo Road*, Issue 6, Mai Hsoong, Air KBZ, pp. 44–47.

Roher, Finlo, *What's a Little Debt between Friends*? BBC, 10 May 2006.

U Vum Ko Hau, *The Spirit of Panglong*, Burma Radio, 4 February 1947, Bogyoke Aung San's broadcast to the nation.

Index

Note: Page numbers in *italics* refer to figures.

CPSIA information can be obtained
at www.ICGtesting.com
Printed in the USA
LVHW050259230623
750591LV00005B/165

9 781350 147577